States and Regions in the European Union
Institutional Adaptation in Germany and Spain

Tanja Börzel argues that the effect of Europeanization on the politics and institutions of member states depends on the degree of conflict between European and domestic policies and rules. If the differences are marked, there will be pressure on a country's institutions to adapt. The extent of this change will then depend upon the domestic framework within which the institutions operate. The book examines the relationship between the central state and regions in Germany and Spain, showing how Europeanization has served to weaken the powers of the regions. In both countries, the regions were forced to cooperate more closely with the centre, but the institutional impact in the two countries has been strikingly different. In Germany the existing cooperative federal system was reinforced, but in Spain the traditional competitive relationship between the levels of government could not continue. Europeanization has led to a significant change in the pattern of Spanish politics, turning rivalry into cooperation. This book thus presents an important analysis of the impact of Europeanization on domestic politics, and of the relationship between states and regions in particular.

TANJA A. BÖRZEL is a Senior Researcher at the Max-Planck-Project Group on the Study of Common Goods in Bonn. Her research interests include comparative politics, comparative federalism and the implementation of European policies.

Themes in European Governance

Series editors
Andreas Føllesdal
Johan P. Olsen

Editorial board
Stefano Bartolini   Beate Kohler-Koch   Percy Lehning
Andrew Moravscik   Ulrich Preuss   Thomas Risse
Fritz W. Scharpf   Philip Schlesinger   Helen Wallace
Albert Weale   J.H.H. Weiler

The evolving European systems of governance, in particular the European Union, challenge and transform the state, the most important locus of governance and political identity and loyalty over the last 200 years. The series *Themes in European Governance* aims to publish the best theoretical and analytical scholarship on the impact of European governance on the core institutions, policies and identities of nation-states. It focuses upon the implications of issues such as citizenship, welfare, political decision-making, and economic, monetary, and fiscal policies. An initiative of Cambridge University Press and the Program on Advanced Research on the Europeanisation of the Nation-State (ARENA), Norway, the series includes contributions in the social sciences, humanities and law. The series aims to provide theoretically oriented, empirically informed studies analysing key issues both at the European level and within European states. Volumes in the series will be of interest to scholars and students of Europe both within Europe and worldwide. It will be of particular relevance to those interested in the development of sovereignty and governance of European states and in the issues raised by multilevel governance and multinational integration throughout the world.

States and Regions in the European Union

Institutional Adaptation in Germany and Spain

Tanja A. Börzel

CAMBRIDGE
UNIVERSITY PRESS

PUBLISHED BY THE PRESS SYNDICATE OF THE UNIVERSITY OF CAMBRIDGE
The Pitt Building, Trumpington Street, Cambridge, United Kingdom

CAMBRIDGE UNIVERSITY PRESS
The Edinburgh Building, Cambridge CB2 2RU, UK
40 West 20th Street, New York, NY 10011-4211, USA
477 Williamstown Road, Port Melbourne, VIC 3207, Australia
Ruiz de Alarcón 13, 28014 Madrid, Spain
Dock House, The Waterfront, Cape Town 8001, South Africa

http://www.cambridge.org

First published 2002

Printed in the United Kingdom at the University Press, Cambridge

Typeface Plantin 10/12 pt.   *System* LaTeX 2$_\varepsilon$ [TB]

A catalogue record for this book is available from the British Library.

Library of Congress Cataloguing in Publication Data
Börzel, Tanja A.
States and regions in the European Union: institutional adaptation in
Germany and Spain / Tanja A. Börzel.
    p.   cm. – (Themes in European governance)
Includes bibliographical references and index.
ISBN 0 521 80381 0 – ISBN 0 521 00860 3 (pbk)
1. Federal government – Germany.   2. Central–local government
relations – Germany.   3. European Union – Germany.   4. Federal
government – Spain.   5. Central–local government relations – Spain.
6. European Union – Spain.   I. Title.   II. Series.
JN3971.A38 S8195   2001
320.443'049 – dc21   2001035701

ISBN 0 521 80381 0 hardback
ISBN 0 521 00860 3 paperback

Contents

Part III Transforming competitive regionalism: Institutional adaptation to Europeanization in Spain

Part IV   Sharing versus shifting the costs of adaptation: The Europeanization of environmental policy-making in Germany and Spain

Figures

Tables

Acknowledgements

A colleague once told me that writing a book is like giving birth to a child. Although I do not have this experience, I have always felt that the construction of a house is a more appropriate metaphor to describe the whole process. You design a plan with the help of a series of good construction books. Once the plan is finished, you search for construction material and reliable suppliers. When you finally start building, you realize that some of your ideas are not feasible, and go back to the drawing board. But no matter how often you redesign your plan, there are always some parts that are shaky or do not fit the overall construction. The work goes slowly, and sometimes stalls, because you lack material or you have the wrong equipment. There are moments when you fear that your whole construction will collapse. But when the last brick is set and the construction holds, you realize how much you have accomplished. You can then move in.

There are many people who were involved in the construction of my book and to whom I am enormously grateful. Adrienne Héritier and Yves Mény assisted me in designing the plan. Jeff Checkel, Thomas Christiansen, Liesbet Hooghe, Patrick Le Galès, and Martin Rhodes convinced me to build a house with sound foundations, rather than a castle, for which I did not have the necessary building material. Bastiaan van Apeldoorn, Thomas König, Andrea Lenschow, Andy Moravcsik, Iver Neumann, Rod Rhodes, Fritz Scharpf, Alec Stone Sweet, and Marlene Wind helped me to cope with specific difficulties that I confronted in the building process. My special thanks go to Alberta Sbragia and to Christine Ingebritsen who, respectively, encouraged me to pay attention to fine details and showed me how to integrate them into the overall construction.

I collected most of the construction material myself. However, I had some very important suppliers whom I would also like to thank. The people whom I interviewed in the regional administrations of Spain and Germany as well as their colleagues at the national level were very patient in introducing me to the world of intergovernmental relations and environmental policy-making in their respective countries. I am also grateful to my Spanish friends, César Colino, Mireia Creús Grau, Manual Jimenéz, and Nacho Molina for helping me to understand their country better.

Dominik Böllhoff, David Cameron, Jim Caporaso, Maria Green Cowles, Michelle Egan, Gerda Falkner, Jürgen Grote, Markus Jachtenfuchs, Bart Kerremans, Hans Dieter Klingemann, Francesc Morata, Wayne Sandholtz, Susanne Schmidt, Vivien Schmidt, Cornelia Ulbert, Ole Wæver, Wolfgang Wessels, and Antje Wiener read various chapters and/or commented on my project on different occasions. My thanks go to all of them. I also presented papers and tossed around ideas at a variety of places. The presentations in the Working Group of International Relations and the Luncheon Seminar of the Robert Schuman Centre, European University Institute, as well as the meetings of the American Political Science Association, the Council of European Studies, and the European Consortium for Political Research were important for me to test my theoretical argumentation and the empirical findings of the study. I am particularly indebted to the participants of the research project "Europeanization and Domestic Change" for their helpful comments and criticisms. I am also most grateful to Adrienne Héritier, Yves Mény, Alberta Sbragia, Fritz Scharpf, Johan Olsen, and two anonymous reviewers who read the whole manuscript.

The empirical data for the policy study of Part IV were partly collected within a research project on the implementation of various European environmental policies in five different member states. My thanks go to the European Commission for funding the project as well as to Christoph Knill who coordinated it.

Finally, Thomas persistently tested the soundness of the foundations of my construction. He was always there when I feared that it could crumble. He made me feel confident that no matter how much redesigning I had to do and no matter how many parts I had to rebuild, the house would ultimately stand.

The book is dedicated to my mother, Anita Börzel, from whom I learned an important, if not the most important, quality for writing a book: the ability to stick things out.

Tanja A. Börzel
Bonn, July 2001

Abbreviations

AGBAR	*Societat General d'Aigues de Barcelona*
AI	Access to Information
ARE	Assembly of the Regions in Europe
Art.	Article
BAT(NEEC)	Best Available Technology (Not Entailing Excessive Costs)
BGBl.	*Bundesgesetsblatt*
BJC	*Boletín de Jurisprudencia Constitucional*
BOE	*Boletín Oficial de España*
BR-Drs.	*Bundesrat-Drucksache*
BT-Drs.	*Bundestag-Drucksache*
BVerfGE	*Bundesverfassungsgerichtsentscheidung*
CA	*Comunidad Autónoma*
CCAA	*Comunidades Autónomas*
CDU	*Christlich Demokratische Union*
CE	*Constitución Española*
CiU	*Convergència i Unió*
CoR	Committee of the Regions
COREPER	*Comité des Représentants Permanents*
DG	*Dirección General/Directorate General*
DM	*Deutsche Mark* (German marks)
DMA	*Departament di Medi Ambient*
EC	European Community; also refers to the Treaty establishing the European Community as it stands after May 1, 1999
ECJ	European Court of Justice
ECSC	European Coal and Steel Community
EEA-G	*Gesetz vom 19. Dezember 1986 zur Einheitlichen Europäischen Akte vom 28. Februar 1986*
EIA	Environmental Impact Assessment

EMAS	Eco-Management and Audit Scheme
EMK	*Europaminister-Konferenz (Ständige Konferenz der Europaminister)*
EP	European Parliament
EU	European Union; also refers to the Treaty of the European Union
EuGH	*Europäischer Gerichtshof*
EUZBLG	*Gesetz über die Zusammenarbeit von Bund und Ländern in Angelegenheiten der Europäischen Union*
FCI	*Fondo de Compensación Interterritorial* (an interregional compensation fund)
FMC	*Federació de Municipis de Catalonia*
GG	*Grundgesetz* (Basic Law)
IDM	Institution Dependency Model
IGC	Intergovernmental Conference
IPPC	Integrated Pollution Prevention and Control
JPPs	Joint Plans and Programs
LOFAGE	*Ley de Organización y Funcionamiento de la Administración General del Estado*
LPA	*Ley del Proceso Autonómico*
MAP	*Ministerio para las Administraciones Públicas*
MAT	*Ministerio para las Administraciones Territoriales*
MIMA	*Ministerio de Medio Ambiente*
OJ	Official Journal of the European Communities
PNV	*Partido Nacionalista Vasco*
PP	*Partido Popular*
PSOE	*Partido Socialista Obrero Español*
Rs.	*Rechtssache*
SEA	Single European Act
STC	*Sentencia de Tribunal Constitucional*
UCD	*Unión del Centro Democrático*
UIG	*Umweltinformationsgesetz*
UMK	*Umweltministerkonferenz*
UVPG	*Umweltverträglichkeitsprüfungsgesetz*
UWWT	Urban Waste Water Treatment

Introduction

In 1992 a change in the German Constitution provided the German regions (*Länder*) with comprehensive co-decision rights in European policy-making. That change made it possible for the *Länder* not only to determine the German bargaining position if their legislative or administrative competencies were affected, but the *Länder* were also permitted to sit at the negotiation table in the Council of Ministers for the very first time. If a European issue falls within the area of their exclusive competencies, it is a *Länder* Minister, and not a member of the German government, who represents the Federal Republic of Germany in the European decision-making process.

Two years later, in 1994, the Spanish government and the 17 Spanish regions (*Comunidades Autónomas*) agreed on a formal procedure through which the *Comunidades Autónomas* were to participate in the decision-making and implementation of European policies. The procedure was further developed and became law in 1997. Unlike the German *Länder*, the *Comunidades Autónomas* do not have access to the Council of Ministers. But they can determine the Spanish bargaining position if their exclusive competencies are affected. For the very first time the *Comunidades Autónomas* have the right to participate directly in central-state decision-making.

The participation of the German and Spanish regions in European policy-making is a clear example of how Europeanization may affect the institutions of the member states. In both cases, we observe a formal institutional change, which aims to counterbalance the progressive transfer of regional competencies to the European level. As compensation for their loss of power, the regions are granted co-decision rights in the formulation and representation of the national bargaining position. Yet, in Germany the constitutional change of 1992 has merely expanded the existing institutions of cooperative federalism to the realm of European policy-making. European issues are subject to the same rules of decision-making and co-ordination procedures as domestic issues. In Spain, on the contrary, the participation of the *Comunidades Autónomas* in European policy-making has introduced a rule structure which is completely new to Spanish inter-governmental relations. European issues are subject to separate rules of decision-making and procedures. Unlike in domestic policy-making, the *Comunidades Autónomas* have direct co-decision powers in central-state decision-making concerning Europe. While in Germany Europeanization has resulted in flexible adjustment and ultimately in the reinforcement of existing territorial institutions, in the Spanish system of intergovernmental relations it has been an impetus for profound institutional change.

How can we explain such variation in the effect of Europeanization on the institutions of the member states? Why do some states undergo more profound change than others do? How does Europeanization interact with national institutions? Are we likely to see some convergence among the member states, or will institutional differences prevail?

The differential impact of Europe: Resource dependency versus institution dependency

In addressing these issues, this book attempts to establish the following claims: the domestic impact of Europe is differential because it is "institution dependent"; the extent to which Europeanization changes the institutions of the member states depends on these very institutions. First, Europeanization affects federal or regionalized member states in a different way than more centralized member states. When regional competencies were Europeanized, the Spanish and German regions lost much more power vis-à-vis their central states than their French or Dutch counterparts. Due to distinct institutional cultures, however, the German and Spanish regions chose opposing strategies to regain their powers. German cooperative federalism entails strong norms of cooperation and consensus-seeking. Accordingly, the German *Länder* demanded co-decision powers in European policy-making as a compensation for their losses. Whenever former regional competencies are affected, the federal government and *Länder* cooperate in formulating and representing the German bargaining position. Spanish competitive regionalism, by contrast, has been characterized by conflict and distrust. The *Comunidades Autónomas* compete rather than cooperate with the central state. Consequently, the regions attempted to bypass the Spanish government in European policy-making. Direct relations with European policy-makers were designed to make up for their losses in autonomous decision-making powers. The different strategies which the Spanish and German regions chose in responding to Europeanization resulted in varying degrees of domestic change. In both member states institutional adaptation ultimately reached a similar outcome. The regions participate in European policy-making by cooperating with their central government. But in Germany intergovernmental cooperation in European affairs simply reinforces the existing territorial institutions of cooperative federalism. In Spain, on the contrary, a new institutional framework had to be installed because up until then competitive regionalism had prevented the emergence of the cooperative institutions necessary for the regions to participate in European policy-making.

Moreover, I argue that the dominant approaches in the literature provide insufficient explanations for the differential effects of Europeanization on the institutions of the member states. Most studies rely on some sort of "resource-dependency" model. The European Union is conceived of as a "political opportunity structure", which provides new resources to some actors, while constraining others. This can cause a significant redistribution of power among domestic actors and result in institutional change. While they agree on the underlying logic of change, resource-dependency approaches present contradictory expectations about outcomes. Some claim that Europeanization strengthens the national governments vis-à-vis other domestic actors because – as the representatives of the member states – they are the key players in the European policy arena (Hoffmann 1966, 1982; Taylor 1991; Milward 1992; Moravcsik 1994). Others argue exactly the opposite: namely, that the European opportunity structure weakens the role of member-state governments because domestic actors can bypass or circumvent them by establishing direct relations with European institutions (Sandholtz and Zysman 1989; Marks 1992, 1993; Cameron 1995; Sandholtz 1996). A third group of scholars does not expect either a "withering away of the nation-state" or its "obstinate resilience" but, instead, a fundamental transformation. In the European system of multilevel governance, European, national and subnational actors share rather than compete for power resources. The fact that they are mutually dependent on resources results in the emergence of cooperative or interactive forms of governance (Kooiman 1993; Kohler-Koch 1996, 1998; Rhodes 1997). In light of these contradictory propositions, resource-dependency approaches appear to be indeterminate as to which actors benefit most from the Europe-induced redistribution of power resources.

I suggest that resource dependency needs to be embedded in an institutionalist understanding of Europeanization in order to explain when and how Europe affects the institutions of its member states. First, domestic institutions influence the distribution of resources among actors. The European Union can be conceived of as a political opportunity structure (Marks and McAdam 1996). Yet, the ability of domestic regions, interest groups, bureaucracies, or parties to explore new opportunities, or to avoid additional constraints, depends on their organizational capacities (resources); domestic institutions provide actors with different financial means, different scopes of access to the public sphere and the political decision-making apparatus, information, and legitimacy (Kitschelt 1986; Marks *et al.* 1996a). Powerful domestic actors – like the German *Länder* or the Spanish *Comunidades Autónomas* – are more capable of exploring new European opportunities, and avoiding additional constraints, because their national constitutions grant them considerable resources. Institutionally less-entrenched actors – like the French *régions* or the Dutch *provincies* – often lack the money, personnel, expertise, and the legal rights to interact directly with European institutions. Likewise, multinational companies are better represented at the European level than small- and medium-sized enterprises.

Second, member-state institutions influence the degree to which Europeanization changes the distribution of resources among domestic actors. The more European institutional rules and procedures challenge those at the national level, the greater the potential changes in the distribution of resources among domestic actors and the higher the pressure for institutional adaptation. The shift of the policy-making arena from the domestic to the European level tends to favor national governments vis-à-vis other domestic actors in the first place. Member-state governments enjoy privileged access to European decision-making through the European Council and the Council of the European Union (Moravcsik 1994, 1998a). But while Europeanization might initially enhance the autonomy of national executives, "strengthening the state" brings about a bigger institutional misfit for those member states whose institutions provide (some) actors with strong influence on domestic policy-making. The *Länder* and the *Comunidades Autónomas* have more power to lose than their French or Dutch counterparts simply because their Constitutions give them more legislative and executive responsibilities. By the same token, business association of countries with corporatist institutions of interest intermediation lose their privileged access to the policy-making process once policy competencies are transferred to the European level. This is less of a problem in states like France or Spain, where business associations are not formally involved in national decision-making processes.

Third, member-state institutions affect the way in which domestic actors respond to the gains and losses of resources caused by their failure to fit with European institutions. The adaptational strategies which actors choose do not only depend on their general capacity of action (resources). Institutions entail informal presuppositions about appropriate behavior within a given formal rule structure (March and Olsen 1989; Powell and DiMaggio 1991: 28; Hall and Taylor 1996: 965). These collective understandings – the institutional culture – influence the dominant strategy employed by actors as they respond to adaptational pressure exerted by Europeanization. The German *Länder* and the Spanish *Comunidades Autónomas* have similar resources. But they have pursued opposing strategies in their attempts to redress the balance of power that has been upset by Europeanization. Cooperative federalism induced the German *Länder* to pursue a strategy of cooperation with the state, which aimed at securing co-decision rights in the formulation and representation of the German bargaining position. The result of competitive regionalism in Spain, by contrast, was that the *Comunidades Autónomas* assumed a confrontational strategy which resorted to constitutional conflict and "circumventing the state" in order to prevent further losses of power.

Actors' strategies play a crucial role in facilitating or prohibiting the institutional adaptation to Europeanization. Adapting institutions is costly. Cooperative strategies are more successful in reducing adaptational costs because the winners and losers of change are willing to share them. The more costs are shared, the more actors will support the changes necessary to maintain or re-establish the institutional equilibrium that has been disturbed by a Euro-induced redistribution of power. Because the need for consensus is high, cost-sharing strategies are likely to result in a flexible adjustment of the existing institutions rather than in their profound transformation (Katzenstein 1984, 1985; Olsen 1996). In Germany Europeanization upset the institutional equilibrium of cooperative federalism because the *Länder* lost power. Such territorial centralization in itself constitutes some formal institutional change, if domestic actors do not adapt their institutions accordingly. But the cooperative strategy of the German *Länder* allowed for a flexible redressing of the institutional balance of power. The existing structures of joint decision-making and interlocking politics were simply extended to the realm of European policy-making. As a result, Europeanization reinforced rather than transformed cooperative federalism. Confrontational strategies, by contrast, prohibit institutional adaptation. Actors strive to shift the costs to each other, which prevents the adjustments needed to re-establish the institutional equilibrium. In Spain as in Germany, Europeanization led to a significant redistribution of power and one which was to the detriment of the regions. However, the confrontational strategy of the Spanish *Comunidades Autónomas* did not succeed in redressing the institutional balance of power. The attempt of the regions to cut their losses by confronting and circumventing the Spanish government in European policy-making proved futile. Only when the *Comunidades Autónomas* embraced a more cooperative strategy did they manage to re-establish the institutional equilibrium. The strategy change of the Spanish regions gave rise to the first framework for joint decision-making in Spanish intergovernmental relations. The formal participation of the Spanish regions in European policy-making constitutes a significant institutional change that is also likely to affect the underlying culture of competitive regionalism.

To sum up, there are two features of institutions which impact on the likelihood that Europeanization will lead to domestic institutional change, and the degree of that change. On the one hand, the formal rule structures define the "goodness of fit" (Risse *et al.* 2001) between European and member-state institutions. *The less the institutions fit, the higher is the pressure for adaptation and the more likely is change.* In other words, without pressure for adaptation, there is no need to expect change. On the other hand, the informal collective understandings of what is considered appropriate behavior within a given rule structure influences how domestic actors respond to pressure for adaptation in their attempt to reduce adaptational costs. *If institutions entail a cooperative culture inducing actors to pursue a strategy of cost-sharing, this will facilitate flexible adjustment and result in reinforcing domestic institutions rather than in fundamentally changing them.* In contrast, non-cooperative strategies of cost-shifting prohibit adaptation. A high degree of pressure for adaptation coupled with a lack of adaptability result in formal institutional change, as the old institutional equilibrium is not re-established. *But if domestic actors change their initial strategy – because it increases rather than decreases adaptational costs – this may trigger domestic change which is also likely to affect the institutional culture.*

This book concentrates on the effect of Europeanization on the institutions of the member states. Europeanization is defined as a process by which domestic policy areas become increasingly subject to European policy-making.[1] This process is essentially driven by the transfer of policy competencies from the member state to the European level. I do not attempt to explain the origins and underlying dynamics of this process. Nor do I explore the feedback effects that the domestic impact of Europeanization has on its very process. I acknowledge that the causal processes go both ways (cf. Olsen 1997). But there is only so much that one book can accomplish.

---

[1] Some refer to this process as "Europeification" (Andersen and Eliassen 1993) and/or save the term "Europeanization" for the repercussions which the transfer of policy competencies from the national to the European level has on the domestic institutions of the member states (Ladrech 1994; Goetz 1995; Olsen 1997). For a broader conceptualization of the term see Risse *et al.* 2001.

Contributions to the field

The study on the effect of Europeanization on Germany and Spain contributes to various theoretical and empirical debates in the field of European studies. First, there is the ongoing dispute in European integration theory between intergovernmentalist, neofunctionalist, and multilevel governance approaches.[2] These approaches have mostly been used to explain the dynamics and outcomes of the European integration process. But they have also been applied in a "second image reversed" perspective, exploring the effect of European integration on the institutions of the member states.[3] This study challenges the different propositions which the three approaches to European integration put forward with respect to the domestic impact of Europe. It is argued that neither liberal intergovernmentalism nor neofunctionlism/supranationalism nor multilevel governance can account for the differential effect of Europeanization on the member states. Rather than engaging in further debates over whether European integration strengthens (Moravcsik 1994), weakens (Marks 1993), or transforms the "state" (Grande 1996; Kohler-Koch 1996), we should focus on the conditions under which the "state" is strengthened, weakened, or transformed. The theoretical model developed in the second part of this book identifies some conditions under which Europeanization is likely to trigger domestic institutional change.

The second debate to which this book contributes concerns the analysis of institutional change. The effect of Europeanization on the institutions of the member states can be conceived of as a process by which the member states adapt their institutions to new practices, rules, and structures that emanate from the emergence of a European system of multilevel governance (Olsen 1996, 1997; Ladrech 1994). Olsen identifies various patterns of institutional change which could be used to interpret the effect of Europeanization on the nation-state (March and Olsen 1989, 1995; Olsen 1992, 1996). From a rationalist perspective, institutional change arises from shifting political purposes, reasoning, and power. Rational actors change institutions if they no longer facilitate the maximization of their self-interests. As national governments strive to preserve their autonomy vis-à-vis domestic actors, they establish European institutions to which they transfer national policy competencies (Moravcsik 1994). From a sociological institutionalist perspective, institutional change can

[2] See, for instance, Sandholtz and Zysman 1989; Moravcsik 1991, 1993, 1998a; George 1993; Wincott 1995; Risse-Kappen 1996; Marks et al. 1996; Kohler-Koch 1996; Zürn 1996; Stone Sweet and Sandholtz 1998.
[3] See, for example, Marks 1992, 1993, 1997; Burley and Mattli 1993; Moravcsik 1994, 1997; Goetz 1995b; Grande 1996; Sandholtz 1996; Börzel 1997.

be conceived of as a path-dependent response to functional and normative changes in the environment. As domestic and European institutions increasingly interact, domestic actors adopt new practices, rules, structures of meaning, and resources through a process of experiential learning, imitation, and diffusion (Olsen 1997).

The study in this book does not test different perspectives on institutional change in an attempt to adjudicate between them. Rather, a model is developed which combines rationalist and sociological institutionalist accounts to identify one causal mechanism through which external challenges, such as Europeanization, trigger domestic change. The primary driving force behind institutional change follows the instrumental logic of consequentiality emphasized by rational-choice institutionalism. Domestic actors have a general interest in maximizing, or at least in preserving, their power resources in responding to European opportunities and constraints. However, their response to Europeanization is influenced by the institutions in which they are embedded. Formal institutions define the range of possible strategies because they delimit the number of resources which actors have available (capacity of action). The institutional culture, in turn, guides actors in their ultimate choice of strategy. Collectively shared understandings of what constitutes appropriate behavior in a given situation may rule out certain strategies because they are considered to be socially unacceptable. Thus, the German *Länder* – more than other regions – have the necessary resources to circumvent their national government in European policy-making. Yet, the culture of cooperative federalism has prevented them from using direct access to European institutions in a way that would undermine the power of the national government. Competitive regionalism in Spain, on the other hand, prevented the *Comunidades Autónomas* from cooperating with the central state in order to compensate for their loss of powers. They resorted to their traditional strategy of confronting and circumventing the state.

Moreover, the actors' initial response to Europeanization is usually not the result of a conscious evaluation of alternative strategies and their respective consequences. Although actors are purposeful, they do not constantly engage in cost–benefit calculations. Rather, they tend to follow certain standard operating procedures and rules of appropriateness, which emerged from their experiences with similar situations in the past. Initially the *Comunidades Autónomas* did not weigh the costs against the benefits of cooperating with the central state and then decide to follow their traditional strategy of confrontation and non-cooperation. The Spanish regions only started to doubt their standard operating procedures and rules of appropriate behavior in dealing with the central state when those failed to preserve their institutional autonomy. Likewise, the *Länder* responded to their Europe-induced losses of power in the same way as they had been reacting to previous challenges to their institutional autonomy such as the federalization of their competencies in the 1960s and 1970s. Given its success, the *Länder* have never seriously questioned their cooperative strategy.

As institutions influence strategies, strategies may feed back to institutions. This book argues that one major source of institutional change is a shift in the strategies by which actors respond to Europeanization pressures. Such strategy changes result from a gradual process of "experiential learning" (Olsen and Peters 1986; Olsen 1997). Domestic actors increasingly realize that their initial strategy does not succeed in preserving, or maximizing, their power resources. They start to try out alternative strategies, which, if successful, increasingly replace the strategies initially embraced. The gradual shift of strategy is driven by the (positive) experience which actors have and see other actors have. The "success" of the *Länder* has been an important factor in moving the *Comunidades Autónomas* toward more cooperation with the central state. The realization of a new strategy, however, may require different domestic institutions. There was no institutional framework on which the Spanish *Comunidades Autónomas* could rely to facilitate the cooperation with the central government on European affairs, to which they had agreed. Central state and regions had to set up new formal institutions, which are also likely to affect the underlying institutional culture in the long run. Regular cooperation, reinforced by a positive experience with its outcome, gives rise to new practices, which may become taken for granted and enter the "cultural repertoire" of socially accepted behavior.

The third area to which this study contributes concerns the empirical analysis of the domestic impact of Europe. There is a growing literature which explores the effect of Europeanization on a particular set of domestic institutions or policies.[4] However, to date, only some empirical studies have systematically traced the causal mechanisms through which Europeanization may bring about domestic change. Even fewer have generated propositions on why, how and under what conditions Europeanization affects the institutions of the member states. The empirical study of this book not only describes, analyzes, and explains the adaptation of territorial institutions to Europeanization in Germany and Spain; the section on Spain also presents some new insights on Spanish intergovernmental relations and environmental policy-making,

---

[4] See, for instance, Anderson 1990; Goetz 1995; Bache *et al.* 1996; Mény *et al.* 1996; Schmidt 1996; Jeffery 1997c; Kohler-Koch 1998; Cowles *et al.* 2001, Héritier *et al.* 2001.

particularly as the literature on both subjects has mostly been written from a legal rather than political science perspective.[5]

Finally, the findings of the book have some important implications for the policy debate on the democratic deficit of the European Union. The "Europe of the Regions", where the regions of the member states constitute a "third level of government", next to the member states and the European institutions, is seen as offering one possible way of increasing the democratic accountability and transparency of European policymaking. But the regions have come to rely on the cooperation with their national governments to represent their interests in the European policy process. European institutions with regional representation, like the Committee of the Regions or the Assembly of the Regions in Europe, merely complement the domestic participation of the regions in European policy-making. If even the most resourceful regions of Europe, like the German and Austrian *Länder*, the Spanish *Comunidades Autónomas* and the Belgian *communautés/gemeenschappen* and *régions/gewesten* (regions), prefer to act jointly with their national governments rather than independently from them, the prospects for an independent and unified regional level of government in the European Union are rather gloomy.

Moreover, if regions choose to participate in European policy-making by cooperating with their national governments, this may exacerbate existing concerns about accountability and transparency. The cooperation between the regions and the central state on European affairs is dominated by intergovernmental networks. Regional parliaments have hardly any influence on the formulation and representation of the national bargaining position. While domestic legislative powers are transferred to the European level, the compensatory regional co-decision rights in European policy-making offer little benefit because they benefit the regional executives, not the legislatures. The erosion of the political power of regional parliaments reinforces the general trend of departamentarization, which is a trend that has come along with Europeanization. Rather than compensating for the insufficiency of democratic institutions in European policy-making, the "Europe of the Regions" raises additional problems of accountability and transparency.

The structure of the book

This book is divided into four parts. In Part I, I develop a model of Europeanization and domestic change. The model embeds the concept

---

[5] But, on Spanish environmental policy-making, see Aguilar Fernández 1993, 1994a, 1997; Font Borras 1996; on Spanish territorial politics, see Morata 1987, 1995; Morata and Muñoz 1997.

of resource dependency in an institutionalist understanding of Europeanization. It explains why, when, and how Europeanization can affect the institutions of the member states.

In Parts II and III, I test the major hypotheses of my model in a comparative study on the effect of Europeanization on the territorial institutions of Germany (Part II) and Spain (Part III). The empirical study is a structured, focused comparison (George 1979) which follows the most similar systems design (Przeworski and Teune 1970: Chapter 2). The territorial institutions of Germany and Spain face comparable pressures of adaptation due to their similar degree of decentralization. This makes it possible to keep the necessary condition of domestic change (adaptational pressure) constant. But Germany and Spain differ with respect to their institutional culture, as a result of which the regions have pursued opposite strategies in responding to the adaptational pressure. I analyze to what extent Europeanization has challenged the territorial institutions of Germany and Spain, how the German *Länder* and the Spanish *Comunidades Autónomas* have responded to the similar European challenges, and to what extent their adaptational strategies have succeeded in reducing costs.

Primary sources and secondary literature provided the major sources for the empirical studies. In order to trace more recent developments, particularly in the case of the major institutional changes in Spain, I conducted over 100 interviews with public and private actors on the regional and national level in both Germany and Spain between 1995 and 2000 (for a detailed interview list, see Börzel 1999).

Part IV contains a policy study on the Europeanization of environmental policy-making in Germany and Spain, which explores in greater detail the effect of Europeanization on the institutions of the two member states. Environmental policy is a regulatory policy which imposes serious costs on resourceful regions because not only do they lose competencies, but they also have to bear the lion's share of implementation costs. At the same time, however, Europeanization also provides some opportunities, particularly in terms of financial resources (Cohesion and Structural Funds). The "making" of different EU environmental policies illustrates the adaptational pressure, which Spain and Germany have been facing. The implementation of the various policies demonstrates how the different strategy choices of the Spanish and German regions failed and succeeded, respectively, in reducing adaptational costs. Finally, the policy study provides a more detailed analysis of the institutional changes that resulted from the change of strategy by the Spanish regions as opposed to the flexible adjustment of existing institutions in Germany.

The conclusion summarizes the empirical findings in light of the theoretical expectations of my model. I then discuss the generalizability of my findings. Do the findings only hold for certain policy areas? Does my model also apply to member states with less powerful regions, such as France and the United Kingdom? Is my model applicable to other dimensions of domestic institutions such as state–society relations? I maintain that the model is, in principle, general enough to analyze the effect of Europeanization across different policy areas, member states, and sets of domestic institutions. I also propose some avenues for further research. I conclude with some considerations on the policy consequences of my study for tackling the democratic deficit of the European Union. The findings of the book present some rather "sceptical reflections on a Europe of the Regions" (Anderson 1990) and its capacity of providing an institutional solution to the lack of accountability and transparency in European policy-making.

Europeanization and domestic institutional change: A historical institutionalist approach

Part I provides the theoretical framework of the book and presents the propositions to be evaluated in the comparative study. I briefly discuss the two major approaches to the study of the domestic impact of Europe dominating the literature: "resource dependency" and "institutional adaptation". The two approaches entail different understandings of how institutions affect actors' behavior. Resource dependency usually draws on some form of rational choice institutionalism, which conceives of institutions as constraining and enabling specific choices and strategies of rational actors striving to maximize their self-interests. Institutional adaptation is firmly rooted in sociological institutionalism, which emphasizes the social or cultural aspect of institutions. Institutions do not only constrain and enable actors' behavior. Institutions entail collectively shared systems of meanings (institutional culture), which constitute actors by providing them with fundamental understandings of what their interests and identities are.

Due to their distinct understanding of institutions, resource dependency and institutional adaptation identify different causal mechanisms by which Europeanization affects the institutions of the member states. They generate different empirical validity claims on the conditions of change, the process of change, and the degree and outcome of change. But rather than testing these empirical validity claims against each other, I strive to combine theoretical assumptions of resource dependency and institutional adaptation in a historical institutionalist approach to Europeanization and domestic institutional change. I argue that both the instrumental and the cultural dimension of institutions have to be taken into account in order to understand Europeanization and its domestic impact. The model, which I develop on the basis of this approach, generates its own propositions on why, when, and how Europeanization is affecting the domestic institutions, which are tested in the empirical parts of this book.

1 Europeanization as a process of institutionalization and institutional change

Europeanization can be conceived of as a two-fold process. It involves the evolution at the European level of a distinct governance system, a new set of political structures and processes, which interact with the established ones of the member states. Hence, Europeanization entails a "bottom-up" and a "top-down" dimension. The former emphasizes the emergence of European institutions as a set of new practices and rules, structures of meaning, and resources, while the latter refers to the effect of these new institutions on the institutions of the member states. The causal processes of Europeanization entail both dimensions. However, most studies distinguish between them analytically, focusing on either of the two dimensions.

For a long time, research on Europeanization focused on the "bottom-up" dimension, which has also been referred to as "Europeification" (Andersen and Eliassen 1993) or "*Vergemeinschaftung*" (communitariza-tion). Europeanization is analyzed as a process of institution-building at the European level driven by the progressive transfer of competencies from the member states to the European Union (formerly European Community). Theoretical and empirical studies focus on the role and interaction of different actors, both European (European Commission, European Parliament, European Court of Justice, Committee of the Regions, EU interest groups) and national (member state governments, interest groups, regions) in European policy-making. The underlying dynamics, the nature, and the final outcome of the emerging European system of governance have been the main dependent variable.[6]

---

[6] Given the large number of studies, it is impossible to provide a complete overview of the existing literature. See, for example, Scharpf 1988, 1993; Sandholtz and Zysman 1989; Moravcsik 1991, 1993, 1998a; Sbragia 1992; Schmitter 1992; Andersen and Eliassen 1993; Burley and Mattli 1993; Cafruny and Rosenthal 1993; Mazey and Richardson 1993; Sandholtz 1993; Cameron 1995; Cowles 1995; Héritier *et al.* 1996; Héritier 1999; Jachtenfuchs and Kohler-Koch 1996; Majone 1996; Marks *et al.* 1996; Marks *et al.* 1996b; Risse-Kappen 1996; Wallace and Wallace 1996; Stone Sweet and Sandholtz 1998.

In recent years, however, scholars have increasingly focused on the potential effects, which the evolving European system of governance has on the institutions of the member states ("top-down"). A growing number of studies started to explore whether and to what extent European policy-making has affected:

- domestic systems of interest intermediation (Schmidt 1996; Cowles 2001; Héritier et al. 2001);
- territorial politics (Jones and Keating 1995; Hooghe 1996; Jeffery 1997c; Kohler-Koch et al. 1998);
- national bureaucracies (Page and Wouters 1995);
- administrative structures (Wright 1994; Rometsch and Wessels 1996; Héritier 2000; Knill forthcoming);
- regulatory structures (Majone 1997; Schneider 2001; Héritier et al. 2001);
- the relationship between executive and legislature (Andersen and Burns 1996; Norton 1996);
- electoral and party politics (Featherstone 1988; Greven 1992; Van der Eijk et al. 1996);
- judicial structures (Caporaso and Jupille 2001; Conant 2001);
- macro-economic institutions (Dyson and Featherstone 1996, 1999; Dyson forthcoming); and
- national identities (Checkel 2001; Risse 2001).

This book follows the "top-down", or, "second image reversed" (Gourevitch 1978) approach to Europeanization. For the sake of clarity, the definition of Europeanization is limited to the process by which domestic policy areas become increasingly subject to European policy-making. This process is essentially driven by the transfer of policy competencies from the member-state to the European level. As I am concerned with the domestic effect of Europeanization, I do not attempt to explain the origins and the underlying dynamics of this process. Nor does the scope of this book allow me to explore the feedback effects of domestic institutional change caused by Europeanization on its very process. Finally, as my dependent variable is domestic institutional change, I am less concerned with changes in domestic policy or politics. Policy change is an important source of changes in political institutions (Börzel 1998a; Héritier 2001; Héritier et al. 2001; Knill and Lenschow 2001; Schneider 2001). More-over, alterations in policy preferences and dominant actor coalitions can also have major implications for political institutions (Keohane and Milner 1996). Yet, this book is about how institutions may change institutions, whereby institutions are defined as a set of formal and informal rules and practices that constrain and enable actors' activity by allocating resources and providing a collective understanding of what constitutes appropriate behavior in specific situations (March and Olsen 1984, 1989, 1995). As such, institutions structure the relationships between actors. I am interested in why, when, and how the evolving set of rules and practices at the European level may change the ones established in the member states.

2 Conceptualizing the domestic impact of Europe: Resource dependency versus institutional adaptation

In order to conceptualize, describe, and explain the effect of Europeanization on the domestic institutions of the member states, most studies draw on two major strands of theory. They either embrace some sort of resource-dependency approach, which conceives of the European system of governance as a new political opportunity structure that changes the distribution of power resources among domestic actors. Or they resort to organizational theories of institutional change, which understand the domestic impact of Europe as a process of institutional adaptation in which domestic actors adopt and internalize new rules and practices. I argue that the two approaches are embedded in different forms of institutionalism and therefore vary in their expectations of whether, when, and how Europeanization effects the institutions of the member states.

The following two sections discuss resource dependency and institutional adaptation with respect to their capacity for explaining the domestic impact of Europe. Rather than embarking on an ideal-type metatheoretical discussion of different institutionalisms, I contrast the two approaches according to:

- the major propositions which resource dependency and institutional adaptation pose on how actors behave, how institutions affect actors' behavior, and why institutions change;
- the expectations which the two approaches generate about the conditions, the process, the degree, and the outcome of domestic institutional change caused by Europeanization.

The domestic impact of Europe as a resource-dependent process

Resource-dependency approaches[7] are usually based on some sort of rational choice institutionalism as defined by James March and Johan

---

[7] For different resource-dependency approaches see, for example, Pizzorno 1978; Simeon 1979; Rhodes 1981, 1997; Kitschelt 1986; Putnam 1988; Parri 1989; Marin 1991; Kriesi *et al.* 1992; Marks and McAdam 1996; Moravcsik 1998a.

Olsen (March and Olsen 1995: Chapter 2) and Peter Hall and Rosemary Taylor (Hall and Taylor 1996). Resource dependency assumes that actors are rational, goal-oriented, and purposeful. They have a fixed and ordered set of preferences, and they act instrumentally in order to maximize their expected utilities by deploying the resources at their disposal. As any individual or corporate actor is dependent on others to achieve his or her goals, actors have to exchange their resources to produce desired outcomes. The resource exchange is based on the mutual assessment of resources, strategies, and interests. Actors will engage in strategic interaction using their resources to maximize influence over outcomes, while trying to become as little dependent as possible on the others with whom they interact. The strategy by which actors strive to maximize their utilities – i.e. the decision about which actors exchange what kind of resources – depends on the availability and relative value of their own resources, as well as the estimated value of the resources and the anticipated exchange behavior (interests and strategies) of others.

Institutions constrain and facilitate actors' activities in two fundamental ways. First, institutions provide a political opportunity structure that allocates resources among political actors such as information, decision-making competencies, financial means, or legitimacy. The distribution of resources in a given political system defines the strategy options that political actors have at their disposal to pursue their interests (Rhodes 1981; Kitschelt 1986; Kriesi *et al.* 1992; Mayntz and Scharpf 1995: 47–48).

Second, institutions set the "rules of the game" (Rhodes 1981: 106). They embody rules and procedures, which regulate the process of resource exchange (North 1990; Garrett and Weingast 1993). They allow regulation of conflicts which arise in situations of mutual dependence and competition (Coleman 1986; Windhoff-Héritier 1991), and they help in overcoming problems of collective action (Ostrom 1990). Institutions affect actors' behavior by economizing on transaction costs (costs of negotiation, execution, and enforcement), providing information on the interests and strategy of other actors, and by reducing opportunism. Institutions create stable expectations and thus reduce uncertainty about the corresponding behavior of others.

For rational choice institutionalism, institutions arise and change as a result of problem-solving and conflict resolution among purposeful actors. Institutional change is likely if institutions no longer serve the purposes of relevant actors. Actors may consider institutions as ineffective because, first, they may have changed their preferences (Keohane and Milner 1996), second, the distribution of power among them may have changed (Keohane 1984), and, third, major changes in the environment may have occurred which are associated with "punctuated equilibria" (Krasner 1984) or "critical junctures" (Collier and Collier 1991) to which institutions have to be adapted to maintain their efficiency (cf. Stein 1983).

Resource dependency emphasizes the second source of institutional change. Institutions change as the result of a redistribution of power resources which changes the dependencies among actors and restructures their relationships. The causes of a redistribution of resources are related to alterations in the political opportunity structure, which provides some actors with new resources while depriving others. Factors that may alter the political opportunity structure are political reform (Rhodes 1997), economic crisis, shifting political coalitions, and the opening-up of cleavages (Tarrow 1995), or the emergence of a new political opportunity structure such as the European Union (Marks and McAdam 1996).

Europeanization as a new political opportunity structure: Strengthening, weakening, or transformation of the state?

Resource-dependency approaches conceive of the European Union as a new political opportunity structure that offers additional resources to some actors, while imposing constraints on others, thereby changing the distribution of power resources in the member states. Although they agree on the redistribution of resources as the major driving force of institutional change, resource-dependency approaches arrive at competing expectations on both the degree and the outcome of institutional change.

Proponents of liberal intergovernmentalist approaches predict that the Europe-induced redistribution of resources results in an overall strengthening of traditional state power. By transferring policy competencies to the European level, national governments can increase their control over policy outcomes as they gate-keep or monopolize the access to European policy-making (Milward 1992; Moravcsik 1994, 1998a; Kohler-Koch 1996; Grande 1996).[8] But while national governments become more independent of domestic actors (such as regions, parliaments, or interest groups), the "net effect" on domestic institutions is relatively low (Moravcsik 1998b).

Advocates of neofunctionalist and supranationalist approaches, on the other hand, expect Europeanization to have a more profound effect on the domestic institutions of the member states. The European political opportunity structure enables domestic actors (such as regions or interest

---

[8] For earlier versions of this "paradox of weakness" argument (states gaining power by giving up sovereignty), see Hoffmann 1966, 1982, 1989; Taylor 1991.

groups) to enhance their control over policy outcomes by circumventing or bypassing the national government in European policy-making (Sandholtz and Zysman 1989; Marks 1992, 1993; Cameron 1992, 1995; Sandholtz 1996). As a result, the role of the state in providing collective policy outcomes is increasingly weakened. State functions are more and more taken over by supranational and subnational actors and institutions (Bell 1988).

Finally, the multilevel governance literature does not expect either a withering away of the state or its obstinate resilience. Rather, it suggests a profound transformation of the state. Europeanization does not strengthen one group of actors at the expense of the others but increases their mutual dependence on each other's resources. The increasing interdependence of public and private actors at all levels of government results in the emergence of cooperative governance and subsequently undermines the key principles of statehood, territoriality, and state sovereignty (Schmitter 1991; Christiansen 1994, 1997; Jachtenfuchs and Kohler-Koch 1995; Grande 1996; Kohler-Koch 1996; Rhodes 1997).

Despite a general disagreement on the concrete impact of Europeanization, all three resource-dependency approaches suggest that there will be some sort of convergence among the member states leading to either a strengthening, a weakening, or a transformation of the state. Yet, comparative studies on the effect of Europeanization have not so far found much empirical evidence for convergence. The debate on the future of the state in the European Union has produced sufficient empirical evidence to prove that the effect of Europeanization on the institutions of the member states is highly diverse (Mény et al. 1996; Jeffery 1997c; Cowles et al. 2001; Héritier et al. 2001). Europeanization does not systematically favor one particular group of domestic actors over others. For instance, while French firms gained more autonomy vis-à-vis their national government by circumventing (Schmidt 1996), Spanish firms did not (Aguilar Fernández 1997). Equally striving to exploit European resources, the Italian regions have been far less able to ascertain their domestic power than their Austrian counterparts (Desideri and Santantonio 1997; Morass 1997). While the Spanish territorial system is undergoing profound change, German federalism has been reinforced by Europeanization.

None of the three resource-dependency approaches is able to account for the variations on the domestic impact of Europe. The strengthening, weakening, or transformation of the state propositions may provide an account of why and how Europeanization causes domestic institutional change. They do not, however, present testable hypotheses because neither specifies conditions under which its assumptions hold.

Table 1 *Resource-dependency expectations about the domestic impact of Europe*

Condition of change	Process of change	Degree of change	Outcome of change
New opportunities and constraints for domestic actors	Redistribution of resources among domestic actors	• Liberal intergovernmentalism: marginal • Neofunctionalism/ supranationalism: significant • Multilevel governance: significant	• Liberal intergovernmentalism: strengthening the state • Neofunctionalism/ supranationalism: weakening the state • Multilevel governance: transformation of the state

Table 1 summarizes the expectations of resource-dependency approaches with respect to the conditions, the process, the degree, and the outcome of domestic change.

The domestic impact of Europe as a process of institutional adaptation

The concept of institutional adaptation, as it is used here, is drawn from organizational theory. It refers to the "long-term substitution of existing practices and structures with new ones" (Olsen 1997: 159). Organizational theory identifies different causal mechanisms through which institutional adaptation can evolve. They draw on a sociological institutionalist understanding of actors' behavior and the nature of institutions (March and Olsen 1984, 1989, 1995; Powell and DiMaggio 1991).

Sociological institutionalism does not necessarily deny that actors are purposeful, goal-oriented, and rational. Yet, actors' behavior is not fully strategic either. Actors do not merely act upon cost–benefit calculations of the expected utility of present behavioral alternatives to attain a certain goal or outcome. They are guided by collectively shared understandings of what constitutes proper behavior in specific situations. The individual logic of instrumentality or consequentiality, on which rational choice institutionalism draws, is contrasted with a social logic of appropriateness (March and Olsen 1989: 160–162) which impacts on the way in which actors define their goals and on what they perceive as rational action. Rather than maximizing their subjective desires, actors strive to fulfill the social expectations in a given situation, i.e. to "do the right thing". For example, it would be rational for a commuter who is exhausted after a long working day to keep his or her seat on the train ride home. However, many people would yield their seat to elderly or pregnant women because this is what "good citizens" are expected to do.

Sociological institutionalists have a far broader notion of institutions than their rational choice counterparts. Institutions are defined not just as (formal) rules, procedures, or norms, but as "the symbol systems, cognitive scripts, and moral templates that provide the frames of meaning guiding human action" (Hall and Taylor 1996: 947). They are the enactment of general cultural rules and accounts, not individual purposes and choices. Institutions do not simply regulate actors' behavior by prescribing what an actor should do or by sanctioning a specific behavior rendering certain choices more costly than others. Institutions constitute actors by providing them with a fundamental understanding of what their interests are and what the appropriate means may be to pursue these interests. Without institutions, actors are not able to perceive their preferences nor can they make choices on how to achieve them. Consequently, actors do not adhere to institutional rules and norms as a matter of choice, i.e. because it makes them better off. Rather, they internalize rules and norms and follow them out of habit, taking them for granted (Berger and Luckmann 1966).

Institutional change then may be conceived of as a process of institutional adaptation through which new rules, norms, and practices are incorporated, (partially) replacing existing norms and practices. The major causal mechanism of institutional adaptation identified by sociological institutionalism is isomorphism (DiMaggio and Powell 1991; Scott 1991; Olsen 1997). Institutional isomorphism suggests that institutions that frequently interact, that are exposed to each other, or that are located in a similar environment, over time develop similarities in formal organizational structures, principles of resource allocation, practices, meaning structures, and reform patterns (DiMaggio and Powell 1991; Meyer and Rowan 1991; Scott and Meyer 1994). Yet, provided that institutions are exposed to such an environment, they are supposed to respond by similar changes in their institutional structure. This poses serious problems in explaining variation in institutional adaptation to a similar environment.

Some sociological institutionalists have addressed this problem by pointing at the "inefficiency of history" in matching institutional practices and structures to environments and reforms (March and Olsen 1989: 54–56, 1995: 40–44). Institutions develop a robustness toward changes in their functional and normative environments. The "inefficiency of history" assumption has two important implications for the process of institutional adaptation. First, institutional adaptation takes place along institutional paths. Existing institutions are not simply to be replaced or harmonized with new rules, norms, and practices. Profound and abrupt transformation – with a sudden elimination and replacement of established practices, meanings, and resource allocations – should be expected only under special circumstances (Olsen 1997: 162). Institutional adaptation is more likely to be incremental. Second, the more new institutional rules, norms, and practices are institutionalized, and the more they "match" the constituting principles of existing institutions, the more likely institutions are to incorporate these new rules, norms, and practices (Olsen 1997: 161). Variation in institutional adaptation is explained by the different degrees to which new and existing institutions match each other. If institutional isomorphy is to evolve, it is the result of a long-term process in which some institutions have to undergo deeper change than others do.

Europeanization as an emerging set of new institutions: Convergence or divergence?

A sociological institutionalist approach goes beyond the conception of Europeanization as the emergence of a new political opportunity structure, which provides additional resources and constraints to domestic actors. European institutions also entail new rules, norms, practices, and structures of meaning which domestic institutions have to incorporate. Such processes of internalization give rise to different degrees of institutional adaptation, depending on the match between European and corresponding domestic institutions.

Authors relying on sociological institutionalist approaches have focused on the dissemination of new ideas and concepts through European institutions, such as the principle of cooperative governance (Kohler-Koch *et al.* 1998), of new norms, like European citizenship (Checkel 2001), or of national identities (Risse 2001).

The effect of the ideational or cognitive dimensions of Europeanization on the domestic institutions is expected to vary according to the degree of fit. The more that European norms, ideas, structures of meaning, or practices resonate with those at the domestic level, the more likely will they be incorporated into existing domestic institutions (Olsen 1996: 272). While cognitive and normative fit facilitates institutional adaptation, it also results in less profound institutional change than in cases of "misfit". Moreover, domestic institutions are not simply replaced or harmonized by European norms, rules, and practices. Institutional adaptation to Europeanization is incremental and takes place along historically

Table 2 *Institutional adaptation expectations about the domestic impact of Europe*

Conditions of change	Process of change	Degree of change	Outcome of change
• High degree of institutionalization at the European level • Fit/resonance between European and domestic institutions	• Internalization of new norms, rules, practices, and shared meanings	• Low institutional fit: marginal • Institutional fit: incremental but affecting institutional culture	• Middle term: institutional divergence • Long term: convergence (institutional isomorphism)

developed national paths. As a result, institutional divergence among member states is likely to prevail. The question whether the emergence of new European institutions will ultimately lead to institutional convergence (isomorphy) in the long-run, however, remains an open one (Jachtenfuchs and Kohler-Koch 1995). Table 2 summarizes the expectations of institutional adaptation approaches about the conditions, the process, the degree, and the outcome of domestic change.

Unlike rational choice institutionalism and resource dependency, sociological institutionalism and institutional adaptation are able to generate hypotheses on the expected domestic effect of Europeanization which account for variation in degree and outcome of institutional change. Variations in domestic change are essentially explained as a function of the "goodness of fit" (Risse *et al.* 2001) between European and member-state institutions. Yet, empirical evidence shows that even if domestic institutions face similar degrees of misfit, they may still vary in the extent to which they adapt. European deregulation of the transport sector profoundly challenged both the corresponding German and Italian institutions. But while Germany underwent albeit painful reform in order to adapt, Italy has so far resisted any significant adaptation (Héritier 2001; Héritier *et al.* 2001). Or, Europeanization challenges the nation-state identities of both France and the United Kingdom. Whereas the UK nation-state identity has so far largely resisted Europeanization, there is increasingly more space for Europe in French identity (Risse 2001).

I argue that the weakness of sociological institutionalism in explaining variation in domestic institutional adaptation under conditions of similar degree of cognitive or normative misfit is related to its neglect of agency and politics. While rational choice institutionalism overemphasizes the role of agency in creating and changing institutions, sociological institutionalism tends to slight the extent to which processes of institutionalization and institutional adaptation provoke and entail a clash of power among actors with competing interests (agency). In order to understand and explain the domestic impact of Europe, both agency and structure are needed. Which new rules, norms, practices, principles of resource allocation, or structures of meaning are incorporated into existing institutions is not only a question of cognitive or normative fit. It is also influenced by the (competing) interests, the power, and the strategies of actors, which have to adapt the institutions in which they are embedded. Even if actors are exposed to the same institutions, they may pursue different interests and strategies. Moreover, actors may embrace European ideas and identities for purely instrumental reasons, e.g. to legitimize political reforms, as the French socialists did in the mid-1980s (Risse 2001) and the Italian leadership did on the verge of the European Economic and Monetary Union (Sbragia 2001), or to bolster demands for more political power, as the German *Länder* did with the idea of the "Europe of the Regions" in the late 1980s (see Part II, Chapter 2).

3   The domestic impact of Europe
as an "institution-dependent" process

Rational choice and sociological institutionalism both understand the effect of Europeanization on the member states as a process of institutional change. The conceptions of the domestic impact of Europe as a resource-dependent process and a process of institutional adaptation, respectively, generate different propositions on the conditions, the process, the degree, and the outcome of domestic change. But neither resource dependency nor institutional adaptation provide a sufficient explanation for variation at the domestic level. Why do domestic actors respond differently to the opportunities and constraints provided by Europeanization, be they material or ideational? Why do some member-state institutions undergo more profound institutional change than others do, even if they face similar degrees of institutional misfit?

In order to address these questions, I combine assumptions (1) of rational choice and socio-logical institutionalism, (2) of resource dependency and institutional adaptation, and (3) of agency and structure within a historical institutionalist framework. This framework emphasizes the role of institutions in mediating the domestic impact of Europe (institution dependency).

Institution dependency denotes, first, that institutional adaptation to environmental changes is influenced by the strategies that actors choose in response and, second, that the choice of adaptational strategies depends on the institutions in which actors are embedded. This definition of institution dependency entails an understanding of actors' behavior and its relationship to institutions which is informed by historical institutionalism (Steinmo *et al.* 1992; Hall and Taylor 1996). Historical institutionalism has been mainly concerned with the question of how institutions structure a nation-state's response to new environmental challenges. It assumes that environmental effects are mediated by historically grown institutions "pushing historical development along a set of 'paths'" (Hall 1993: 957; Krasner 1988; cf. Collier and Collier 1991).

Historical institutionalism seizes the middle ground between rational choice and sociological institutionalism, particularly with respect to assumptions about actors' behavior and the role of institutions in affecting actors' behavior. Since historical institutionalism brings together a wide variety of approaches, I briefly outline my historical institutionalist understanding of two major cornerstones that are used for building an institution dependency model of Europeanization and domestic change.

Actors' behavior: Purposeful but socially constrained

The Institution Dependency Model (IDM) treats actors as purposeful in the sense that they strive to maximize their preferences. Although I do not deny the possibility of preference change, my model takes certain preferences as given. Thus, I consciously assume that corporate domestic actors have a principal self-interest in organizational survival, autonomy, and growth (Scharpf 1997: 64). While I consider this preference of institutional survival and autonomy as stable, I do not intend to exogenize or bracket preferences as rational choice institutionalists do. Actors' preferences are predominantly shaped by institutions. Institutions do not provide actors solely with resources: they also define the purposes for which it is legitimate to use these resources (see below). The Spanish and German constitutions constitute the *Comunidades Autónomas* and the *Länder*, respectively, by defining them as territorial entities whose purpose is to provide the political representation of historical nationalities and/or to ensure political decentralization and democracy. In order to fulfill their purpose, the regions of both countries are attributed significant resources (legislative, administrative, and fiscal powers). It is plausible to assume that the German and the Spanish regions strive to preserve and enhance their resources in order to protect their institutional autonomy.

Yet, actors' behavior does not exclusively follow the instrumental logic of consequentiality. Actors do not merely base their choices of action on cost–benefit calculations with respect to the expected utilities of alternatives. They are also guided by concerns about what is socially appropriate behavior in a given situation. It might be perfectly rational for the Catalan administration to strike a deal with the Spanish government. It is more difficult to justify such a deal in the eyes of Catalan voters who perceive cooperation with the central state as an act of betrayal to the "Catalan cause" – irrespective of the material benefits. In other words, it is simply inappropriate for a Catalan government to cooperate with the central state because many Catalans consider it a compromise on the political autonomy of Catalonia. Moreover, although actors are purposeful, they do not constantly engage in means-end or cost–benefit calculations. Instead of consciously evaluating alternative strategies and their respective consequences, actors tend to follow certain standard operating procedures and rules of appropriateness, which emerged from experiences with similar situations in the past. Thus, the *Länder* responded to their Europe-induced losses of power in the same way as they used to do when faced with a centralization of their competencies at the federal level in the 1960s and 1970s. And the *Comunidades Autónomas* started to question their traditional strategy of confronting and circumventing the central state only when it proved increasingly ineffective in protecting their institutional autonomy.

Institutions: Formal and informal rule structures which constitute actors and regulate their behavior

Unlike rational choice institutionalism, the IDM assumes that institutions influence actors' behavior not only by stabilizing expectations about what others will do in terms of what should be instrumentally viable but also by what should seem to be socially appropriate to them. Institutions, then, do not only include sanctioned rules, which change the costs, and benefits that an actor can expect from choosing a certain course of action. They also entail social norms "that actors will generally respect and whose violation will be sanctioned by loss of reputation, social disapproval, withdrawal of co-operation and rewards, or even ostracism" (Scharpf 1997: 38). Thus, institutions do not only constrain and facilitate actors' behavior by rendering some causes of action more costly than others, but they also entail collective understandings of what constitutes appropriate or legitimate behavior for an actor in a given situation, rendering some causes of action socially unacceptable.

But institutions do not only regulate actors' behavior. They also constitute actors in the sense that corporate or collective actors "may be said to exist only to the extent that the individuals acting within and for them are able to coordinate their choices within a common frame of references that is constituted by institutional rules" (Scharpf 1997: 39). They define not only the membership of composite actors and the resources they can draw upon. Institutions also prescribe the purposes for which actors are to deploy the resources, i.e. outline ways of legitimate use of resources.

In sum, institutions affect actors' behavior by influencing their preferences, capabilities, and strategy choices (Hall 1986; Thelen and Steinmo 1992). The IDM focuses on the last two dimensions of actors' behavior. In order to analyze the regulatory effect of institutions on actors' capabilities and strategies, I distinguish between two institutional dimensions: formal institutions and informal institutions.

Formal institutions

Formal institutions refer to explicit – that is, written – norms, rules, and procedures codified in the Constitution, laws, treaties, agreements, etc., which create resources and regulate their exchange. Hence, formal institutions impact on the distribution of resources among actors. Resources are defined as "any attribute, circumstance or possession that increases the ability of its holder to influence a person or a group because this person or group depends on this resource" (Rogers 1974: 1425). More specifically, resources are factors, which allow actors to influence political outcomes. Whether and which resources are effective instruments of political influence is contingent upon the specific context (Scharpf 1997: 51). But one can identify certain types of resources, which have the potential of providing political influence.

- legal resources: codified or formalized rules and procedures which allocate rights of autonomous decision-making (legal and administrative competencies), participation, and veto;
- financial resources: formal rights to funding as well as the control over the distribution of finances;
- organizational resources: human resources, expertise, information;
- political resources (legitimacy): the capacity to mobilize political consensus or social support in favor or against a political decision as well as the capacity to increase (decrease) efficiency and transparency of policy-making processes.

The distribution of resources in an institutional setting results in a certain power constellation which largely defines the range of strategy options among which actors may choose to pursue their interests as function of their own preferences and capabilities as well as the perceived preferences and capabilities of others.

Informal institutions

Informal institutions refer to implicit – that is, unwritten and uncodified – rules and collective understandings of what constitutes appropriate, i.e. socially acceptable, behavior in a given situation (socially shared meanings of appropriateness). While formal institutions impact on the distribution of resources, informal institutions – or institutional culture – define how to use the available resources in a legitimate way. Consequently, the ultimate strategy choice of an actor within the range of options defined by the distribution of resources is not only a question of available resources and the cost–benefit calculation of the expected utility of present alternative

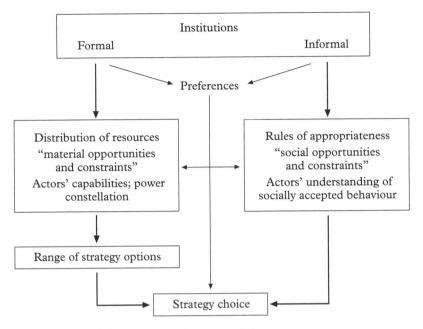

Figure 1 Institutions and strategy choice

strategies depending on the preferences and strategy options of the other actors. The socially shared meanings or rules of appropriateness embedded in the institutional culture favor or discredit certain strategy choices because they would be considered as inappropriate behavior. Thus, actors can be expected to use a strategy which resonates with established routines, familiar patterns of behavior, and shared meanings of appropriateness in order to attain their purposes (Hattam 1993). Most of the time, actors do not even consider alternative strategies and then discredit them as being socially inappropriate. Rather, they employ those strategies which they are used to invoking in comparable situations. See Figure 1.

Europeanization as a challenge to domestic institutions: Facilitating or prohibiting adaptation?

Europeanization has been defined as a process by which domestic policy areas become increasingly subject to European policy-making through a transfer of policy competencies from the domestic to the European level. The European institutions emerging from this process constitute a new political opportunity structure, which may significantly challenge the institutions of the member states by providing some domestic actors with new opportunities while imposing constraints on others.

The degree to which Europeanization results in a redistribution of resources among domestic actors causing significant pressure for adaptation depends on the formal and informal institutions of the member states. Domestic institutions mediate the domestic effect of Europeanization in three fundamental ways:

1 Domestic institutions define the distribution of resources among domestic actors (action capacity)

European institutions provide resources to domestic actors while depriving others. Yet, the ability of domestic actors to exploit additional resources, or avoid new constraints, depends on their action capacity, i.e. the resources which domestic formal institutions attribute to them.

The constitutional and legal norms, rules, and procedures of a member state impact on the distribution of power resources between the central state and the regions. As opposed to unitary or weakly decentralized states, the regions in federal or regionalized states have considerable resources in terms of policy competencies, financial revenue, organizational capacity, and political legitimacy. On the one hand, these resources enable the regions to exploit new European opportunities, while regions in non-decentralized or weakly decentralized states often lack the capacity to do so. On the other hand, resourceful regions might benefit less from European opportunities, such as direct contacts with European institutions, as they do not provide a substitute for the losses of formal domestic powers which Europeanization imposes on them as significant constraints on their institutional autonomy.

2 Domestic institutions impact on the degree to which Europeanization changes the distribution of resources among domestic actors (pressure for adaptation)

As domestic institutions differ with respect to their internal distribution of power, they are not equally affected by changes in the political opportunity structure and, hence, face different degrees of pressure for institutional adaptation. The more European institutional rules and procedures challenge those at the domestic level, the greater the potential changes in the distribution of resources among domestic actors and the higher the pressure for institutional adaptation.

The degree of centralization or decentralization of domestic institutions is crucial for the "goodness of fit" (Risse *et al.* 2001) with European institutions. For regions of unitary and weakly decentralized states, Europeanization may offer additional opportunities which could strengthen their autonomy vis-à-vis the central state, although less resourceful regions often lack the resources to fully exploit these opportunities. In highly decentralized member states, on the contrary, regions suffer a significant loss of their legislative and administrative competencies from Europeanization, which results in an uneven distribution of "say and pay" between the central state and the regions. On the one hand, the central state gains access to regional competencies, which it did not have at the domestic level. When regional competencies are transferred to the European Union, the central-state governments decide on how these competencies are exercised in the Council of the European Union, while the regions are left without any influence (known as "say") since most of them are not formally represented in the European decision-making process. On the other hand, the regions are in many policy areas the main implementers of European law. They often have to bear the lion's share of implementation costs (known as "pay") of policies in whose formulation and decision-making they do not participate.

For highly decentralized states, this uneven distribution of "say and pay" (pay without say) constitutes a major misfit between European and domestic decision rules and procedures. The centralization of decision powers in the hands of the member-state governments (say) and the shifting of implementation costs onto the subnational level (pay) results in a redistribution of resources in those member states where the regions either share decision powers and implementation costs with the central state, like in Germany, or the regions enjoy strong autonomy in both decision-making and implementation, like in Spain.

In sum, the pressure for adaptation caused by Europeanization should be higher in decentralized than in centralized member states where domestic actors (e.g. regions, interest groups) have more resources to lose. While Europeanization may provide new opportunities for actors in centralized member states, they often lack the capacity to exploit them, as a result of which the domestic distribution of resources remains largely unchanged.

3 Domestic institutions guide the way in which domestic actors respond to the misfit between European and domestic institutions, facilitating or prohibiting institutional adaptation (adaptability)

Even if domestic institutions face similar adaptational pressure (redistribution of resources due to institutional misfit), they may still differ in their capacity to accommodate it (adaptability). Some institutions can easily absorb adaptational pressure by incremental adjustments, while others undergo profound transformation. The adaptability of domestic institutions is a function of the strategies which actors pursue in response to changes in the domestic distribution of power.

Adaptational strategies

The redistribution of resources imposes costs on some domestic actors as they lose power. Domestic actors pursue different strategies to avoid or reduce such costs by trying to rebalance the domestic distribution of resources. Regional authorities (but also other domestic actors) may pursue two basic strategies to redress the balance of power, which Europeanization changed in favor of the central state (cf. Rhodes 1986; Morass 1994; Jeffery 1997b):

1 A cooperative strategy of sharing the costs with the central state, which aims at redressing the territorial balance of power by a "compensation-through-participation"

The central state compensates the regions for their losses of power by sharing with them its decision powers in European policy-making, on the one hand, and the costs for implementing European policies, on the other hand. This cost-sharing strategy presupposes the cooperation of the regions both with each other and with the central state. While intrastate participation (mediated by the central state) of the regions in European policy-making does not preclude direct contacts between the regions and the European institutions, such extrastate participation (independent from the central state) serves the regions as a complement to rather than a substitute for their cooperation with central state.

2 A non-cooperative or competitive/confrontational strategy of shifting costs, which aims at redressing the territorial balance of power by "ring-fencing" regional competencies and by circumventing the central state

This strategy entails a zero-sum-game type of competition for resources between the different levels of government. In order to ring-fence their institutional autonomy, the regions resort to constitutional litigation against European interventions in their spheres of competencies. They also minimize cooperation with the central state because such cooperation is perceived as an attempt by the central state to intervene in their sphere of competencies. Instead, the regions strive to circumvent or bypass the central state by establishing direct relations with European institutions and therefore to gain extrastate participation in European policy-making. The costs for the central state are twofold: On the one hand, the costs of constitutional conflict over the distribution of responsibilities and the refusal of the regions to cooperate in European policy-making often lead to implementation failure; after all, it is the central state which is legally responsible to the European Union for the effective application and enforcement of European policies. On the other hand, the costs of the "parallel diplomacy" of the regions at the European level may undermine the bargaining capacity of the central state (government).

Strategy choice

The strategy choice of domestic actors is guided by the formal and informal domestic institutions in which they are embedded. The formal institutions define the range of strategy options among which actors may chose. A non-cooperative strategy of circumventing the state, for instance, is not feasible for regions, which lack the necessary resources to access directly the European policy arena. But even if domestic actors have the necessary resources, a cooperative institutional culture may still discredit such a strategy.

Cooperative institutional culture does not imply that actors have harmonious relationships or only pursue altruistic interests. Nor does it preclude conflict and contention. Rather, cooperative cultures entail rules of appropriateness that induce actors to search for solutions to problems and conflicts, accommodating the interests of all actors involved. Collectively shared rules of conflict-avoidance and consensus-seeking render strategies which discriminate against third actors within the same institution less acceptable. If environmental changes exert pressure for adaptation, actors tend to refrain from outcomes which unilaterally shift the costs on a particular group of actors. Rather, they strive to reach a solution which allows for the compensation of potential losers. The losers will ask the winners for compensation for their losses, which the winners will be likely to grant, e.g. by sharing their (gained) resources with the losers.

Non-cooperative institutional cultures, which lack cooperative norms and rules, induce actors to pursue non-cooperative or confrontational strategies which aim at a shifting of adaptational costs. In order to redress the balance of power, the losers will try to win back resources from the winners; the latter are, however, likely to defend their newly gained powers, resulting in additional conflict and competition over resources. The losers will also strive to gain new resources outside their institution in order to regain power vis-à-vis the winners.

In states like Spain, Italy, and Belgium, ethnic, religious, and socio-economic cleavages gave rise to competitive regionalism where the collective understanding of the regions about their behavior toward the central state is based on competition and confrontation rather than cooperation. The regions tend to protect their institutional autonomy by constitutional litigation and strive to deal with the central state on a bilateral rather than multilateral level. An institutional culture of confrontation, competition, and bilateralism largely precludes cooperative strategies, which aim at a sharing of adaptational costs with the central state through intrastate participation in European policy-making. Rather, it favors a non-cooperative strategy of ring-fencing regional competencies by constitutional conflict and circumventing the state. In states like Germany and Austria, on the other hand, where we observe cooperative federalism, the behavior of the regions toward the central state is based on a collective understanding that multilateral bargaining and consensus-seeking are the most appropriate way of dealing with intergovernmental problems. Such an institutional culture is hostile to non-cooperative strategies and is far more conducive to a sharing rather than a shifting of adaptational costs.

Adaptability

I suggest that the strategy by which actors strive to avoid or reduce adaptational costs plays a crucial role in facilitating or prohibiting institutional adaptation to Europeanization. As Peter Katzenstein argued, states with cooperative institutions have a higher adaptability to external pressures because the costs are shared between the winners and losers of change (Katzenstein 1984, 1985; Olsen 1997). If regions strive to reduce adaptational costs by sharing them with the central state (cooperative strategy), this will facilitate the redressing of the territorial balance of power (institutional adaptation). Central state and regions share both decision powers and implementation costs in European policy-making, which compensates the regions for their losses. This outcome is most likely in states like Germany and Austria, where the culture of territorial institutions entails cooperative norms, rules, and practices which promote a sharing of the costs between central state and regions and thus facilitate a redressing of the territorial balance of power.

If, by contrast, regions try to shift adaptational costs onto the central state (non-cooperative strategy), this will prohibit the redressing of the territorial balance of power (institutional adaptation). The regions attempt to cut their losses by denying the central state the power to interfere in their sphere of competencies (constitutional conflict and non-cooperation) and by gaining the capacity to pursue their interests in European policy-making independently from the central state (circumventing). This type of activity is expected in countries with non-cooperative institutional cultures like Spain and Italy, which prevent a sharing of adaptational costs between central state and regions and, hence, hinder a redressing of the territorial balance of power.

Institutional change

Domestic institutions with a high adaptability (cooperative institutional culture) are able to accommodate Europe-induced adaptational pressure by adjusting flexibly . The degree of institutional change is rather limited. In this case the extent to which the lack of adaptability (non-cooperative institutional culture) results in institutional change depends on the degree of pressure for adaptation. The higher the pressure for adaptation (redistribution of resources) and the lower the adaptability of domestic institution (non-cooperative institutional culture), the greater the formal institutional changes (changes in the balance of power). For highly decentralized states, Europeanization exerts significant pressure for adaptation because the transfer of domestic competencies to the European level changes the territorial distribution of power to the detriment of the regions. If regional strategies fail to redress the territorial balance of power because they strive to shift rather than share the adaptational costs, Europeanization results in significant territorial centralization, which constitutes formal institutional change of some kind. Yet the losers can be expected to reconsider their adaptational strategy if it does not succeed in redressing the balance of power. If the regions experience direct access to European policy-making as an insufficient substitute for the loss of formal decision-making powers, then they may begin to seek some form of cooperation with the national government in order to inject their interests in the European policy process. In other words, the logic of appropriateness which guides actors in their initial response to external challenges is replaced by the logic of consequentiality as actors start to search for more effective ways or strategies in reducing adaptational costs. Such strategy changes which contradict the institutional culture (e.g. a cooperative strategy in a competitive culture) evolve from an incremental process of "experiential learning" (Olsen and Peters 1986; Olsen 1997). Before engaging in a strategy change, the Spanish regions first had to appreciate that their initial strategy of non-cooperation was ineffective in redressing the territorial balance of power. Rather than consciously calculating the costs and benefits of such a change, however, the *Comunidades Autónomas* started to try out elements of alternative, more cooperative strategies. This gradual shift of strategy was driven by the (positive) experience which they had and which they saw other regions like the German *Länder* had with cooperative strategies.

As institutions define strategies, strategies feed back to institutions. If the dominant strategy reflects the underlying formal and informal institutions, substantial strategy change is likely to result in institutional change, because existing institutions, formal and informal, are no longer compatible with the new strategy. Cooperative strategies require cooperative institutions, while confrontational strategies are difficult to reconcile with cooperative institutions. While Spain, Italy, and Belgium suffer from a traditional lack of formal institutions in which the regions could cooperate with the national government on European issues, the formal institutions of joint decision-making and interlocking politics in Germany and Austria make a strict delimitation of regional competencies (ring-fencing) or regional unilateralism (*Alleingänge*) difficult. As strategy changes are driven by a predominantly instrumental logic of consequentiality, they are likely to affect formal institutions in the first place. Actors will create formal rules and procedures which are necessary to make their strategy work. Yet, as formal and informal institutions mutually influence each other, formal institutional changes may, in the long run, also affect institutional culture. Given that the initial strategy of the regions was strongly influenced by the territorial institutional culture, their strategy change is also likely to have an impact on collectively shared rules and meanings of appropriateness. If formal institutions require the regions and the central state to cooperate on a regular scale, then they are likely to develop more cooperative patterns of behavior. These patterns of behavior may be reinforced by a positive experience with the new rules and procedures and, over time, be taken for granted as they enter the "cultural repertoire" of socially accepted behavior. See Figure 2.

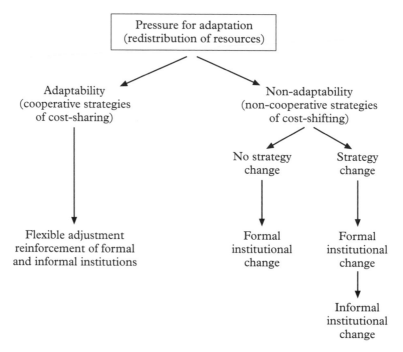

Figure 2 The causal chain of institutional change

To sum up, there are two features of member-state institutions which impact on the likelihood and the degree to which Europeanization leads to domestic institutional change. On the one hand, the formal institutions which influence the distribution of resources among domestic actors, define the "goodness of fit" between European and member-state institutions, giving rise to differing degrees of pressure for adaptation:

The more that formal norms, rules, and procedures at the European level challenge those at the domestic level (misfit), the greater the changes in the distribution of resources among domestic actors (pressure for adaptation), and the more likely domestic institutional change will occur.

On the other hand, the informal collective understandings of what is considered appropriate behavior within a given rule structure (institutional culture) influences how domestic actors respond to pressure for adaptation, facilitating or prohibiting institutional adaptation (adaptability):

Given a similar degree of pressure for adaptation, those domestic institutions which entail a cooperative institutional culture possess a higher adaptability. They are, therefore, less likely to undergo significant institutional change than those entailing a competitive and confrontational institutional culture.

The propositions of the Institution Dependency Model of Europeanization and Domestic Institutional Change are summarized in Figure 3. The IDM allows a prediction to be made as to when Europeanization is most likely to cause substantial domestic institutional change as opposed to mere flexible adjustment and reinforcement (degree of change). It is less powerful in predicting concrete outcomes. The IDM suggests that member states with similar formal and informal institutions are likely to converge around similar outcomes. First, they face the same pressure for adaptation. The European Union provides domestic actors with comparable resources with the same opportunities and constraints. Regions in highly decentralized member states have suffered more losses from Europeanization than their counterparts in centralized unitary states. The pluralist structure of the European Union offers more opportunities to interest groups of statist countries where they have only limited access to the political system. Second, similar institutional cultures induce actors to pursue related strategies in responding to new opportunities and constraints. Cooperative federalism in Germany and Austria induced the regions to push for a sharing of decision powers and implementation costs in European policy-making while competitive regionalism in Spain, Belgium, and Italy provoked a confrontational response by the regions. Third, actors who face the same pressure for adaptation are likely to learn from each other. The regions of the five strongly decentralized states

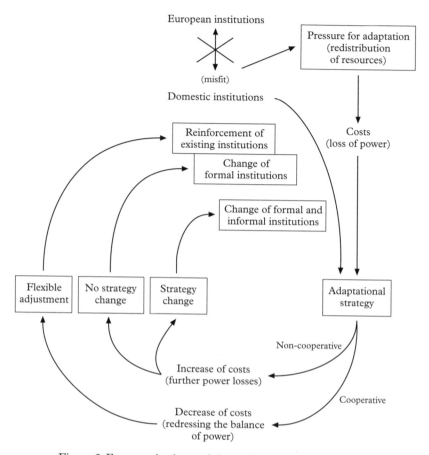

Figure 3 Europeanization and domestic institutional change

ultimately opted for the German model of cooperation with the central state in European policy-making in order to redress the territorial balance of power. For the Spanish, Belgian, and Italian regions this implied a significant strategy change, which was partly motivated by the positive experience of the German *Länder*. As the member states differ in their formal and informal institutions, we would expect only partial or, at best, some "clustered convergence" where some member states converge toward similar outcomes, but others do not.

Table 3 contrasts the IDM expectations about the conditions, the process, the degree, and the outcome of change with those generated by the resource-dependency approach and institutional adaptation approach.

Table 3 *Expectations about the domestic impact of Europe in comparison*

	Resource dependency	Institution dependency	Institutional adaptation
Conditions of change	• New opportunities and constraints for domestic actors	• Misfit between European and domestic institutions (pressure for adaptation) • Non-cooperative domestic institutional culture which prohibits institutional adaptation (non-adaptability)	• High degree of institutionalization at the European level • Fit/resonance between European and domestic institutions
Process of change	• Redistribution of resources	• Redistribution of resources • Change/non-change of adaptational strategies	• Internalization of new norms, rules, practices, and shared meanings
Degree of change	• Liberal intergovernmentalism: marginal • Neofunctionalism/ supranationalism/ transactionism: significant • Multilevel governance: significant	• No pressure for adaptation: marginal • High pressure for adaptation and: – adaptability: marginal – no adaptability: significant change in formal institutions – no adaptability and strategy change: significant change in formal and informal institutions	• Low fit/resonance between European and domestic institutions: marginal • Fit/resonance between European and domestic institutions: incremental but affecting institutional culture
Outcome of change	• Convergence	• "Clustered convergence" • Convergence among similar institutions	• Middle term: divergence • Long term: convergence?

The following chapters evaluate the theoretical propositions of the Institution Dependency Model in a comparative study on the impact of Europeanization on the territorial institutions of Germany and Spain (Parts II and III). The territorial institutions of Germany and Spain faced similar pressure for adaptation but induced the regions to pursue different strategies in response to the adaptational pressure. This resulted in different degrees of institutional change. A policy study on the Europeanization of Spanish and German environmental policy-making (Part IV) makes it possible to trace the causal mechanism of domestic institutional change on a more concrete level.

Part II

Reinforcing cooperative federalism: Institutional adaptation to Europeanization in Germany

The first empirical part of this book analyzes the effect of Europeanization on German territorial institutions. Chapter 4 briefly maps the formal and informal institutions of the German federal system. I argue that the institutional culture of multilateral bargaining and consensus-seeking induces the *Länder* to pursue a cooperative strategy of "compensation-through-participation" in responding to centralization as the major challenge to their institutional autonomy. The *Länder* have always aimed to be compensated for their losses of regional self-determination through co-determination rights in federal decision-making. This sharing of adaptational costs has allowed for a redressing of the territorial balance of power through an incremental process of flexible adjustment avoiding structural reforms.

Chapter 5 starts by exploring the extent to which Europeanization has exerted pressure for adaptation on German territorial institutions. The transfer of domestic policy competencies to the European level has caused an uneven distribution of "say and pay" for the *Länder* which has seriously challenged the territorial balance of power in German federalism (1). Then, I show how the *Länder* have subsequently pushed for comprehensive co-decision powers in the formulation and representation of the German bargaining position in European policy-making in order to redress the territorial balance of power (2). I argue that this compensation-through-participation strategy of the *Länder* has succeeded in redressing the territorial balance of power (3) which facilitated a flexible adjustment of German territorial institutions to Europeanization. The existing territorial institutions were extended to the realm of European policy-making, as a result of which German cooperative federalism has been reinforced rather than transformed (4).

4 The Federal Republic of Germany as a model of cooperative federalism

This chapter outlines the major formal and informal institutions of German federalism. In particular, it shows how the institutional culture of multilateral bargaining and consensus-seeking have induced the *Länder* to confront the centralization of their autonomous competencies by a cooperative strategy of cost-sharing. Rather than invoking constitutional conflict, they demanded a compensation for their power losses in the form of participatory rights in federal decision-making. This has allowed for a flexible redressing of the territorial balance of power.

Functional division of labor, strong bicameralism, and fiscal equalization as the major formal institutions of German federalism

The Federal Republic of Germany comes close to a prototype of cooperative federalism. Unlike dual or competitive federalism as seen in the United States, the German Federal State was never meant to accommodate territorial plurality. In the post-war German Constitution, the federal structure fulfills two major purposes. First, it provides a vertical dimension of separation of power. A powerful regional level of government was designed to prevent the re-emergence of a strong central state (Hesse 1962). Second, the federal structure was designed to ensure a certain uniformity of living conditions for all Germans, as demanded by the *Sozialstaatsprinzip* (welfare state principle) enshrined in Art. 20 I of the *Grundgesetz* (GG; Basic Law) (Böckenförde 1980). The three major formal institutions of the German federal system are designed to balance the normative prescriptions for decentralization (separation of powers) and centralization (uniform living conditions).

Marble-cake federalism and the problem of centralization

Unlike in dual federal systems, where each level of government has its own sphere of responsibilities for which it holds both legislative and

45

executive competencies, cooperative federalism is based on a functional division of labor between central state and regions. While legislation is concentrated at the federal level, execution and administration are largely entrusted to the *Länder*. What prevents the German *Länder* from being downgraded to mere administrative units of the *Bund* (Federation), is the discretion that the *Länder* have in the execution and administration of federal laws. More importantly, the *Länder* have a considerable political weight in federal legislation through their participation in central-state decision-making. The representation of the *Länder* executives in the *Bundesrat*, the second chamber of the German Parliament, prevents a shift in the German federal system toward centralization, despite the preponderance of the central state in legislation (Benz 1991b).[9] Most importantly, the *Länder* could be compensated for the increasing transfer of their self-determination rights to the federal level by co-decision powers in federal policy-making (see below). This "compensation-through-participation" gave rise to an extensive system of interlocking politics and joint decision-making (*Politikverflechtung*), where *Bund* and *Länder* share and jointly exercise policy competencies.

Interlocking politics and executive federalism

A major corollary of the functional division of labor between *Bund* and *Länder* with its high degree of legislative centralization, on the one hand, and extensive administrative decentralization, on the other hand, is the increased importance of ensuring both intergovernmental cooperation and consultation of the views of the administering governments when central-state legislation is being formulated. Such vertical intergovernmental cooperation is provided by the participation of the *Länder* in the federal legislation and administration through the *Bundesrat*, the second chamber of the national parliament. Their representation in the *Bundesrat* allows the *Länder* to bring in their political interests and administrative experience in the federal legislation. The *Bundesrat* has the right to legal initiative (Art. 76 I GG). Any federal law that affects the interest or duties of the *Länder* or lays down administrative procedures for them in their function of implementing federal legislation requires the explicit consent of the *Bundesrat*. Otherwise, the *Bundesrat* has a suspensive veto, which can be overridden by an equal majority of the first chamber of parliament, the *Bundestag* (Art. 77 IV GG). About three quarters of all federal laws as well as many federal ordinances (*Rechtsverordnungen*) require the consent of the *Bundesrat* (Blanke 1991: 50).

---

[9] For contending views see Hesse and Renzsch 1991; Klatt 1991; Abromeit 1992.

The interlocking of federal and *Länder* decision-making competencies through the participation of the *Bundesrat* in federal legislation, gave rise to a whole variety of formal institutions of vertical and horizontal intergovernmental cooperation in which *Bund* and *Länder*, and also the *Länder* among themselves, coordinate their interests. There are three levels of intergovernmental cooperation:

- First, the *Gesamtstaat* (Whole State), i.e. the level which comprises institutions in which both the *Bund* and the *Länder* are represented on terms of equal status. At this level, the most important institutions are the regular conferences between the heads of the *Bund* and *Länder* governments, and the top-level coordinating bodies of the political parties.
- Second, the *Bundesstaat* (Federation), i.e. the constitutionally organized structure of interrelationships between *Bund* and *Länder*, whose decisions are usually subject to majority voting rules. Here, we find the greatest number of cooperative institutions, which are organized under the umbrella of the *Bundesrat*.
- And, third, the "third level" of horizontal coordination between the *Länder* themselves, formally excluding the *Bund*, of which the most important coordination bodies are the *Länderministerkonferenzen* (conferences of *Länder* ministers) in the various policy areas (cf. Leonardy 1991).

The functional distribution of labor and strong bicameralism has resulted in a growing interdependence of *Bund* and *Länder* in public policy-making and gave rise to a high level of multilateral coordination and cooperation among the executives of the federal and the *Länder* level. The *Länder* parliaments are largely excluded from this joint decision-making process. Their political power is restricted to approving or disapproving the results of intergovernmental negotiations. Cooperative federalism thereby entails a double disempowerment of the regional legislatures: first, through the transfer of *Länder* competencies to the federal level and, second, through the logic of joint decision-making which is based on intergovernmental and interadministrative negotiations. German cooperative federalism is executive federalism in which the role of the *Länder* parliaments is increasingly one of "*staatsnotarielle Ratifikationsämter*" (Lenz 1977), state notary's offices merely ratifying executive decisions (Hesse 1962; Ossenbühl 1990). Executive federalism not only undermines the political power of parliaments, it also constrains party competition. The need for cross-party agreement if the political opposition controls the majority of the *Länder* in the *Bundesrat* favors consensus-seeking rather than competition and confrontation among the political parties (Lehmbruch 1976). While executive federalism may prevent territorial centralization, it promotes deparliamentarization. As we see in the next chapter, this ambivalent logic of executive federalism has been reinforced by Europeanization.

Fiscal solidarity: Vertical and horizontal equalization

The functional division of labor implies a strong decentralization of public tasks. Unless the *Länder* execute a task on behalf of the *Bund* (*Bundesauftragsverwaltung*), they have to bear the implementation costs themselves (Art. 104a GG). The more public tasks are decentralized, the more the differing spending power of the *Länder* becomes apparent. The *Länder* differ considerably in size, population, per capita income, and administrative capacity. The provision of similar living conditions therefore requires a fiscal system of vertical and horizontal equalization which allows for a balance of resources between the two levels of government as well as among the *Länder* themselves (Art. 106 GG).

Unlike the USA, German fiscal federalism does not favor competition in performing public tasks among the federal units, which have the right to levy their own taxes. Instead, the *Grundgesetz* opted for a combination of *Steuerverbund* (joint tax system) and *Finanzausgleich* (fiscal equalization). The most important taxes – income, corporation and turnover tax – are joint taxes, whose revenues *Bund* and *Länder* roughly share by half. The system of joint or shared taxes is completed by a financial equalization among the *Länder* (*Länderfinanzausgleich*), which levels out the differences in spending power among the *Länder*. The criteria for the resource transfer among the *Länder* are rather complicated and are beyond the scope of this book (see, however, Ellwein and Hesse 1987: 535–542).

The introduction of the joint tasks (*Gemeinschaftsaufgaben*) as an instrument of co-financing and mixed financing in 1969 further strengthened the fiscal interlocking of *Bund* and *Länder*. Joint tasks are concerned with economic and structural matters of general interest that require heavy public investments of the *Länder* and municipalities, above all in infrastructure projects. The joint tasks preview a financial participation of the *Bund* of at least 50%, depending on the task (Art, 91a IV GG; cf. Scharpf *et al.* 1976; Patzig 1981).

Multilateral bargaining and consensus-seeking as the dominant institutional culture of German federalism

The formal institutions of German federalism are embedded in an institutional culture which favors multilateral bargaining and consensus-seeking as the most appropriate behavior in territorial politics. This cooperative culture is reflected in the dominant approach of *Bund* and *Länder* to intergovernmental problem-solving and conflict resolution.

While at the "third level" (horizontal self-coordination of the *Länder*) all decisions have to be agreed unanimously, *Bundesrat* decisions are subject to majority rule. Yet, particularly at the working level where federal and *Länder* administrators hammer out political agreements before they enter the final decision-making process in the *Bundesrat*, there is a strong sense of conflict avoidance and consensus-seeking. In many *Bund–Länder* negotiations, decisions are taken unanimously even where formal rules and procedures would allow for majority or unilateral decisions (cf. Scharpf 1989). Moreover, *Länder* that would benefit from a particular policy outcome usually refrain from voting with the federal government as long as there is no almost unanimous agreement among all the *Länder* (Scharpf 1988; Renzsch 1995; cf. Scharpf *et al.* 1976). A situation in which the federal government is able to play off the interests of some *Länder* against the others is the exception rather than the rule. The *Länder* tend to be careful in forming coalitions with the *Bund* against the others. By cooperating at the "third level", the *Länder* try to find a common position which accommodates the interests of all and which is then negotiated with the *Bund* (cf. Scharpf 1989). Horizontal self-coordination among the *Länder* is facilitated by certain rules of appropriateness, like the rule of non-intervention according to which those *Länder* whose interests are not directly affected abstain from the decision-making process. A strong sense of *Länder* solidarity discourages individual *Länder* from defecting from a joint position once accepted by all *Länder*.

Conflict resolution between *Bund* and *Länder* also relies on intergovernmental agreement. Resorting to the Constitutional Court as an arbiter in *Bund–Länder* disputes has been the exception rather than the rule in German federalism. The number of intergovernmental conflicts taken to the Constitutional Court is low, particularly if compared with countries like Spain, Belgium or Italy (Blair 1991). Moreover, disputes between *Bund* and *Länder* are often not truly federal disputes but conflicts between political alignments within the federal state which are cast in the guise of federal disputes and settled by recourse to constitutional litigation (Hesse 1962; cf. Blair 1991).

One might argue that the institutional culture of multilateral bargaining and consensus-seeking is merely the outcome of the opportunities and constraints provided by the formal institutions of German federalism. The mutual resource dependency of *Bund* and *Länder* in public policy-making has certainly nourished a collective understanding of multilateral bargaining and consensus-seeking as the most appropriate way of intergovernmental problem-solving. At the same time, however, formal institutions often codify traditional shared meanings, norms and values. Moreover, while formal and informal institutions do not exist independently from each other, they differ in the way in which they affect actors' behavior. Thus, formal institutions may offer the *Länder* the opportunity (resources) to appeal to the Constitutional Court in order to solve intergovernmental problems or conflicts in their interest. However, although the *Länder* won most of the constitutional conflicts against the federal government, they prefer political solutions, even if this means timely bargaining and outcomes often being considered as ineffective (interview NRW$_{18}$; for details of this and other interviews, see Börzel 1999). Instrumental cost–benefit calculations do not always render court appeals prohibitive. Very often such considerations are, at best, indeterminate. The same is true for majority decisions or striking winning coalitions with the federal government against other *Länder*. Finally, non-cooperative strategies are usually only "a second-best choice" of the *Länder*, if considered at all (interview Bay$_{13}$). The aversion against open conflict, which is a general feature of German political culture (Sontheimer 1990), and the solidarity among the *Länder* render constitutional conflict, minimal winning coalitions with the federal government, and special deals negotiated between the federal government and only some *Länder* unacceptable.

Adapting to centralization: The *Länder* strategy of cooperation and cost-sharing

Centralization and its compensation-through-participation

The first 20 years of German federalism witnessed a process of subsequent centralization challenging the institutional autonomy of the *Länder*. A number of constitutional amendments between 1965 and 1976 transferred a substantial amount of regional legislative competencies to the federal level (cf. Barschel 1982; Klatt 1989).

The driving force of centralization has been the pressure for ever greater uniformity in the provision of government services, coordinated planning for efficient use of resources, and centralized overseeing of public expenditure having regard to the needs of economic management. The German *Länder* did not oppose the subsequent centralization of their legislative, and partly also administrative, competencies. The *Bundesrat* approved all constitutional amendments with the necessary two-thirds majority. Appeals to the Constitutional Court by the *Länder* against federal interventions into their sphere of competencies have been the exception rather than the rule. The *Länder* had come to accept their overall inability, particularly with respect to spending power, to deal adequately with certain responsibilities. The smaller or economically weaker *Länder* have always had a clear preference toward transferring cost-intensive public functions to the central-state level. The larger and wealthier *Länder*, on the contrary, would have favored fiscal redistribution to enable the *Länder* to fulfill even cost-intensive public functions. Yet, fiscal redistribution would have been only possible if the large differences in size and financial power between the *Länder* had been leveled out by a *Länderneugliederung* (territorial reorganization), which has been opposed by the smaller *Länder* for the last 50 years (Benz 1991a; Scharpf and Benz 1991). Given the heterogeneity of the *Länder*, on the one hand, and the normative prescription for uniform living conditions and *Länder* solidarity, on the other hand, centralization appeared to be the only solution.

At the same time, however, the larger *Länder* would not approve any expansion of federal competencies without being granted a co-decision right in the exercise of these at the central-state level. In order to protect their institutional autonomy vis-à-vis the central state, the *Länder* pursued a strategy of balancing their legislative competencies against participatory rights in federal decision-making on policies. Thus, *Bund* and *Länder* share the costs for ensuring uniform living conditions under circumstances of strong regional heterogeneity by substituting regional self-determination by co-decision. This "compensation-through-participation" strategy of the *Länder*, which constitutes a compromise between the concerns of the poorer and the richer *Länder*, has contributed considerably to the political and fiscal interlocking between *Bund* and *Länder*. Inversely, cooperative federalism allowed for such a strategy in the first place. Without the formal and informal institutions of vertical and horizontal intergovernmental cooperation, the subsequent expansion of *Länder* co-decision rights in federal decision-making would not only have caused policy inefficiencies, but also a major blockage and ultimate break-down of the whole federal system. At the same time, compensation-through-participation allowed the German federal system to maintain its institutional equilibrium without having to undergo fundamental reform (cf. Benz 1985).

"Gemeinsam sind wir stark": Regional coalition building vis-à-vis the federal government

The compensation-through-participation strategy as the response of the *Länder* to centralization has rested upon the *Länder* presenting a united front toward the federal government. Despite diverging interests, the *Länder* have attempted most of the time to present a joint position in negotiations with the central state instead of pursuing their individual interests bilaterally, at least when their institutional autonomy is at stake. From the very beginning, the *Kooperation auf der dritten Ebene* (cooperation at the third level) has been a major strategy of the *Länder* in protecting their institutional autonomy against encroachments of the central state; this has given rise to a whole range of institutions of horizontal self-coordination (cf. Pietzcker 1988).

The *Länder* cartel vis-à-vis the *Bund* has been stronger at some points in time and weaker at others; the level of strength has depended on the balance of power in the *Bundestag* and *Bundesrat* (cf. Scharpf 1991). German unification put *Länder* solidarity to a hard test. But the *Länder* ultimately formed an interest cartel vis-à-vis the *Bund* in the negotiations on the new regulations on fiscal equalization in 1993. They successfully pressed the *Bund* to pay a major contribution to financing German unification, instead of calling specifically on the financially strong *Länder* (Renzsch 1994). The recent appeal of Bavaria (Bayern), Baden-Württemberg, and Hesse (Hessen) before the Constitutional Court was not intended as an assault against the institution of fiscal equalization as such. Rather, the three financially strongest *Länder* resorted to the Constitutional Court in order to bring the *Länder* with lower spending power back to the negotiation table in order to settle for a more balanced redistribution of fiscal resources. By ruling the current system of fiscal equalization unconstitutional in November 1999, the Constitutional Court has forced the *Länder* to negotiate a political compromise; this was achieved in June 2001.[10]

---

[10] For earlier articles on this issue, see Ende der heiteren Gelassenheit; Tür zu Verhandlungen offen, *Süddeutsche Zeitung*, 12.11.1999; Geber und Nehmer sehen neue Chances, *Süddeutsche Zeitung*, 13.11.1999.

5 The *rinascimento* of cooperative federalism: The impact of Europeanization on the territorial institutions of Germany

This chapter demonstrates how, over a period of more than 40 years, the *Länder* have pulled together in pursuing a compensation-through-participation strategy in responding to the challenges of Europeanization. Their cooperative strategy facilitated a sharing of adaptational costs, which allowed for a flexible redressing of the territorial balance of power and resulted in a reinforcement and certain revival (*rinascimento*) of German cooperative federalism.

The double loss of competencies and the uneven distribution of "say and pay"

Europeanization is, alongside German unification, the most important challenge that cooperative federalism has been faced with so far. After the constitutional amendments in the 1960s and 1970s, the transfer of domestic competencies to the European caused the second major push toward territorial centralization. Unlike joint tasks and mixed financing, however, Europeanization entails a gradual erosion of regional autonomy, which increases as European integration proceeds. Moreover, Europeanization entails a twofold logic of centralization: the *Länder* lose competencies both at the regional and the federal level, which fundamentally alters the territorial balance of power in favor of the central state.

Like all institutionally well-entrenched regions, the *Länder* lose policy competencies in the area of their exclusive responsibilities as a consequence of Europeanization. Unlike in domestic policy-making, the *Länder* do not receive any compensation for such losses. Once their competencies are transferred to the European level, the *Länder* do not have any direct input on decisions taken in these areas. The number of exclusive *Länder* competencies is, however, rather small (culture, media, education, justice and home affairs). The *Länder* have been far more affected by the transfer of federal and shared competencies to the European level, because they are deprived of their co-determination rights in federal decision-making, which they exercise through the *Bundesrat*.

53

European Regulations have a direct impact, i.e. they do not require transposition into national law in which the *Bundesrat* could intervene if regional competencies were affected. European Directives must be transposed into domestic law. But *Bundestag* and *Bundesrat* have limited discretion in the legal implementation as European Directives set binding objectives and often provide very detailed regulations on how to implement these objectives. As in executive federalism, the role of the member-state legislatures is reduced to the formal ratification and practical application of European policies. They have hardly any formal influence on the formulation and decision-making of European policies. The *Bundesrat* as the Second Chamber of the German legislature used to have as little influence on European policy-making as the *Bundestag*.

But Europeanization does not only cause a twofold loss of self-determination and co-decision powers for the German *Länder*: Their double loss of competencies resulted in a "double shift of competencies" in favor of the central state (Hailbronner 1990: 149; cf. Ress 1986; Schröder 1986; Vitzthum 1990; Wiedmann 1992; Morawitz and Kaiser 1994).

First, Art. 24 I GG served as an *Integrationshebel* (Integration lever; Tomuschat 1988: 23), which allowed the *Bund* not only to transfer its own competencies but also shared and exclusive competencies of the *Länder* to the European level without even requiring the consent of the *Bundesrat*. When exclusive *Länder* competencies are Europeanized, the *Länder* are deprived of any formal influence on the exercise of these competencies. The *Bund*, however, whose executive represents Germany in the Council of the European Union and the European Council, is directly involved in the policy formulation and decision-making. As a result, the *Bund* gains access to regional competencies that the German Constitution placed beyond its reach. Europeanization allowed the *Bund*, for instance, to break into one of the last resorts of exclusive *Länder* competencies, the *Kulturhoheit* (cultural sovereignty).

Second, when federal or shared competencies are transferred to the European level in whose exercise the *Bundesrat* used to be involved, the formal input of the *Länder* is reduced from a co-determination right in formulation and decision-making (legal initiative and veto power) to mere participation in the implementation of European policies (ratification and practical application). The central state, however, which also loses decision-making power, still has a major influence on policy formulation and adoption through its representation in the Council of the European Union.

This double shift of *Länder* competencies led to a subsequent centralization, which applies to most policy areas since the vast majority of policy competencies are either shared or exclusive *Länder* competencies. The *Länder* have been particularly affected in culture, educational and vocational training, media, research and technology, transport, environment, regional and structural policy (cf. Blanke 1991: 242–249; Borkenhagen *et al.* 1992; Friebe 1992: 70–96).

But the *Länder* do not only lose decision-making competencies. Due to the functional distribution of labor in German federalism, the *Länder* have the responsibility for implementing the bulk of European policies (cf. Kössinger 1989). Europeanization must not change the internal distribution of competencies. Neither the *Integrationshebel* of Art. 24 I GG nor the federal foreign-policy prerogative of Art. 32 I GG legitimize a general competence of the *Bund* in the execution of European law. Unlike Spain, the federal government has never claimed such a general competence. The implementation of European policies follows the distribution of competencies in domestic policy-making, and hence falls under the general responsibility of the *Länder* (Art. 83ff. GG).[11] Yet, Europeanization has challenged the organization of policy implementation in Germany.

In domestic policy-making, the *Länder* enjoy a considerable legal and administrative discretion in implementation. More importantly, the *Länder* are usually involved in the policy formulation and decision-making of federal laws, which allows them to bring in both their administrative expertise and their interests. While the *Länder*, in principle, carry the burden of implementation, their participation in the formulation and decision-making stage offers the possibility of allocating implementation costs between the two levels. Rather than shifting the costs to the subordinate level, the *Bund* strives to share them with the *Länder*. First, federal policies that rest on the agreement of *Bund* and *Länder* are unlikely to incur prohibitive implementation costs. The *Länder* will not accept policies that impose costs they are not willing to bear, or for which they are not compensated. At the same time, joint decision-making grants a certain homogeneity in implementation across the *Länder*. Uniform implementation is also promoted by the horizontal self-coordination of the *Länder* in the practical application of policies. If the *Bund* does not provide for a uniform policy to be implemented by all *Länder*, the *Länder* strive to harmonize the rules for practical application and enforcement among themselves (Ossenbühl 1990: 159). Cooperative federalism prevents individual *Länder* from initiating policy implementation in order to gain a competitive advantage over other *Länder*.

---

[11] See Ipsen 1972: 220; Kössinger 1989: 46; Blanke 1991: 293–297.

Second, the *Bund* usually takes a share in the implementation costs. If the *Länder* carry out policies on behalf of the *Bund* (*Bundesauftragsverwaltung*), the *Bund* covers the expenses (Art. 104a II GG). Moreover, the joint tasks (*Gemeinschaftsaufgaben*) preview the co-financing of certain policies through the central state (Art. 91a; 104a IV GG). *Bund–Länder* programs may offer additional financial support for the realization of policies. However, *Bund* and *Länder* not only often share the financial burden; they also pool their expertise in the numerous *Bund–Länder* committees, which prepare the policies to be adopted by the *Bundestag* and *Bundesrat*.

The logic of European policy-making seriously undermines the principle of *Länder* discretion and "sharing the burden of implementation". On the one hand, the *Länder* have increasingly less discretion in implementing European policies. European Regulations do not allow the *Länder* to implement legislation as they see fit, contrary to the principles of German legislation (Art. 38 GG; cf. Bulmer and Paterson 1987: 190–191). With respect to the implementation of Directives, the European Commission has been striving to develop a proper administrative law, which is to harmonize administrative procedures as well as material principles of administrative law across the member states (Hailbronner 1990). The choice of how legally to implement European policies is only one example. Germany has been subject to several infringement procedures for not effectively implementing European law because German administration resorted to the traditional form of administrative directives (*Verwaltungsvorschriften*). The Commission successfully argued that administrative directives do not effectively implement European law as they are only internally binding and do not have a legal effect outside the administration (see Part IV). The *Bundesoberbehörden* and *Bundesanstalten*, proper bodies of Federal administration (Art. 87 III GG), which the *Bund* created in order to ensure its involvement in the execution of European law, also impinge on the discretion of the *Länder* in implementation (cf. Grabitz 1986).

On the other hand, the allocation of implementation costs in European policy-making is left to the member states. According to Art. 104a I GG, the *Länder* have to carry the financial burden in the implementation of European policies. There are three sorts of expenses which European policies may impose on the *Länder*. First, European policies can preview the obligatory (partial) financing through the member states; for example, the structural agriculture policy. Second, European policies can oblige the *Länder* to forgo certain revenue, like the fees for examining imported meat (*Einfuhruntersuchungsgebühren*). Germany brought four cases before the European Court of Justice (ECJ) to defend these fees because their abolition caused the *Länder* a loss of income of about

DM 40 million (US$ 17.9 million) per year (Morawitz 1981: 64–65). Third, the implementation of European policies imposes an additional work-load on the *Länder* administration, which can result in considerable costs. Not surprisingly, the *Länder* rejected the application of the domestic principle of burden allocation (*Lastenabgrenzung*) in European policy-making. They argued that the *Bund* had to pay for the implementation of European policies because the *Länder* did not participate in the decision-making process.[12] The federal government rejected this legal point of view (cf. Morawitz 1981: 13–14).

Finally, as the *Länder* have no veto in the formulation and decision-making of European policies, their interests are not systematically accommodated. The *Länder* have no opportunity effectively to prevent European policies that impose significant costs for them in their implementation. For obvious reasons, European policies do not allow for the kind of side-payments and issue linkages that could compensate the *Länder* for their implementation costs.

The erosion of the federal state?

Both a nucleus of autonomous jurisdiction (*Hausgut*) and the participation of the *Länder* in central-state decision-making constitute the essence of the state quality of the German *Länder*, which is subject to the "eternity clause" (*Ewigkeitsgarantie*) of the German Constitution (Art. 79 III GG). Most legal scholars agree that Europeanization has challenged both elements of the state quality of the *Länder*. But the Federal Constitutional Court and the German jurisprudence (Haas 1988; Bethge 1989; Kewenig 1990) have not found any unconstitutional intrusion of the European Union in the *Hausgut* of the *Länder* yet.

Whether Europeanization ultimately undermines the state quality of the *Länder*, and hence the substance of the German Federal State as a whole, is a legal question. From the perspective of the approach taken in this study, the subsequent erosion of the formal co-determination powers of the *Länder* is the most serious challenge which Europeanization poses to cooperative federalism. This is not because it reduces the state quality of the *Länder per se*, but because it undermines the territorial balance of power and, hence, the overall stability of cooperative federalism. As pointed out in the previous chapter, the institutional equilibrium of the German federal system has rested on the possibility of counterbalancing territorial centralization by regional co-determination. Whenever *Länder* competencies are transferred to the federal level, the *Länder* are

---

[12] *BR-Drs. 600/73, vom 30.11.1973.*

compensated through the participation of the *Bundesrat* in the formulation of and decision-making on federal policies. Reducing formal codetermination powers of the *Länder* to the implementation of European policies significantly devalues this compensation. Joint policy formulation and decision-making is replaced by joint implementation. The formal exclusion of the *Länder* from the formulation and decision-making of European policies constitutes a serious misfit between European and domestic institutions. The loss of formal decision-making powers both at the federal and the regional level results in a significant redistribution of power, altering the territorial balance of power in favor of the central state.

"The *Länder* strike back"[13]

From the very beginning of European integration the German *Länder* had been aware of the danger of losing institutional autonomy. As early as 1951 the *Minister-President* (Prime Minister) of North Rhine–Westphalia, Karl Arnold, warned the *Länder* that they could lose their state quality and find themselves degraded to purely administrative units of the central state as a consequence of European integration.[14] Despite this early warning, it took the *Länder* more than 30 years to bring Europe-induced centralization to a halt.

"Rein in" versus "Roll back":
The compensation-through-participation strategy

The *Länder* had two basic options in redressing the territorial balance of power that was undermined by Europeanization. They could pursue a non-cooperative strategy of "rolling back" Europeanization (Jeffery and Yates 1993). The "roll back" strategy of the *Länder* would be based on, first, the attempt to ring-fence their nucleus of autonomous responsibilities as well as their co-decision powers in federal policy-making by demanding a strict separation of European, national and regional competencies in the application of the principle of subsidiarity. Moreover, the *Länder* would appeal to the Federal Constitutional Court against intrusions of the *Bund* in their sphere of competencies. Likewise, they would use the right to appeal to the European Court of Justice against intrusions by the EU. And, second, the *Länder* would try to circumvent the federal government in European policy-making by establishing direct,

---

[13] Jeffery 1994.
[14] Proceedings of the sessions of the *Bundesrat*, 27.7.1951: 445.

unmediated access to the European policy arena through direct bilateral or multilateral contacts with European institutions.

Alternatively, the *Länder* could opt for a cooperative strategy of "reining in" Europeanization. The *Länder* would ask the *Bund* to compensate their costs of Europeanization (power losses and implementation costs) by sharing with them its decision powers in European policy-making as well as the costs of implementing European policies. The *Länder* would essentially push for comprehensive co-decision rights in the formulation and representation of the German bargaining position. Such a "rein in" or "compensation-through-participation" strategy presupposes the cooperation of the *Länder* with the federal government as well as among each other.

The *Länder* have sufficient resources to pursue both strategies. Their spending power and administrative capacity enable the *Länder* to establish direct channels of access to the European policy arena. Unlike many regions of other member states, the *Länder* not only have the organizational strength to be present at the European level, but they also have a lot of expertise and information that they can offer to European institutions in exchange for access to the policy process. Moreover, the *Bund* has no legal right to prevent the *Länder* from maintaining direct contact with European institutions, as long as they do not claim diplomatic status. Finally, direct participation in European policy-making appears increasingly legitimate in light of the emerging idea of the "Europe of the Regions", forcefully promoted by the European Commission and the European Parliament in the 1980s (see below).

At the same time, their participation in federal policy-making through the *Bundesrat* and other institutions of joint decision-making provides the *Länder* with the tool box as well as the experience to make a "rein in" strategy work. They can draw on already existing mechanisms of intergovernmental cooperation to participate in the formulation and representation of the German bargaining position. The "rein in" strategy would also follow the general practice in German federalism of compensating regional losses of competencies through co-determination powers.

The veto power of the *Länder* in ratifying European treaties gives them a powerful tool to push either strategy. As we will see, both strategies have been present in the attempt of the *Länder* to protect their institutional autonomy against Europeanization and to redress the territorial balance of power. Yet, from the very start of European integration, the "rein in" or "compensation-through-participation" strategy has clearly prevailed. The "roll back" strategy was only seriously considered by the *Länder* in the 1980s and has never been carried through.

1951–1986: The dominance of the Bund *in European policy-making*

Even before the ratification of the Treaty of the European Coal and Steel Community (ECSC), the *Bundesrat* had already demanded its participation in the definition of the German bargaining position.[15] A corresponding initiative of the conservative coalition, however, was defeated in the *Bundestag* (Jaspert 1988: 92). Instead, Chancellor Adenauer agreed to inform a subcommittee of the *Bundesrat* about ongoing issues in the ECSC and to consult (individual) *Länder* if their specific interests were affected.[16] And while particularly those *Länder*, along with the coal and steel industry, had hoped to have some influence on the decisions of the High Commission and the Council of Ministers, Adenauer only informally committed himself to consulting those *Länder* on the appointment of one of the two German members of the High Commission.

Prior to the negotiations on the Treaty of Rome, the *Bundesrat* repeated its claims to the right of being consulted by the federal government in the formulation of the German bargaining position.[17] As in 1951 the federal government rejected the claims as an unconstitutional intervention into its foreign policy prerogative. But the *Länder* were allowed to participate in the negotiations by being permitted to send two representatives as part of the German delegation; these representatives enjoyed observer status (Stöger 1988: 102). After the conclusion of the Treaty of Rome, the federal government agreed to notify the *Bundesrat* on European issues according to its obligation under Art. 53 (3) GG to inform the *Bundesrat* and *Bundestag* on the ongoing affairs of the government. The *Länder* were granted a first formal right to information on European policy-making; this was institutionalized through the *Zuleitungsverfahren* (information procedure) in Art. 2 of the law ratifying the Treaty of Rome.

The Zuleitungsverfahren *of 1957:*   According to the *Zuleitungsverfahren*, the federal government was obliged to constantly inform *Bundestag* and *Bundesrat* about ongoing developments at the European level. If a European decision required transposition into German law or deployed a direct legal effect at the domestic level, the *Bundesrat* had to be notified before the decision was taken in the Council of Ministers. The federal government would transmit all Community proposals (500–600 per year) in order to give the *Bundesrat* the opportunity to make recommendations. These recommendations were not binding, but the federal

---

[15] *61. Sitzung des Bundesrates vom 27.7.1951, BR-Drs. 470/51 Ziff. 5 vom 27.7.1951.*
[16] *Sitzungsbericht des Bundesrates vom 1.2.1952: Ziff. VI.*
[17] *BR-Drs. 146/57 vom 3.5.1957.*

government had to take them into account according to the principle of Federal Comity.

Although not granting the *Länder* much influence, the *Zuleitungsverfahren* laid the foundations for the further participation of the *Länder* in European policy-making. It already carried the major weakness of intrastate participation: the disempowerment of the *Länder* parliaments. The *Zuleitungsverfahren* as well as any subsequent participatory procedure did not provide for any role of the *Länder* legislatures. From the very beginning the *Länder* participation in European policy-making has been monopolized by the *Länder* executives. Europeanization was to become a major factor in promoting deparliamentarization at the regional level.

The Länder *Observer:* The first official representation of the *Länder* at the European level was the *Länderbeobachter* (*Länder* Observer) whose position was created in 1957. For more than 30 years, the existence of the *Länder* Observer was not formally established, but was based on a "gentlemen's agreement". It was not until 1988 that the *Länder* signed an agreement to regulate formally the tasks, the organizational structure and the financing of the *Länder* Observer (cf. Morawitz and Kaiser 1994: 128). The *Länder* Observer is appointed by the Conference of Ministers on Economic Affairs of the *Länder*. His/her main task is to inform the *Länder* as early as possible about all developments at the European level that could have an impact on them. He/she can participate in the sessions of the Council of Ministers and other European decision-making bodies as a passive member (neither voice nor vote) of the German delegation. He/she also takes part in meetings organized by the Federal Ministry of Economic Affairs that prepare the German bargaining position for the Council meetings. Even though he/she is a member of the German delegation, the *Bund* has no authority over the *Länder* Observer. With the *Länder-beteiligungsverfahren* of 1979 (see below) the *Länder* Observer became the official focal point for the exchange of information between *Bund* and *Länder*. He/she receives all the Council documents at the same time as member-state governments. The federal government sends him/her draft documents for the Council meetings as well as reports on the results of the meetings. The *Länder* Observer reports to the *Bundesrat* on the meetings of the European decision-making bodies and informs the respective committees of the *Bundesrat* and the *Länder*. He/she is also the official interlocutor of the *Länder* with the European Commission. As a member of the German delegation, the *Länder* Observer enjoys official status and the formal support of the federal government when dealing with European institutions (Morawitz 1981: 33).

The *Länder* Observer provides the *Länder* with access to virtually all the information officially available to the federal government. Through his/her participation in the European decision-making body, the *Länder* have control over whether the federal government takes their views into consideration and whether the reasons given for a derogation are justified. Nevertheless, the role of the *Länder* Observer is often characterized as "very modest" (Strohmeier 1988: 635) due to his/her limited resources (cf. Morass 1994: 110–113). Since the *Länder* received extensive access to European decision-making bodies in 1992, they have further curtailed the resources of their Observer.[18]

Independent of the *Zuleitungsverfahren*, *Bund* and *Länder* started to debate practical issues of intergovernmental cooperation in the area of foreign policy. The so-called *Kramer/Heubel* consultations, which took place between 1964 and 1967, resulted in an informal agreement in which the federal government committed itself to the participation of *Länder* representatives in international negotiations as members of the German delegation, if their competencies or essential interests were affected. In theory, the agreement also enabled the *Länder* to participate in European Community (EC) negotiations if issues fell under their exclusive responsibilities. But it was never applied in European policy-making (Morawitz and Kaiser 1994: 52). Rather, *Bund* and *Länder* started to develop an informal practice in the 1970s which provided ample participation of *Länder* representatives in decision-making on various European issues, also in areas outside the exclusive *Länder* competencies.[19] Before 1992 the *Länder* formally had only a passive status; however, in practice their representatives were often allowed to participate actively in the EU decision-making bodies (with voice but without vote; Birke 1973: 44). In 1983 *Länder* representatives also gained access to the Council of Ministers (Culture and Education).[20]

Although the *Zuleitungsverfahren* developed into substantial cooperation between *Bund* and *Länder* on European issues (cf. Ziller 1986), it was ultimately no more than the application of the constitutional obligation of the federal government to inform the *Bundesrat* on its activities (Art. 53 (3) GG). The procedure did not constitute substantial participation. Moreover, the *Länder* made the criticism that the federal government did not provide them with comprehensive information on negotiations in Brussels, as a result of which the recommendations of the *Bundesrat*

---

[18] *Beschluß der Europaministerkonferenz vom 4. Juni 1997* (http://www.europaminister.de).
[19] For an overview, see Morawitz 1981: 42–55.
[20] Protocol Declaration of the Federal Chancellor of May 19, 1983 on the occasion of a conference of the heads of government of *Bund* and *Länder* on the "Solemn Declaration on the European Union".

often came too late or did not reflect the current stage of the negotiations. The *Länder* also complained that the federal government frequently ignored the recommendations of the *Bundesrat* altogether (Jaspert 1988). Finally, the *Länder* had great difficulties in processing the floods of information that they received from the Commission, the Council, the federal government and the *Länder* Observer (Hannaleck and Schumann 1983; Oschatz and Risse 1988). In 1977 the *Länder* therefore requested negotiations with the federal government with the aim of establishing more effective participation of the *Länder* in European policy-making; this resulted in the *Länderbeteiligungsverfahren* of 1979.

The Länderbeteiligungsverfahren *of 1979:* In September 1975 the *Länder* established a working group to examine *Bund–Länder* cooperation on European issues affecting the exclusive competencies of the *Länder*. With Bavaria taking the lead, six *Länder* prepared a proposal for an agreement with the *Bund*, which the Conference of Minister-Presidents approved in Munich in October 1976. In order to prevent the centralization of their autonomous competencies at the federal level, the *Länder* essentially requested a determining influence on the formulation of the German bargaining position if their autonomous competencies were affected. They backed their demand by referring to the *Lindauer Abkommen* (Lindan Agreement) of 1957 (cf. Morawitz 1981: 14–25).[21] The *Bund* rejected these claims on the grounds of its exclusive competence for European integration (Art. 24 I GG) and its foreign policy prerogative (Art. 32 I GG). Despite this fundamental disagreement, *Bund* and *Länder* were able to negotiate a pragmatic solution.

After two years of negotiations, an exchange between Chancellor Schmidt and the Head of the Conference of Minister-Presidents, Johannes Rau, established a legally *non*-binding procedure, which gave the *Länder* the possibility of formulating joint recommendations on European issues which fell under their exclusive responsibility. The federal government was only allowed to depart from these recommendations for irrefutable reasons affecting foreign and integration policy goals, and these reasons had to be communicated to the *Länder*. The federal government would also inform the *Länder* of all Community initiatives (not only official proposals) affecting their exclusive competencies as soon as possible. Finally, in these cases, the *Bund* would allow two *Länder*

---

[21] The *Lindauer Abkommen* refers to cases in which international agreements affect exclusive *Länder* competencies. As the *Bund* has the foreign-policy prerogative, the *Länder* delegate their competencies to the *Bund* so that it can exercise them on their behalf in concluding international agreements. However, the *Bund* has to have the unanimous consent of the *Länder*.

delegates to participate in the consultative bodies of the Commission and the Council working groups whenever it was possible and the *Länder* wished to participate.

Since the *Länderbeteiligungsverfahren* applied to issues subject to exclusive *Länder* competencies, the *Länder* had to agree on a joint position by unanimity; this is in contrast to the *Bundesrat* where decisions are taken by majority. The high requirement for consensus and the complicated process of horizontal coordination rendered the new procedure ineffective. Between 1979 and 1986, the *Länder* formulated 37 recommendations of which only one was transmitted to the federal government (Einert 1986: 44–45; Morawitz 1988: 46–49).

All in all, during the first 30 years of European integration, the *Länder* had succeeded in subsequently expanding their rights to information, consultation, and participation in European policy-making. The increasing involvement of the *Länder* in European policy-making was the result of a consequent "rein in" strategy of "compensation-through-participation". Unlike the Spanish regions, the *Länder* have never contested the exclusive right of the *Bund* (federal government) to represent Germany at the European level. Hence, the *Länder* have not requested an independent representation at the European negotiation table. The participation of *Länder* representatives in European decision-making bodies is exclusively mediated through the central state since they are members of the German delegation. Nor have the *Länder* challenged the exclusive competence of the *Bund* to transfer their competencies to the European level.

While the *Länder* appeared willing to accept the Europeanization of their autonomous jurisdiction, they opposed the centralization of their competencies at the federal level. But instead of ring-fencing their competencies, the *Länder* continuously pushed for formal co-determination rights in defining the German bargaining position whenever European issues affected their competencies or essential interests. The *Bund*, in turn, rejected the right of the *Länder* to make binding recommendations, citing its foreign-policy prerogative. Despite a serious conflict of interests, similar to those between the Spanish government and the *Comunidades Autónomas*, the *Länder* did not resort to the Constitutional Court to settle the issue. Nor did individual *Länder* start to circumvent the central state by trying to establish direct, extrastate relations with European institutions as an alternative to their multilateral intrastate participation in European policy-making (see below). Rather, *Bund* and *Länder* informally agreed on pragmatic cooperation on European affairs.

In sum, the *Länder* pursued a "rein in" or "compensation-through-participation" strategy, which they successfully used to expand their influence on European policy-making in order to redress the territorial balance of power. Yet, by the beginning of the 1980s, the *Länder* had still not achieved formal and binding participatory rights in European policy-making, which they considered necessary as an adequate compensation for their losses (Morawitz and Kaiser 1994: 52). The *Bund* had dominated the *Länder* in European policy-making throughout the first 30 years of European integration (cf. Börzel 1997). The largely informal level of information, consultation, and participation, which the *Länder* had enjoyed in European policy-making until 1986, was by no means sufficient to compensate them for their double loss of formal decision-making rights at the domestic level. As a result, Europeanization significantly changed the territorial balance of power in favor of the central state by undermining the institutional autonomy of the *Länder*.

However, Europeanization did not only alter the territorial balance of power between *Bund* and *Länder*. It also affected the relationship between executive and legislature. While the *Länder* had not been able to achieve full compensation for their losses of power, their information and consultation rights as well as their informal participation constituted the first steps in redressing the territorial balance of power. Yet, these first inceptions of intrastate participation were exclusively limited to the *Länder* executives. The *Länder* parliaments (*Landtage*) had no role to play in European policy-making. Nor was the exclusion of the *Landtage* considered to be a problem at the time. The issue of deparliamentarization emerged only after the conclusion of the Single European Act.

1986–87: Starting to get even

Although not required by the German Constitution (before 1992), the federal government requested the *Bundesrat* to ratify the treaty reforms concluded in the Single European Act (SEA). The *Länder* decided to use their veto power as a window of opportunity to push through their demands for "real," that is formal and binding, participatory rights in European policy-making. For the very first time, the *Länder* officially took the offensive against the federal government by linking their consent on the ratification of the SEA in the *Bundesrat* to the institutionalization of a series of participatory rights in European policy-making, which the *Länder* had jointly formulated and adopted in the *Bundesrat*.[22] The *Länder* justified their claims on the grounds that, again, the federal government in the negotiations on the Treaty reform had not consulted them. More importantly, they perceived the transfer of

---

[22] *BR-Drs. 150/86 vom 16.5.1986.*

competencies decided in the SEA as a serious threat to their state quality.[23]

Despite their veto threat, the *Länder* did not fully succeed in pushing through their joint demands (see below). After a heated debate with the *Länder* on its foreign-policy prerogative, the federal government was, however, finally willing to acknowledge that European policy could no longer be classified as traditional foreign policy. This made room for a formal participation of the *Länder* in European policy-making (Morawitz and Kaiser 1994: 66). The German law ratifying the SEA[24] introduced the *Bundesratverfahren*, a formal procedure which would allow for an intrastate participation of the *Länder* in European policy-making organized exclusively through the *Bundesrat*. The federal government was obliged to comprehensively inform the *Bundesrat* as early as possible regarding all issues of *Länder* interest. Instead of an informal hearing, the *Bundesrat* was entitled to make formal recommendations on European issues that affected the exclusive jurisdiction or essential concerns of the *Länder*. The federal government could depart from these recommendations only for irrefutable reasons of foreign or integration policy goals that had to be justified in the *Bundesrat*. Finally, the federal government had to call in *Länder* representatives to negotiations in European decision-making bodies if the *Bundesrat* had the right to make a recommendation.

In order to deal with urgent or confidential Community proposals, the *Bundesrat* established a special "EC Chamber" (*Kammer für die Vorlagen der Europäischen Gemeinschaft*) in 1988. The EC Chamber constitutes a "*Bundesrat en miniature*" (Haas 1988: 619), which can convene within one week and is allowed to take decisions for the *Bundesrat* plenum (cf. Oschatz and Risse 1989). The EC Chamber is dedicated to dealing exclusively with European issues and is as such a unique institution in German federalism.

The *Bundesratverfahren* was a major step in redressing the territorial balance of power upset by Europeanization. For the first time, the *Länder* received formal participatory rights in European policy-making. But it was only the *Länder* executives that would benefit from these new powers. The *Landtage* were, again, the real losers of Europeanization because they did not gain any role in European policy-making.

By forming a unified front against the federal government in the *Bundesrat*, the *Länder* had been able to push through negotiations on their

---

[23] See the various debates in the *Bundesrat* on the SEA (*BR-Drs. 31/86 vom 31.1.1986; BR-Drs. 50/86 vom 21.2.1986; BR-Drs. 150/86 vom 16.5.1986*; cf. Stoiber 1987; Engholm 1989).

[24] *Gesetz vom 19. Dezember 1986 zur Einheitlichen Europäischen Akte vom 28. Februar 1986 (EEA-G), BGBl. 1986 II: 1102.*

formal participation in European policy-making. While having fought a
first political victory against the *Bund*, the *Länder* lost the battle in the public debate. Politicians and academic observers alike heavily criticized the
Länder for their *Kleinstaaterei* (particularism) and *Provinzialismus* (provin-
cialism). Some even accused the *Länder* of *Integrationsfeindlichkeit* (hostility toward European integration).[25] The European Commission also
voiced doubts about *Länder* support for European integration.[26] The
Länder Junktim (conditional link) between the ratification of the SEA
and more participatory rights did not only lead to a heated debate with
the federal government: The *Länder* felt themselves exposed to a *"Sturm
der Entrüstung"* (an "outcry of indignation") in the public media, where
people talked about *"Nebenaußenpolitik, von europafeindlich, von Kleinstaaterei, von Kirchturmspolitik, von Obstruktion [und] von ersehnter Sper-
rfunktion des Bundesrates in EG-Angelegenheiten"*.[27]

While *Bund* and *Länder* finally reached an agreement, the *Länder* did
not succeed in obtaining legally binding co-decision rights in European
policy-making. The federal government was obliged only to give the
Bundesrat recommendations due consideration. Nor did the *Länder* obtain a veto right on the transfer of domestic competencies to the European
level. Due to the general public support for the SEA in Germany, on the
one hand (Platzer and Ruhland 1994: 28–32), and the strong public criticism of the *Länder Junktim*, on the other hand, the *Länder* could simply
not veto the SEA ratification.

For the first time, the *Länder* strategy, in responding to the challenges
of Europeanization, showed some conflicting elements. Yet, the principal components of the compensation-through-participation strategy remained unchanged. The *Länder* used their veto power in negotiations with
the federal government only to push for more participatory rights, that
is, cooperation with the federal government. Their veto threat was only
credible if the *Länder* formulated a joint position which they would jointly

---

25 See Noch mehr Köche, *Kölner Stadtanzeiger*, 23.4.1986; Degenerierter Föderalismus, *Die Welt*, 10.5.1986; Hrbek, Rudolf: Die Bundesländer im Bremserhäus-
chen, *Europäische Zeitung*, 1.5.1986; Zundel, Rolf; Das doppelte Lottchen in Brüssel,
Die Zeit, 15.5.1986; Wieder Kleinstaaterei, *Handelsblatt*, 20.5.1986; Eschenburg,
Theodor: Bundesstaat im Staatenbund. Bahnt sich ein Verfassungskonflikt an?, *Die Zeit*,
24.10.1986; Hellwig 1987; Hrbek 1986, 1987; Meier 1987; Nass 1986; Delors 1988;
Magiera 1988.
26 Jacques Delors in his speech to the *Länder* Minister-Presidents on May 19, 1988, published in: Europa Archiv 41, 12: D 341–343 (341).
27 Minister Einert in the *Bundesrat* session of May 16, 1986, *Protokoll: 303*. See also *BR-
Sitzung vom 19.12.1986, Protokoll (Anlage): 755*). In order to refute reproaches of *Integrationsfeindlichkeit*, the *Länder* repeatedly referred to their commitments to European
integration (Minister Schmidhuber, *BR-Sitzung vom 31.1.1986, Protokoll: 31*; Minister
Einert, Senator Kahns and Minister Hahn, *BR-Sitzung vom 21.2.1986, Protokoll: 108,
109 and 113*).

defend vis-à-vis the federal government. The reason why the *Länder* nevertheless did not fully succeed with their claims was not the weakness of the *Länder* coalition (note that in 1986 the incumbent conservative party of Chancellor Kohl also controlled the majority of the *Länder* governments): It was the heavy public criticism as well as the general aversion to conflict in German intergovernmental relations that prevented the *Länder* from exercising their veto power in the ratification of the SEA.

Experience with the ratification of the SEA had important implications for the strategy that the *Länder* subsequently pursued in their attempt to redress the territorial balance of power. In 1992 they would again invoke their veto power in the ratification of the Maastricht Treaty in order to push for legally binding participatory rights in European policy-making. Yet, for the first time, the *Länder* employed a two-fold strategy; this strategy complemented their previous strategy of "reining in" with some elements of "rolling back".

1992–93: Redressing the territorial balance of power

In order to be not passed over again in a major revision of the European Treaties, as early as 1990 the *Länder* formulated a catalogue of demands, which they presented to the federal government to take into account in negotiations on the Maastricht Treaty. The various *Länder* statements on the revision of the European Treaties were prepared by the *Länder Staats- und Senatskanzleien* (state chancelleries), were debated and adopted by the Conference of *Länder* Minister-Presidents, and were formally decided by the *Bundesrat*. The *Länder* essentially presented the federal government with five major points upon which they made conditional the ratification of the Treaty revisions in the *Bundesrat*:

1. the inclusion of the principle of subsidiarity in the EU Treaty;
2. the creation of a regional body at European level (equivalent to the recognition of the regions as a third level of government of the European Union);
3. the right of the regions to appeal to the European Court of Justice (ECJ) in case of violations of their jurisdiction by the EU;
4. the direct participation of regional representatives in the Council of Ministers; and
5. the participation of the *Länder* in the Intergovernmental Conference.[28]

---

[28] See the following decisions of the *Bundesrat*: *BR-Drs. 198/90*; *BR-Drs. 220/90*; *BR-Drs. 550/90*; *BR-Drs. 780/90*; *BR-Drs. 680/91*.

The catalogue of *Länder* demands reflected a change in strategy in two respects. First, the principle of subsidiarity, the regional body, and the right of the regions to appeal to the ECJ would provide a barrier against the "self-aggrandizing" tendencies of the Community in (over)using its competencies. This constituted a "roll back" element, which was new to the strategy of the German *Länder*.

Second, the *Länder* extended their "rein in" strategy to the European level by requesting a general participation of all regions in European policy-making through a proper institution of regional representation. The demand for an active political participation of the regions in European integration was based on the idea that both the efficiency and legitimacy of European policy-making could be increased only by building a "Europe of the Regions", which implied a strengthening of the regions as the "third level" of the European Union.[29]

The Europeanization of their compensation-through-participation strategy was an attempt by the *Länder* to prevent a similar wave of criticism to that which they had faced when they had linked the ratification of the SEA to their demands for legally binding co-decision rights in European policy-making. By embedding their claims in the broader concept of a "Europe of the Regions", the *Länder* not only avoided the impression that their demands were particularistic claims of the German regions (*deutsche Sonderwünsche*), but they were also able to mobilize additional support for their claims from other regions as well as the European Commission and the European Parliament.

On the one hand, the *Länder* took advantage of the increasing responsiveness of EC institutions toward regional interests. When the President of the Commission, Jacques Delors, met the *Länder* Minister-Presidents in 1988, he assured them that he was a "defender of the principle of subsidiarity" and that the EC had a "vital interest in the preservation of the German federal system" (Delors 1988: D 338; my translation). In 1988, the European Parliament passed the Community Charter on Regionalization, which called for a comprehensive regionalization of the member states. The member states were asked to establish or maintain the regions as a third level of government which should adequately participate in the domestic formulation of the national bargaining position and whose competencies would be respected in European policy-making.[30] The *Länder* repeatedly referred to the Community Charter in the formulation of their demands for the Intergovernmental Conference[31] while

---

[29] Cf. Späth 1989; Rau 1990; Clement 1991; Teufel 1992.
[30] OJ C 326, 19/12/1988: 296–301.
[31] *BR-Drs. 279/89; BR-Drs. 550/90.*

the European Parliament adopted the four general claims of the *Länder* in its resolutions on the Intergovernmental Conference.[32]

On the other hand, the *Länder* strove to gain support for their demands from the regions in other member states. The Bavarian Minister-President Streibel initiated the "European Conference of the Regions", which was designed as a forum for institutionally well-entrenched regions such as the German *Länder*, the Spanish *Comunidades Autónomas*, or the Belgian regions. At their first meeting in Munich on October 18–19, 1989, the Conference adopted a resolution that contained the key demands of the German *Länder* for the Intergovernmental Conference (IGC).[33] The resolution of the third Conference of October 25, 1990[34] is largely the same as the resolution that the *Bundesrat* adopted on August 24, 1990 on the IGC.[35] The Assembly of the Regions in Europe also passed a similar resolution on September 6, 1990 on the institutional participation of the regional level in European policy-making.[36]

All in all, the *Länder* succeeded in framing their demands for a broader and more effective participation in European policy-making as part of a "Europe of the Regions" concept, which stood as a remedy against the centralism of the Brussels bureaucracy as well as a means for achieving greater democracy and transparency in general. The "Europe of the Regions" not only gained the support of the European Commission and the European Parliament: After the negative reactions to the Maastricht Treaty in Denmark and France, the European Council also recognized the importance of the "Europe of the Regions" and the principle of subsidiarity in promoting democracy and transparency in the European Union.[37]

Despite initial objections from the federal government, the *Länder* managed to participate in both the formulation of the German bargaining position and the negotiation process for the Maastricht Treaty, except for the final decision-making stage in the European Council (cf. Borchmann and Kaiser 1992; Kalbfleisch-Kottsieper 1993). Due to pressure from the *Länder*, the federal government brought the principle of subsidiarity

---

[32] See the resolution of the European Parliament of July 11, 1990 (Colombo Report and Martin Report), OJ C 231, 11/7/1990: 95–101 and the resolution of the European Parliament on the Second Conference of the European Parliament on "Regions of Europe", Strasbourg, November 27–29, 1991, which contains the four general claims of the *Länder* for the IGC (4 DOC/DE/RRdececonf.2de: ciff. 5–7).

[33] The resolution is published in Borchmann 1990.

[34] The resolution is published in Hrbek and Weyand 1994: Appendix 5.

[35] *BR-Drs. 550/90 vom 24.8.1990.*

[36] The resolution is published in Hrbek and Weyand 1994: Appendix 4.

[37] "Resolution on Transparency and Democracy in the Community" of the European Council, Birmingham, October 18, 1992 (Conclusion of the Presidency, Appendix 1: Point 4).

and the European body of regional representation onto the negotiating agenda. It refused, however, to place the other two *Länder* demands – court access for the regions and direct access of regional representatives to the Council of Ministers – on the agenda, arguing that those were particularistic German claims. The final issue, however, was introduced into the negotiations by Belgium – as a result of pressure from the Belgian regions (Borchmann and Kaiser, 1992: 42–43).

Having prepared the ground by calling for a general participation of the regions in European policy-making, when the Maastricht Treaty came up for ratification, the *Länder* presented their demands for constitutional co-determination rights in the formulation and representation of the German bargaining position in European decision-making. Although both *Bund* and *Länder* considered the participation of the *Länder* through the *Bundesratverfahren* to be effective,[38] the *Länder* argued that only binding participatory rights provided adequate compensation for the Europeanization of their competencies.[39] Amendments to the Basic Law which became necessary after German unification and the conclusion of the Maastricht Treaty provided a window of opportunity to the *Länder* to maximize their claims, because any change to the Basic Law has to be approved by a majority of two-thirds in the *Bundesrat*.

The new "*Europa-Artikel*" of the Basic Law – Art. 23 revised (n.F.) GG – provides the *Länder* with comprehensive, legally binding co-determination powers in EU policy-making. For the first time, the transfer of both national and regional competencies to the EU requires the consent of the *Bundesrat*. A majority of two-thirds in the *Bundestag* and *Bundesrat* has to ratify any changes to the EU Treaty, or similar regulations. Unlike in the *Bundesratverfahren* of 1987, the federal government is not only obliged to give *Bundesrat* recommendations due consideration in cases where the *Länder* would participate in the decision on a corresponding domestic issue. The same also applies to European issues that fall under exclusive federal competencies but affect *Länder* interests. Most importantly, when former administrative or legislative *Länder* competencies are involved, the *Bundesrat* has the final decision on the German bargaining position in the Council of Ministers. And whenever exclusive legislative competencies of the *Länder* are at issue, a *Länder* minister represents Germany in the Council negotiations as the head of the German delegation. Moreover, the Law on the Cooperation between *Bund* and

---

[38] *Erfahrungsbericht der Bevollmächtigten der Länder beim Bund über das Beteiligungsverfahren nach Art. 2 EEA-G vom 16.5.1990* (cf. Engholm 1989; Engel and Borrmann 1991); for the federal government see Minister of State Seiters during the session of the *Bundesrat* on November 9, 1990 (*Protokoll: 623*).

[39] For references, see the *Länder* statements on the Intergovernmental Conference quoted in fn. 19.

Länder in European Affairs (EUZBLG), which specifies the provisions of Art. 23 n.F. GG, grants the *Bundesrat* the right to request the federal government to appeal to the European Court of Justice on behalf of the *Länder* if their competencies are affected by the (non-)action of European institutions. The Law also provides a legal basis for direct contact that the *Länder* maintain with European institutions. The *Länder* are allowed to establish official representations in Brussels, which, must not, however, have diplomatic status. Finally, the Law formalizes the right of the *Länder* to participate in the working groups and committees of the Council and the Commission, which, before the Law, had been largely dependent on the goodwill of the federal government.

All in all, the *Länder* finally achieved all the powers that they had considered necessary as a compensation for the Europeanization of their competencies. Despite some criticism of the *Länder* demands, in particular of their threat to veto the Maastricht Treaty,[40] the *Länder* did not face reproaches of *Integrationsfeindlichkeit* (hostility toward European integration) this time.

The new Art. 23 GG redressed the territorial balance of power (see below). It also upgraded the role of the upper chamber of the German parliament, the *Bundestag*, in European policy-making by granting it formal rights to information and participation, which are, however, less powerful than those of the *Bundesrat*. The losers were, once again, the *Länder* parliaments. After the conclusion of the SEA, the *Landtage* finally raised the issue of deparliamentarization at the regional level as a consequence of Europeanization. They began several initiatives to gain influence on the co-decision rights of the *Länder* (executives) in European policy-making.[41] In most *Länder*, however, the *Landtage* only achieved the right to be updated with information from their government on European issues if those issues were relevant to the *Länder*. The *Landtage* of Baden-Württemberg and Saarland are the only *Landtage* which actively use their right to make non-binding recommendations on specific European issues. Some *Länder* parliaments have formulated general demands, e.g. for the Intergovernmental Conference on the Maastricht Treaty, but have so far refrained from commenting on specific issues. In 1990 the Conference of the Presidents of the *Landtage* established a commission to develop suggestions on how to improve the participation of the *Länder* parliaments in European policy-making, so far with little effect (cf. Morass 1994: 138–143).

The compensation for regional loss of power through co-decision rights in European policy-making is the success of a joint strategy of

---

[40] See Brenner 1992; Herdegen 1992; Scharpf 1992; Wiedmann 1992; Everling 1993.
[41] See Thaysen 1985; Schneider 1986; Eicher 1988; Friebe 1992.

compensation-through-participation, which the *Länder* have been pursuing since the very beginning of European integration. Embracing some of the "roll back" elements, in the form of the principle of subsidiarity and the Committee of the Regions, was as important as the expansion of the "compensation-through-participation" strategy to the European level. Negotiations on the revision of the Maastricht Treaty witnessed some reminiscences of the two "innovations" to the *Länder* strategy. But, at the same time, the *Länder* showed little interest in pushing their luck much further.

Post-1993: Resting on the laurels of success

As in 1991, the *Länder* formulated some claims for the revision of the Maastricht Treaty, which was scheduled for 1996 and resulted in the Amsterdam Treaty.[42] The list of issues that the *Länder* sought to place on the agenda of the Intergovernmental Conference of 1996–97 centered around the revision of the principle of subsidiarity (Art. 3b EC Treaty, now Art. 5 EC), a clear delimitation of competencies between the different levels of government (in particular a clear definition of the exclusive competencies of the EU), and more extended competencies for the Committee of the Regions (CoR), including the right to appeal to the ECJ. The *Länder* demands remained far below what the Committee of the Regions[43] and the Assembly of the European Regions (ARE)[44] had asked for. The *Länder* list of demands neither included the upgrading of the CoR into a proper body of the European Union nor did it include a demand for cooperation of the CoR with the Commission.[45] Compared with ambitions voiced by the regions at the European level, the demands of the *Länder* "pa[id] little more than lip-service to the third level ambitions trumpeted during the Maastricht process" (Jeffery 1997a: 73). The *Länder* threatened to veto ratification in the *Bundesrat* if the principle of subsidiarity was not redefined. But the *Junktim* had been a concession to Bavaria's politics of asserting its competence[46] and was only

---

[42] *BR-Drs. 810/92 vom 18.12.1992; BR-Drs. 169/95 vom 31.3.1995; BR-Drs. 667/95 vom 15.12.1995; BR-Drs. 813/96 vom 8.11.1996.*

[43] Resolution of the Committee of the Regions on the Revision of the Treaty on the European Union, April 20-21, 1995, CoR 136/95.

[44] *Versammlung der Regionen Europas, Kommission I: Entwurf: Vorschläge zur Revision des Vertrages über die Europäische Union anläßlich der Regierungskonferenz 1996, vom 24.5.1995.*

[45] The ARE had also requested the transformation of the CoR into a Regional Chamber (in which the municipalities would no longer be represented) with binding co-decision rights.

[46] See for instance the Bavarian "subsidiarity list" of 1996, *Memorandum der Bayerischen Staatsregierung zu den Vorschlägen der Europäischen Kommission in der "Agenda 2000"* (published in: *Euro Aktuell, Nr. 149, 24.9.1997*).

half-heartedly supported by the smaller *Länder* (interview Ba-Wü$_{14}$). The *Länder* not only refrained from pushing the "third level" any further, but they also did not put forward any claims for an extension of their participatory rights in European policy-making at the domestic level, except for a general right to appeal directly to the European Court of Justice.

The joint position of the *Länder* was a fragile compromise between those *Länder*, which, like North Rhine–Westphalia, Baden-Württemberg and particularly Bavaria, hoped to assert regional competencies by strengthening the regions as an autonomous level of government in the EU, on the one hand, and the weaker *Länder*, particularly the new eastern *Länder*, on the other hand, which were very hesitant to support any upgrading of the "third level" or "rolling back" of European interventions in their sphere of competencies because of European subsidies which they received.[47] But even the larger *Länder* started to share some of the skepticism toward the "Europe of the Regions" and the subsequent upgrading of the "third level" (interviews NRW$_{17}$; Ba-Wü$_{14}$). This is at least partly related to the sobering experience that the *Länder* had with the newly established Committee of the Regions.[48] The *Länder* realized that they could not simply control this body in the way in which they had initially thought (Kalbfleisch-Kottsieper 1993). The strong heterogeneity of the regions in terms of their institutional autonomy seriously impairs the efficiency of regional participation in European policy-making through a joint body of representation (Degen 1998).

With respect to domestic participatory rights, the *Länder* felt that they had already reached the maximum level of intrastate participation within the constitutional and institutional framework of German federalism (interviews Bay$_{13}$; NRW$_{17}$; Ba-Wü$_{14}$). Moreover, since German unification, the horizontal self-coordination among the *Länder* had become more difficult because of the stronger heterogeneity of interests (see below). All in all, the *Länder* position on the revision of the Maastricht Treaty reflected the preference of the majority of the *Länder* to improve and make better use of already existing mechanisms of participation and cooperation rather than develop them any further.

The federal government supported, in principle, the claims of the *Länder* in negotiations at the Intergovernmental Conference of 1996–97. It rejected, however, the redefinition of the principle of subsidiarity and

---

[47] Unpublished minutes of the European Ministers' Conference (*Europaministerkonferenz*). The divergence of priorities among the *Länder*, particularly with respect to funding issues, has been present from the moment in which the new eastern *Länder* fully participated in the horizontal self-coordination of the *Länder* on European affairs (Gerster 1993; Jeffery 1997a).

[48] *Der Ausschuß der Regionen vor seiner zweiten Amtsperiode 1998–2002*; unpublished report of the *Länder* members of the Committee of the Regions, September 18, 1997.

the right of the *Länder* as well as of the Committee of the Regions to appeal directly to the European Court of Justice.

The *Länder* participated in the negotiations of the Intergovernmental Conference with two representatives (cf. Blume and Graf von Rex 1998). But their demands on the "third level" were not, or only partially, included in the Treaty revision, due to the opposition of other member-state governments. In the end, the *Länder* had to accept a subsidiarity protocol instead of a revision of the corresponding Treaty provision and settled for an appendix to the protocol, which declared that the principle of subsidiarity also applied to the regional and local level. The attached declaration was signed only by Germany, Belgium, and Austria. Furthermore, a clear delimitation of competencies was also not achieved; nor did the Committee of the Regions receive the right to appeal to the ECJ. Nevertheless, the *Bundesrat* ratified the Amsterdam Treaty unanimously on March 27, 1998.[49]

The unwillingness of the *Länder* to really push the issue of the "third level" in general, and the principle of subsidiarity in particular, reflects the low priority that the majority of the *Länder* attributes to them. The *Länder* appear to be satisfied with the level of (intrastate) participation they have achieved so far (interviews NRW$_{17}$; Ba-Wü$_{14}$).

In the Intergovernmental Conference of 1999–2000, the *Länder* did not put forward any specific claims for an extended regional participation in European policy-making either at the domestic level or the European level. They did voice some concerns about further Europeanization of their competencies, particularly in the areas of justice and home affairs and the provision of public services. Striving to ring-fence their few remaining core competencies, the *Länder* called again for a stricter application of the principle of subsidiarity and a clear delimitation of competencies between the European Union and the member states by means of a "competence catalogue". Moreover, the *Länder* restated their demands for the right of the regions with legislative powers to appeal directly to the European Court of Justice.[50] This time the *Länder* did not even tie the fulfillment of their demands to the ratification of the Treaty revisions in the *Bundesrat* – although the President of the European Commission, Romano Prodi, told the *Länder* in May 2000 that their concerns about a strict delimitation of competencies would not be addressed in this round of intergovernmental negotiations but would be considered in the white book, which the Commission will prepare on "New Governance". Nor did the German government support the *Länder* demands for a

---

[49] *BR Drs. 196/98 vom 27.3.1998.*
[50] *BR-Drs. 61/00 vom 4.2.2000; Ergebnis der Besprechung der Regierungschefs der Länder am 15. Juni 2000 in Berlin.*

regional standing before the ECJ.[51] All in all, the *Länder* played an even more passive role during the Nice Treaty negotiations, concluded in December 2000, than during the Amsterdam Treaty negotiations. Nevertheless, the demands of the *Länder* for a clear delimitation of competencies entered Annex IV of the Nice Treaty as one of the issues to be tackled in the next IGC envisioned for 2004.

Extrastate channels of influence: Complementary to rather than a substitute for intrastate participation

The strong preference of the *Länder* for a "compensation-through-participation" strategy has not prevented them from establishing direct, extrastate channels of access to European policy-making. But while other regions, such as the Spanish *Comunidades Autónomas*, have used these channels to circumvent the central-state level, they have served the *Länder* as a complement to, rather than a substitute for, their cooperation with the federal government in European policy-making (intrastate participation).

The *Länder* started to become active at the European level in the 1970s by establishing unofficial contacts with European institutions. Representatives of the *Länder* traveled to Brussels for information visits at the European Commission, and some *Länder* maintained regular correspondence with the European Commission. *Länder* trips to Brussels had to and still have to be announced to the Federal Foreign Ministry. And the *Länder* must accommodate the interests of the federal government in representing their position to European institutions (Morawitz 1981: 32). Unlike Spain, however, neither of these issues has caused any problems with the *Länder* (interview AA$_2$).

The *Bundesrat* has also established relations with European institutions. Apart from regular contact between the *Bundesrat's* EC Committee and Members of the European Parliament (Morawitz 1981: 35), in 1967 the *Bundesrat* also created a liaison office with the European Parliament for the mutual exchange of information (cf. Jaspert 1988). Moreover, each *Land* maintains regular contact with its regional Members of the European Parliament; these contacts are based mainly on exchange of information. For some *Länder*, however, their representatives in the European Parliament (EP) also have a lobbying function, channeling regional interests through the EP into the European decision-making arena.

It was only in the second half of the 1980s that *Länder* began opening their own offices in Brussels. The main task of these offices (*Länderbüros*) is (1) to survey the European scene for upcoming issues and to inform respective *Länder* governments of all developments at the European level

---

[51] *Ergebnis der Besprechung der Regierungschefs der Länder am 15. Juni 2000 in Berlin.*

that may be of particular interest to the *Land*, (2) to help public institutions and private enterprises of the respective *Land* in establishing links with EU institutions, and (3) to conduct public relations for the *Land*, especially with the Commission (cf. Strohmeier 1988; Fastenrath 1990).

When the *Länder* began opening their own offices in Brussels, they faced several reproaches of pursuing a *"Nebenaußenpolitik"* (parallel foreign policy; Nass 1986; Hellwig 1987). The Federal Foreign Ministry in particular was concerned that the *Länder* might undermine the foreign policy prerogative of the federal government and, hence, the ability of Germany to speak with one voice.

Yet, unlike other member state governments, the federal government was not able, from a legal point of view, to prevent the *Länder* from maintaining direct relations with European institutions. Since 1992 the *Länder* offices have also been able to claim official status (Para. 8 EUZBLG). Some *Länder* changed the name of their offices from *Verbindungsbüro* (liaison office) to *Vertretung* (representation) in order to highlight their understanding of themselves as political actors in their own right in European policy-making.

However, the federal government increasingly recognized the complementary nature of the EU *Länder* activities. Thus, the German Permanent Representation acknowledges that the *Länder* offices may relieve it of certain functions, such as the provision of information to universities, interest groups, and businesses; they may also relieve it of duties to the *Länder* themselves, for instance in the area of structural funds, where the *Länder* often pursue competing interests (Morass 1994: 155). The *Länder* offices not only closely cooperate with the German Permanent Representation; since the 1990s they have also started to engage in institutionalized cooperation among themselves (Knodt 1998: 49–51). Issue-specific joint working groups, in which a member of the German Permanent Representation often also participates, facilitate a division of labor among the *Länder*; these groups also facilitate an exchange of information which avoids the doubling of work. This pooling of resources is more important for less resourceful *Länder* which have to concentrate their European activities on issues that are of particular relevance to their regional interests. The more resourceful *Länder* also recognize that coordination of the *Länder* activities at the EU level is often more effective in influencing the policy process than regional unilateral action (interview Bay[23]). Institutionalized cooperation between the *Bund* and *Länder* representations at the EU level promotes joint action and has brought reproaches of *Nebenaußenpolitik* and regional *Alleingänge* into question.

As well as their direct contact with European institutions, the *Länder* also gained, along with the regions of the other member states, direct representation at the European level through the Council of Regional and Local Territorial Corporations (established by the Commission in 1988) and the Assembly of Regions in Europe/ARE (established in 1989 and replacing the Council of Regions in Europe which was founded in 1985). Due to the strong heterogeneity of member regions and municipalities with respect to their institutional autonomy, the *Länder* only reluctantly joined these institutions. European institutions of regional representation gained importance for *Länder* only when they became potential allies in pursuing their claims for a strong regional participation in European policy-making. While the *Länder* had been very active in pushing through, as well as setting-up, the Committee of the Regions, they started to retreat from it when they realized how difficult it was to reach common positions that could have a significant impact (Benz 1993a; Kalbfleisch-Kottsieper 1993; Clement 1995; Degen 1998). At the start of the twenty-first century many *Länder* have shifted their activities from the European level to the "Fourth Level" of transregional and interregional cooperation in order to build the "Europe of the Regions" from below rather than above (interviews NRW$_{17}$; Ba-Wü$_{12}$).

All in all, the *Länder* have established a series of extrastate relations with European institutions that provide them with direct access to the European policy arena independent of the central state. While the *Länder* have made extensive use of these extrastate channels of access, their European activism has not been to the detriment of either the federal government or the *Länder* as a whole. The *Länder* have basically employed their European resources for three different purposes. First, the individual *Länder* use their direct contacts with European institutions to realize particular interests, such as attracting foreign investment or Community subsidies. Second, the *Länder* lobby European decision-makers for the common position upon which the *Länder* have agreed at the domestic level. They usually co-ordinate such lobbying activities at the European level both among each other and with the central state. Third, the *Länder* make use of their transnational relations with European and other regional figures in order to promote their agenda for co-determination powers in European policy-making at the domestic level, as they did in 1991–92 (see above).

There is a common understanding amongst the *Länder* that extrastate channels must not be used to circumvent or bypass either the *Bund* or common *Länder* positions (interviews Bay$_{20}$; Ba-Wü$_{14}$). Even in cases where the *Länder* do not coordinate their activities at the European level, they avoid pursuing positions that would be counter to the official German bargaining position, or that would severely damage the interests of other *Länder*. The complementary role of intrastate and extrastate channels of influence is also reflected in the division of labor that has emerged between the two. While direct contact with European institutions is the most important aspect for the *Länder* in influencing Eu agenda-setting, participation in formulating the German bargaining position via the *Bundesrat* and in the Council negotiations as members of the German delegation are central in the policy-formulation and decision-making stages of the European policy process.

Redressing the territorial balance of power through sharing the costs of adaptation

As the previous sections have shown, the *Länder* have successfully employed their "compensation-through-participation" strategy in order to expand their intrastate participation in European policy-making. This has given rise to a number of formal institutional changes which culminated in an amendment to the German Constitution in 1992 granting the *Länder* comprehensive co-decision powers in the formulation and representation of the German bargaining position.

The increasing participation of the *Länder* in European policy-making successfully redressed the territorial balance of power in German federalism which had been negatively affected by the uneven distribution of "say and pay" caused by Europeanization. By sharing its decision-making powers with the *Länder*, if their competencies and interests are affected, then the *Bund* takes on a considerable portion of the costs of Europeanization rather than shifting them to the regional level. Co-determination rights in European policy-making compensate the *Länder* for their losses of autonomous and shared competencies. The *Länder* are involved in the formulation and decision-making of essentially every European policy that they have to implement. There are good reasons to argue that the "compensation-through-participation" strategy of the *Länder* has successfully reduced the costs of Europeanization by leveling out the uneven distribution of "say and pay".

One could contend, however, that the intrastate participation of the *Länder* does not provide adequate compensation for their double loss of competencies for two reasons. First, co-determination is no substitute for self-determination. And, second, the *Länder* might not be able to exercise their co-decision powers in European policy-making effectively.

Substituting self-determination for co-determination: The loss of state quality?

It has been repeatedly argued that the compensation for self-determination through co-determination rights undermines the state quality of the *Länder* because their autonomous interests are mediated three times in the formulation of the German bargaining position: first, in the process of horizontal self-coordination among the *Länder* in the *Bundesrat*; second, in the vertical coordination with the *Bund* and, third, in European negotiations with other member states (Voß 1989; Wiedmann 1992; Wuermling 1993). While it might be true that co-determination is no full substitute for self-determination, this issue is a general problem of cooperative federalism rather than of Europeanization. Europeanization only reinforces a logic which is inherent in cooperative federalism: the exchange of autonomous legislative competencies for co-decision rights in central-state legislation. Even without European integration, the *Länder* would have hardly any competencies that could be exercised independently of the *Bund*. Moreover, the *Bund* faces the same problem: if exclusive federal competencies are Europeanized, then the federal government has to share its decision-making powers with the other member states. If Europeanization is challenging anything, then it is challenging the state quality of the German federation as such rather than the state quality of the *Länder*.

With respect to the territorial balance of power between the *Bund* and *Länder*, the important issue is that the new Art. 23 GG effectively prevents the *Bund* from having access to regional competencies that it would not have without Europeanization. On the one hand, the *Bund* can no longer transfer *Länder* competencies to the European level without the consent of the *Bundesrat*. On the other hand, the *Länder* have the right to determine and represent the German bargaining position whenever their exclusive jurisdiction is affected.

Multilevel interlocking politics: A dual joint decision trap?

The effectiveness of the "compensation-through-participation" strategy in reducing the adaptational costs of Europeanization could be impaired because either *Bund* and *Länder* are not able to coordinate their interests in the formulation and representation of the German bargaining position or the *Länder* are not able to agree on a joint position. Several scholars have warned that the participation of the *Länder* in European policy-making has led to a "*doppelte Politikverflechtung*" (double joint decision trap; Hrbek 1986), which would not only damage the capacity of the federal government to represent German interests at the European level because it would lose flexibility in the negotiations (Brenner 1992; Benz 1993a). There was also concern that a "double joint decision trap" would affect the efficiency of European policy-making as a whole (Scharpf 1992; Schultze 1993). More than nine years of practicing Art. 23 n.F. GG show that these concerns were unfounded.

While there is no systematic study of the efficiency of *Bund–Länder* cooperation in European affairs, data that are available indicate that (1) the *Länder* make extensive use of their new participatory rights, and (2) the participation of the *Länder* does not cause any delays or blockages in the European decision-making process.

The *Bundesrat* receives on average 4000 European documents per year, of which around 160 are debated in the *Bundesrat*. In the vast majority of the cases, the debates result in official position statements, of which about 20% are ultimately binding for the federal government (European Parliament 1995; Dewitz 1998).

With respect to the representation of the German bargaining position in the EU decision-making process in cases when their exclusive competencies are affected, the *Länder* have designated nine ministers for five Councils: Research, Education, Culture, Media, and Justice and Home Affairs. With the exception of the Research Council, the *Länder* have had a presence on a regular basis.

Finally, the *Bundesrat* has designated around 450 representatives for participation in EU decision-making bodies. One hundred and fifty *Länder* representatives participate in 90 (of about 200) working groups of the Council. While the *Länder* do not formally participate in the advisory bodies of the Commission in the agenda-setting stage, they appointed about 220 representatives for the Commission working groups dealing with the implementation of EU policies (comitology). Another 50 representatives attend instruction meetings of the federal government for the Committee of Permanent Representatives (COREPER).

It would go beyond the scope of this study to explore the extent to which the federal government accommodates the concerns of the *Länder* in its bargaining position. In any case, *Bund* and *Länder* have been able to achieve a compromise on each European issue on which the *Länder* decided to take a stance within the given time framework. There are no cases where the participation of the *Länder* caused a delay or a blockage in the European decision-making process.

Most of the conflicts between *Bund* and *Länder* have been of a formal rather than substantive nature, centering on the right of the *Länder* to represent Germany in European negotiations. In a few cases, both *Bund* and *Länder* claimed the right to lead the negotiations in the Council because the *Bund* considered these issues outside the exclusive competencies of the *Länder*. Instead of settling the conflict before the Constitutional Court, the *Bund* and *Länder* representatives in the German delegation settled on a pragmatic solution in which *Bund* and *Länder* would jointly exercise the right of representation (*Doppelkopfregelung*). In 1998 *Bund* and *Länder* also agreed on a formal mediation procedure to resolve such conflicts (cf. Dewitz 1998: 77–78).

Despite some conflicts, the review of *Bund–Länder* cooperation in European affairs, as previewed by the *Bund–Länder* Agreement in Art. 23 n.F. GG,[52] resulted in the joint assessment of *Bund* and *Länder* "*daß sich die Regelungen der Vereinbarung durchaus bewährt haben und deshalb kein Bedarf für Änderungen am Text der Bund–Länder-Vereinbarung besteht*" ("that the regulations of the Agreement proved effective at all accounts and that there is therefore now need to change the text of the *Bund–Länder* Agreement"; quoted in Blume and Graf von Rex 1998: 42).[53] The only controversial points were the insistence of the federal government to abstain from Council decisions based on Art. 235 of the EC Treaty (now Art. 308 EC) if there was no agreement with the *Bundesrat* (Para. 5 III EUZBLG), and the issue as to whether the *Länder* would also head the German delegation in the mediation procedure between the European Parliament and the Council of Ministers. The issues were resolved in a *Bund–Länder* protocol, which formed the basis for ratification of the Amsterdam Treaty in the *Bundesrat*. The federal government declared that, if it could not agree on a common position with the *Bundesrat*, it would resort to abstention in the Council only in exceptional cases. It also agreed that the *Länder* would head the German delegation in the mediation procedure between the Parliament and the Council.[54] The issue of *Länder* participation in the German Permanent Representation as well as in the deliberations of COREPER was ultimately dropped, although *Bund* and *Länder* agreed that the *Länder* can delegate two representatives to the German Permanent Representation,

---

[52] *Abschnitt VIII, Ziff. 8* of the *Bund–Länder Vereinbarung vom 29. Oktober 1993* demands a review of the Agreement in light of experience up to July 1, 1996.

[53] For a similar assessment, see *Erfahrungsbericht zur Beteiligung der Länder am Entscheidungsverfahren in europäischen Angelegenheiten*, prepared by the *Ministerium für Bundes- und Europaangelegenheiten des Landes Nordrhein-Westfalen*, March 26, 1996; *Überprüfung der Bund–Länder-Vereinbarung über die Zusammenarbeit in Angelegenheiten der Europäischen Union*, prepared by the *Staatsministerium Baden-Württemberg* and the *Ministerium für Bundes- und Europaangelegenheiten Nordrhein-Westfalen*, April 19, 1996; and the report of the *Bundesrat Ausschuß für Fragen der Europäischen Union* "*Die Praxis der Mitwirkung der Länder und des Bundesrates in Angelegenheiten der Europäischen Union nach dem Inkrafttreten des Vertrages von Maastricht am 1. November 1993*", April 16, 1996; *Beschluß der Europaministerkonferenz vom 27. Februar 1997* (http://www.europaminister.de).

[54] The protocol settled three other controversial issues which had emerged during the Intergovernmental Conference on the revision of the Maastricht Treaty. First, the regulations of the *Bund–Länder* cooperation were extended to the newly established framework decisions in the area of the Third Pillar (Art. 34 II b new EC). Second, *Bund* and *Länder* coordinate their research and development activities at the European level. And, third, the federal government informs *Bundesrat* (and *Bundestag*) on the appointment of ECJ Judges and Attorneys (*Protokoll des Bund/Länder Gesprächs vom 6.2.1998*, approved by the *Ministerpräsidentenkonferenz* on March 18, 1998; unofficial document).

who must, however, not participate in negotiations of COREPER. So far, the *Länder* have one representative, who is in charge of cultural affairs. Given the comprehensive consultation and cooperation between *Bund* and *Länder* in earlier stages of the formulation of the German bargaining position, the *Länder* do not consider their lack of representation in the COREPER affects their participation in European policy-making (Escher 1998).

All in all, *Bund* and *Länder* have chosen a consensual approach in dealing with European affairs. Both sides agree that the participation of the *Länder* has improved the effectiveness of European policy-making because the *Länder* can contribute their administrative expertise in the formulation of European policies, and their involvement in policy formulation and decision-making increases the acceptance and, hence, the effectiveness of implementation (interviews $BMWi_1$; NRW_{17}; Ba-Wü$_{14}$). The coordination of the German bargaining position is facilitated by the fact that European issues appear to be less controversial than domestic issues. The *Bundesrat* has also played a less important role as an instrument of the political opposition in European policy-making (Morass 1994: 131; interview Ba-Wü$_{14}$). Moreover, more than 40 years of *Bund–Länder* coordination in European affairs has given rise to the same kind of routinized, technical, and largely depoliticized inter-personal and inter-institutional relationships, which are typical of cooperative federalism, and which allow for a flexible and pragmatic coordination of *Bund* and *Länder* interests in European policy-making.

If the *Länder* are prevented from fully exploiting their co-decision powers in European policy-making, it is because they have faced difficulties in formulating a joint position among themselves. This problem is directly related to German unification, which increased the heterogeneity of the *Länder* (Schultze 1993; Sturm and Jeffery 1993; Goetz 1995b; Jeffery 1997a).

Particularly the smaller, new, eastern *Länder* lack the administrative capacity to process the flood of information which they receive and to formulate their own position on EU proposals. They often feel powerless in negotiations with resourceful *Länder* like Bavaria, North Rhine–Westphalia, Baden-Württemberg, or Hesse. They find these *Länder* better informed and prepared. Moreover, the cleavage between the (larger) *Länder* striving to assert their competencies against further European interventions, and those (smaller, eastern) *Länder* whose view on European interventions in their affairs are understandably affected by their receipt of considerable EU structural funding has become more pronounced.

Diverging interests and limited information-processing capacities sometimes make the formulation of joint *Länder* positions difficult. But these difficulties do not produce any breakdown in *Länder* coordination and cooperation. Nor do they spill over into the area of vertical intergovernmental coordination with the *Bund*. To date the *Länder* have always been able to present their joint position in due time (or have otherwise refrained from presenting one). Moreover, the formulation of joint positions of the *Bundesrat* on European issues appears to be significantly less controversial than in domestic policy-making (Morass 1994: 127–128). There is, however, a tendency for opinions expressed by the *Bundesrat* to include "soft formulations", which reflect the need for ample compromises in order to accommodate all *Länder* interests but which, at the same time, provide little guidance to *Länder* representatives in European negotiations (interviews, Bay$_{22}$; Ba-Wü$_{35}$; cf. Clostermeyer 1992; Gerster 1993). Time constraints for formulating joint *Länder* positions also seem to grant the stronger *Länder* more influence because of their superior resources in the preparation of their bargaining position (interviews Brem$_{19}$; Ba-Wü$_{14}$).

All in all, intrastate participation of the *Länder* in European policy-making provides a viable solution to the "say" side of the uneven distribution of "say and pay". The question then is how effective the "compensation-through-participation" strategy is in reducing the costs of Europeanization on the "pay" side, that is the costs of implementing European policies.

Sharing the burden of implementation?

Participation of the *Länder* in the formulation and decision-making of European policies is unlikely to grant them more discretion in implementation. The Commission will not change its formalistic approach to implementation just because the *Länder* sit on the bargaining table. Nor will the *Länder* receive any additional payments or package deals at the European level, which would allow them to cover implementation costs. Although the *Länder* participate in the formulation and representation of the German bargaining position, Germany can still be outvoted in the Council.

Yet, while intrastate participation of the *Länder* leaves European implementation costs by and large unchanged, it has had some effect on implementation at the domestic level. The *Länder* are more willing to accept the implementation of costly policies if they are involved in their formulation and decision-making process. Co-decision fosters co-responsibility. Early involvement in the European policy-making process also allows the *Länder* to anticipate implementation costs.

Nevertheless, the "compensation-through-participation" strategy has been more effective on the "say" side of the uneven distribution of "say and pay". As we see in Part IV, *Bund* and *Länder* have developed a joint strategy of "shifting the burden of implementation" on to other member states in order to reduce the costs for the *Länder* on the "pay" side.

Reinforcement through flexible adjustment: The Europeanization of cooperative federalism

In the course of the half century of European integration, the German federal system has undergone a number of formal institutional changes triggered by the dynamics of Europeanization. First, Europeanization brought an uneven distribution of "say and pay" to the detriment of the *Länder*; this caused a redistribution of power in favor of the *Bund* (territorial centralization). Second, in trying to redress the territorial balance of power, the *Länder* subsequently pushed for formal participatory rights in European policy-making (intrastate participation). The consequent pursuit of their "compensation-through-participation" strategy carried the *Länder* from the level of *ad hoc* and informal consultations in 1951, via formal rights to information and consultation in 1957 and 1987, to constitutional co-determination rights in the formulation and representation of the German bargaining position in 1993.

The successful attempts of the *Länder* to reduce the costs of adaptation by sharing them with the central state have resulted in the gradual Europeanization of German cooperative federalism. European policy-making has simply been integrated into the formal institutions of joint decision-making and interlocking politics; or, to be more precise, the institutions of joint decision-making and interlocking politics have been extended flexibly to European affairs, adjusting them to the new tasks. Unlike in Spain, institutional adaptation to Europeanization has not given rise to any substantially new institutions.

The *Länder* have created additional bodies and procedures in order to organize their participation in European policy-making. Alongside the *Europakammer* (Europe Chamber) and the EU Committee of the *Bundesrat*, the *Länder* established a Standing Conference of the Ministers of European Affairs (*Ständige Konferenz der Europaminister* or *EMK*) in 1992 in order to facilitate the exchange of information and the coordination of *Länder* positions on general issues, such as the revision of the Maastricht Treaty (cf. Gerster 1993; http://www.europaminister.de). The *Länder* have also adjusted their administrative structures. Each *Land* has a Plenipotentiary for European Affairs (*Europabeauftragte*) affiliated to either the *Staatskanzlei* (*Länder* Chancellery) or *Staatsministerium* (Ministry of the State), who enjoys either the status of a state secretary or a minister and whose major function is to coordinate the European policy of the *Land* government. He/she is supported in his/her work by European Advisers (*Europareferenten*) in the various sectoral ministries (*Fachministerien*). The *Europareferenten* regularly meet to prepare the *Land* position on European issues, which are often cross-sectoral in nature and, hence, affect the responsibilities of various ministries (cf. Schönberg 1998).

While the Europeanization of cooperative federalism gave rise to a number of institutional changes, we see a flexible adjustment and reinforcement rather than a fundamental transformation of existing territorial institutions. After being adopted, the main institutions of cooperative federalism have remained by and large unchanged. The functional division of labor, strong bicameralism, fiscal equalization, as well as multilateral bargaining and consensus-seeking are foremost in the decision-making on both domestic and European issues. The *Länder* are the main implementers of European policies, and they participate in formulation and decision-making through the *Bundesrat*. The coordination of the joint *Länder* position as well as its integration with the interests of the *Bund* into the German bargaining position proceed through multilateral bargaining and consensus-seeking. While *Bund* and *Länder* have largely relied on existing institutions for coordinating their interest on European issues, the few newly created coordination mechanisms, such as the *Europakammer* or the *EMK*, do not break with existing institutional traditions but adopted similar norms, rules, and procedures. Finally, fiscal equalization provides the weaker *Länder* (to a certain extent at least) with the necessary resources to exercise their competencies in European policy-making.

Europeanization has posed a serious challenge to German territorial institutions. It has ultimately resulted in a reinforcement (Goetz 1995) and maybe even revitalization or *rinascimento* of cooperative federalism. While the beginning of the 1980s witnessed an attempt to disentangle the politics of joint decision-making (cf. Hesse 1986), intrastate participation of the *Länder* in European policy-making has caused a significant push for interlocking politics and joint decision-making, and this is likely to further increase as European integration proceeds. The policy areas in which *Bund* and *Länder* can independently exercise their competencies have almost disappeared. Moreover, *Bund* and *Länder* representatives agree that the cooperation between the two levels has significantly improved since the introduction of the new Art. 23 n.F. GG (interviews NRW$_{15}$; Bay$_{13}$; Ba-Wü$_{14}$; BMWi$_1$). The historical legacy of cooperative federalism in Germany (dating back into the nineteenth century), which has been considerably reinforced by European integration (Benz 1999; Lehmbruch 2000), makes debate on competitive federalism look rather academic.

The Europeanization of cooperative federalism has redressed the territorial balance of power between *Bund* and *Länder*. By balancing the loss of *Länder* competencies through co-decision rights in European policy-making, cooperative federalism has once again proved effective in flexibly adjusting to significant changes in its external environment without undergoing a profound reform of its institutions. The "double joint decision trap" did not materialize. *Bund–Länder* cooperation in European affairs is effective because it is organized through the same institutions as *Bund–Länder* cooperation in domestic policy-making. But while the institutions of joint decision-making and interlocking politics have been reinforced, so have their major deficiencies: executive dominance, lack of transparency, and deparliamentarization.

From the very beginning, *Länder* participation in European policy-making, as weak as it initially was, has been organized through cooperation among the executives of *Bund* and *Länder*. The Europeanization of legislative *Länder* competencies, which are exercised by the *Länder* parliaments, was compensated for by co-decision rights for their executives exercised through the *Bundesrat*. Thus, Europeanization has contributed significantly to the transformation of the German federal system into executive federalism (Lenz 1977; Eicher 1988; Memminger 1992). Art. 23 n.F. GG constitutionally sanctioned the deparliamentarization at the *Länder* level (Herdegen 1992: 594). As long as the *Bundesrat* is the body designated to represent *Länder* participation in European affairs, binding participatory rights of the *Länder* parliaments are constitutionally not feasible. The Federal Constitutional Court explicitly ruled out binding participation of the *Länder* parliaments in *Bundesrat* decisions, because such participation would violate the separation of power between executive and legislature.[55] While the problem of deparliamentarization is less prevalent at the federal level, the *Bundestag* still enjoys far less participatory rights in European policy-making than the *Bundesrat*.

The problem of deparliamentarization both at the national and regional level is sharpened by the strong position of the sectoral administration (*Fachverwaltung*) in European policy-making. As the study on the Europeanization of environmental policy shows in more detail, the experts in the sectoral administrations of *Bund* and *Länder* often form cross-level alliances. They push their sectoral interests vis-à-vis those parts of the *Bund* and *Länder* administrations which pursue a more generalistic, integrated approach to European issues that is oriented more toward legal and political considerations than technical considerations (cf. Part IV, Chapter 1).

To conclude, while *Bund* and *Länder* have not become caught in the "joint decision trap", it seems that policy-making effectiveness in European affairs is paid for by a further loss of democratic legitimacy and accountability in cooperative federalism (Benz 1993b; Classen 1993).

---

[55] *BVerfGE 8, 104: 120/121.*

6   Conclusion

Part II of this book has shown that Europeanization has exerted significant pressure for adaptation on German territorial institutions. European institutions which concentrate decision-making powers in the hands of member-state executives while shifting the implementation costs of European policies to subordinate levels (national, regional, and local) do not match the structure of the formal institutions of German federalism. The latter provide for a sharing of both decision-making powers and implementation costs between central state and regions. As a result of this institutional misfit, Europeanization has caused an uneven distribution of "say and pay" to the detriment of the German *Länder*. On the one hand, the transfer of policy competencies to the European level has not only given the *Bund* access to exclusive *Länder* competencies (which the German Constitution had blocked), but the co-decision powers of the *Länder* in federal policy-making (formulation, decision, and implementation) have also been reduced to the implementation of European policies. On the other hand, the *Länder* have had to implement policies in whose formulation and decision-making they did not formally participate, and this precluded a sharing of implementation costs. The uneven distribution of "say and pay" in European policy-making has led to a redistribution of resources between *Bund* and *Länder* that has changed the territorial balance of power in favor of the central state.

I have argued that the informal institutions of cooperative federalism have facilitated the adaptation of its formal institutions to this Europe-induced shift of power. Unlike less resourceful regions in the EU, the *Länder* had a choice between two major strategies in order to redress the territorial balance of power. They could either try to ring-fence their sphere of competencies against interventions from both the central state and the European Union and circumvent the federal government – by establishing direct, extrastate channels of influence on European policy-making – or they could seek compensation for their loss of power through intrastate participation in the formulation and representation of the German bargaining position. While the *Länder* had sufficient resources to pursue both strategies, the institutional culture of multilateral bargaining and consensus-seeking clearly favored the latter, cooperative, strategy over the former, more confrontational, strategy. From the very beginning, the *Länder* pursued a clear "compensation-through-participation" strategy in order to redress the territorial balance of power. Their cooperative response to the challenges of Europeanization was not the result of a conscious cost–benefit calculation with respect to the two alternative strategies at hand. Rather, the *Länder* followed a line of behavior which in the past had proved successful in dealing with similar challenges to their institutional autonomy (federalization of their competencies). It was not until the 1980s that they started to consider elements of a more confrontational strategy of ring-fencing and circumventing because they felt that their initial strategy of "compensation-through-participation" would not be sufficient to redress the territorial balance of power. Yet, the strong institutional culture of consensus-seeking, multilateral bargaining, and avoiding conflict severely constrained the use of a more confrontational strategy. In the final analysis, ring-fencing and circumventing predominantly served in favor of the *Länder* in their strategy of pushing for "compensation-through-participation".

By sharing the adaptational costs of Europeanization – that is, decision-making powers and implementation costs in European policy-making shared with the *Bund* – the formal institutions of German federalism could be adjusted flexibly by extending them to the realm of European policy-making. As a result, German territorial institutions were reinforced rather than significantly changed.

While the cost-sharing strategy of "compensation-through-participation" facilitated a redressing of the territorial balance of power through flexible adjustment, it promoted a major trend in both European and German policy-making: deparliamentarization. German federalism is executive federalism. The compensation for *Länder* losses of power through the participation of their executives in the formulation and representation of the German bargaining position at the EU level corresponds to and reinforces the logic of cooperative federalism. It subsequently alters the balance of power between executive and legislature, particularly at the regional level. Even compared to the *Bundestag*, the *Landtage* have hardly any role to play in European policy-making. Apart from some general rights to information, the *Länder* parliaments are left with an *ex post* control of the European activities of their governments. Executive dominance in European policy-making – at the regional, national, and European level – is a major reason for the general lack of transparency and accountability in European policy-making.

Transforming competitive regionalism: Institutional adaptation to Europeanization in Spain

Part III of this book explores the effect of Europeanization on Spanish territorial institutions. Chapter 7 outlines the major formal and informal institutions. I argue that the institutional culture of competitive regionalism has shaped the way in which the *Comunidades Autónomas (CCAA)* respond to challenges to their political and institutional autonomy. In order to protect their sphere of autonomy against harmonization and centralization, the *Comunidades Autónomas* have developed a two-fold strategy of constitutional conflict and non-cooperation vis-à-vis the central state.

Chapter 8 starts by showing that Europeanization has posed a similar challenge to Spanish territorial institutions to the one posed in Germany. As in case of the *Länder*, Europeanization has challenged the institutional autonomy of the *Comunidades Autónomas* by causing an uneven distribution of "say and pay" in favor of the central state (1). I demonstrate how the institutional culture of competitive regionalism has encouraged the *CCAA* to pursue a strategy of confrontation against and circumventing of the state (2). I argue that this non-cooperative strategy has hindered a redressing of the territorial balance of power. Facing increasing costs of Europeanization, the *CCAA* started to reconsider their initial strategy and to adopt a more cooperative approach (3). This strategy change by the *CCAA* brought about the first institutional framework of multilateral cooperation in Spanish intergovernmental relations that provides for regional participation in central-state policy-making. The introduction of joint decision-making in Spanish competitive regionalism constitutes a major change in the territorial institutions of Spain (4).

7   The Spanish State of Autonomies as a form of competitive regionalism

This chapter describes the major formal and informal institutions of the Spanish State of Autonomies. I show that the institutional culture of competitive regionalism has shaped the way in which the *Comunidades Autónomas* responded to challenges to their institutional autonomy by choosing a strategy of constitutional conflict and non-cooperation.

Political autonomy, fiscal centralization, and weak intergovernmental cooperation as the major formal institutions of the Spanish State of Autonomies

In an attempt to reconcile the tradition of a unitary-centralist state with the historical, cultural, and socio-economic aspirations for autonomy voiced by regionalists and national minorities, the Fathers of the Spanish Constitution of 1978 designed a system of intergovernmental relations that emphasizes the institutional autonomy of the central state and the subnational level of government. Unlike German federalism, which is based on a fusion of federal and regional powers in public policy-making (joint decision-making), the Spanish State of Autonomies is oriented toward the American model of dual federalism, which emphasizes the separation of central-state and regional powers. The sectoral distribution of competencies, asymmetrical bicameralism as well as the scarce constitutional provision for intergovernmental cooperation and vertical integration reflect an attempt to grant both levels of government a certain level of political and institutional autonomy in order to secure the cultural pluralism of Spain. Fiscal centralization and mechanisms of voluntary intergovernmental cooperation, such as sectoral conferences (*conferencias sectoriales*), should provide a minimum of intergovernmental integration and policy harmonization.

*Layer-cake federalism and the problem of conflict
over competencies*

The sectoral distribution of competencies in the Spanish State of
Autonomies is very different from the functional distribution of power
in German cooperative federalism. The vast majority of competencies
are also shared or concurrent. Yet, unlike cooperative federalism, sharing
competencies does not necessarily entail joint action of the two levels of
government. Rather, the central state authorizes the *CCAA* to "share"
its powers by developing and implementing its framework legislation
(*legislación básica*). The central state legislates without the participation of
the Autonomous Communities. The *CCAA* implement central-state decisions without the central government being able to intervene. Each level
of government is independent in exercising its respective competencies.
The constitution does not prescribe any mechanisms for coordinating
the exercise of shared competencies. As a consequence, the central state
often resorts to detailed framework legislation, which limits the discretion
of the *CCAA* in the creating and fulfillment of legislation and allows the
central state to exercise executive functions that are usually entrusted to
the *CCAA*. The *CCAA* have perceived the exhaustive use of framework
legislation as a continuous attempt by the central state to intervene in
their exclusive sphere of autonomy. This intrusion has been one of the
major sources of constitutional conflict between the central state and the
CCAA (Viver i Pi-Sunyer 1990).

The institutional separation of the two levels of government has resulted in some instances in a duplication of administrative structures
at the subnational level. Unlike Germany, where the implementation of
federal policies is entrusted to the *Länder*, the Spanish central-state
administration has maintained its traditional field services at the subnational level, the *administración periférica del Estado* (cf. Newton 1997:
112–116). This duplication and overlapping of administrative structures
at the subnational level has not only provoked bureaucratic overload,
but the *administración periférica* has also been a constant source of intergovernmental tension. The central state justifies the maintenance of its
administración periférica on the grounds that some *CCAA* have not ac-
quired the full range of competencies granted to them by the Spanish
Constitution, particularly in the fulfillment of central-state policies. The
CCAA, however, perceive the central-state field services as "watchdogs"
of Madrid.

Another source of conflict over competencies is the asymmetric nature of the Spanish State of Autonomies. Recognizing the claims of the
Basques and the Catalans, and to some extent the Galicians, that, for
historical and cultural reasons, they merit preferential status (*el hecho*

diferencial), the Spanish Constitution laid the grounds for an *"asimetría autonómica"* (López Guerra 1993), an "asymmetrical federalism" (González Encinar 1992; Agranoff 1993). Art. 2 of the *Constitución Española* (CE) defines two types of *Comunidades Autónomas*: *nacionalidades* (the Basques, that Catalans and the Galicians), which can claim the status of "historical nations", and *regiones*, which strive for autonomy on the basis of particular historical prerogatives (Navarre), their geography (the Balearics, the Canaries), or for socio-economic reasons (Andalusia, Extremadura, Valencia) (cf. Díaz-López 1985; Moreno 1997). While all *CCAA* have the right to accede to full institutional and political autonomy, the constitution prescribes different routes: a "fast track" procedure for the *nacionalidades* and a "slow track" procedure for the *regiones* (cf. Agranoff and Ramos Gallarín 1997). Ultimately, all *CCAA* opted for full political as opposed to mere administrative autonomy. The attempt of the central state to harmonize the level of autonomy among the *CCAA* has further reduced the privileged status that the three *nacionalidades* had initially enjoyed. The policy of *"café para todos"* (coffee for everyone) as opposed to "champagne for the *nacionalidades*", supported by all national political parties, profoundly challenged preferential status and caused substantial conflicts between the *nacionalidades* and the central state. The claim for privileged rights has also provoked conflict among *CCAA* themselves, as the slow-track *CCAA* reject the claim of the fast-track *CCAA* for privileged powers. But even among the *nacionalidades*, the Catalans complain that the Basques and the Navarese are "given brandy with their coffee" in form of taxation privileges (Agranoff 1993: 5).

*Marble-cake fiscal federalism and the problem
of fiscal centralization*

While the Spanish Constitution provided the regions with (the potential for) strong political autonomy vis-à-vis the central state, it breaks with a major principle of dual federalism: strong fiscal autonomy at the regional level. Authentic autonomy implies control over financial resources. Art. 156 of the Spanish Constitution recognizes the right of the *CCAA* to financial autonomy. The regional governments have been granted considerable tax and spending powers. Yet, unlike Germany, taxation power is exclusively granted to the central state. Any fiscal power must be devolved to the regional level.

The *CCAA* possess their own financial resources in the form of regional taxes, charges, surcharges over and above state taxes, borrowing, and investments. However, with the exception of the Basque Country (*el País Vasco*) and Navarre, which have an autonomous financial system,[56] regional resources constitute only a small percentage of total revenue for any of the other 15 *CCAA* (ca. 14%). Regional tax revenues are far smaller than those of the municipalities, which collect taxes such as property tax, business tax, and vehicle tax. Moreover, the *CCAA* have largely refrained from levying an income tax add-on or surtax to finance their services because of the general unpopularity of such measures.

The bulk of revenue comes from the central government via conditional and unconditional grants (block grants, tax-sharing grants, matching funds, retention/ceding of certain state taxes). The share of the different *CCAA* in state revenue is calculated with a formula based on their population, land area, administrative units, dispersal of population, relative poverty, fiscal pressure, and insularity. Another source of regional income is the *Fondo de Compensación Interritorial* (FCI), an inter-regional compensation fund, which allocates state money designated for the economic development of poorer regions in accordance with a needs formula based on population, income, net emigration, unemployment rate, and geographic size.

The distribution of financial resources has resulted in significant conflict in intergovernmental relations in Spain. On the one hand, the poorer *CCAA* complain that the FCI favors more densely populated regions, such as Madrid, Andalusia, Valencia and, above all, Catalonia on whose support the Spanish government depended for several years in the national parliament. On the other hand, the Basque Country and Catalonia deny that they are "net-payers" of the FCI due to the relatively high level of personal income tax generated in the two *CCAA*. Moreover, the Catalans have constantly protested against the privileged taxation rights of the Basques and the Navarese. Poorer *CCAA* share this critique of what they consider as unfair tax advantages, especially in the case of the Basque Country, which pays a lower share than it otherwise would (cf. Hildebrand 1992).

Asymmetrical bicameralism and the problem of intergovernmental cooperation

While fiscal centralization conflicts with the model of dual federalism, the weak representation of the *CCAA* at the central-state level corresponds to

---

[56] Two special economic agreements, the *concierto económico* for the Basque country and the *convenio económico* for Navarre, grant the three Basque provinces and the single province of Navarre the right to levy and collect taxes, except customs duties and taxes on petroleum products and tobacco. The two *CCAA* have to deduct an annual quota (*cupo*) from their tax income which is paid to the central state for services and responsibilities that the latter retains in the two *CCAA*.

a vertical distribution of power that stresses the independence of the two levels of government. The Spanish Constitution opted for a weak or asymmetrical bicameralism, which follows the *Senado* (Senate) rather than the *Bundesrat* principle (Lijphart 1984). Art. 69.1 CE defines the *Senado* as the "Chamber of territorial representation" of the national parliament. But only 20% of the *senadores* (senators) are drawn from among the members of the regional assemblies. The vast majority is directly elected in the *provincias* (provinces), administrative units below the regional and above the local level, with four *senadores* (senators) assigned to each *provincia* (region). Moreover, unlike the German *Bundesrat*, the *Senado* (the Senate) has only a weak role in central-state decision-making. It enjoys the right to legal initiative (Art. 87 CE), which is, however, rarely invoked, and has only a suspending veto power in the second reading of national draft laws (Art. 90 CE). Due to its composition and weak decision-making powers, the *Senado* does not constitute a real chamber of territorial representation; nor does it provide a means for integrating regional interests into national policy-making (cf. Muñoz Machado 1985; Parejo Alfonso 1993; Albertí Rovira *et al.* 1995). Any attempt to turn the *Senado* into an effective chamber of representation for territorial interests has so far failed since the *CCAA* are unable to agree on its nature and composition (cf. Cienfuegos Mateo 1997).

Given the weak role of the *Senado* and the need to achieve a minimum of cross-regional policy harmonization and a coordinated implementation of state policies in the 17 *CCAA*, the central-state administration has had to resort to alternative mechanisms for intergovernmental coordination. In 1983 the Spanish government presented a draft law to establish the *Conferencias Sectoriales* (sectoral conferences) as "interministerial fora" for intergovernmental coordination.[57] The *CCAA* appealed to the Constitutional Court because they perceived the "imposed" intergovernmental cooperation as an attempt by the central state to curtail their autonomous powers. Their mistrust was fostered by the fact that the *Conferencias* resulted from one of the four *Acuerdos Autonómicos* (autonomic agreements), agreements to which the ruling conservative party (UCD) and the socialist opposition (PSOE) agreed in the aftermath of the attempted coup of 1981 in order to bring the autonomy process under tighter control of the central state. The Constitutional Court approved the sectoral conferences. While the number of sectoral conferences (*Conferencias Sectoriales*) steadily increased over the years, they remained a source of intergovernmental conflict rather than cooperation. The *CCAA* showed a clear disinterest in participating, which in some cases amounted to a

---

[57] *Ley 12/1983, de 14 de octubre, de Proceso Autonómico* (LPA).

de facto boycott of the institution (interview MAP$_{51}$). The attempt to "revitalize" the conferences by formally institutionalizing them in 1992 did not have much of an impact.[58] The effectiveness of the conferences improved only when European issues started to dominate the agenda (see Chapter 8).

The *Planes y Programas Conjuntos* provided another formal institution through which the central government hoped to achieve intergovernmental cooperation. Joint Plans and Programs (JPPs) allow the central state and the *CCAA* to organize joint tasks and activities by formulating common goals, identifying ways to implement them, and setting up the necessary financial arrangements. The number of JPPs has significantly increased over the years, especially since the Community Programs became part of the JPPs. But their number is still relatively small compared with the large number of bilateral intergovernmental agreements (*convenios*) between the central state and individual *CCAA* (see below).

Bilateralism, confrontation, and regional competition as the dominant institutional culture of Spanish regionalism[59]

The ineffectiveness of formal institutions in coordinating the interests and policies of the central state and the *CCAA* can be largely attributed to an institutional culture of bilateralism, confrontation, and competition. The Spanish government and the *CCAA* strive to "solve" problems and to settle intergovernmental conflicts by means of bilateral bargaining and constitutional conflict rather than by multilateral cooperation and consensus-seeking.

The two most important instruments of intergovernmental cooperation in Spain are *Juntas de Cooperación* (bilateral commissions) and *convenios* (intergovernmental agreements). The *Juntas de Cooperación* serve as an informal platform for the exchange of information, the settling of conflicts over competencies, and the discussion of joint activities. They do not have any decision-making powers but prepare joint agreements (such as *convenios*), which are then signed by the governments. Bilateral commissions also exist in specific policy areas, such as public

---

[58] *Ley 30/1992, sobre el Régimen Jurídico de las Administraciones Públicas y del Procedimiento Administrativo Común.*

[59] The role of the party system in intergovernmental relations is left aside here. It follows the tradition of bilateral bargaining in Spanish territorial politics and has not provided a venue for multilateral intergovernmental cooperation (Agranoff and Ramos Gallarín 1997: 32–33).

security, public finance, health, agriculture, forestry, and environment (cf. Albertí Rovira 1990). Even more important than bilateral commissions are the "*cooperación por teléfono*" (cooperation by phone) (Albertí Rovira 1991: 214) and the informal *ad hoc* meetings between higher officials of the central state and the regional administration, where specific problems are tackled and agreements prepared before they enter a bilateral commission (interview Gencat$_{63}$).

Convenios are the major instrument of formal intergovernmental cooperation on specific issues. Unlike most of the bilateral commissions, they have a legal basis. *Convenios* have played a crucial role in the devolution of competencies to the *CCAA* by delimiting competencies and regulating the transfer of corresponding resources and services from the central state to the regional level. Moreover, *convenios* distribute a large proportion of financial resources to the *CCAA*. They are not *per se* bilateral. *Convenios* can be agreed upon between the central-state administration and several, if not all, *CCAA*. Almost all *convenios* are, however, bilateral. Between 1981 and 1999 the Spanish government negotiated around 5000 *convenios* with individual *Comunidades Autónomas*. Other *CCAA* subscribed to about half of them at a later date, that is, the Spanish government bilaterally signed the same agreement with various or all *CCAA*. Genuinely multilateral *convenios*, which are negotiated and agreed upon between the Spanish government and all 17 *CCAA*, are very rare (*Ministerio para las Administraciones Públicas* 1996; unpublished data of MAP, June 2000).

All in all, intergovernmental cooperation between the central state and the *CCAA* has steadily increased over the years but has been predominantly characterized by "*el casuismo, la informalidad y la bilateralidad*" (Albertí Rovira 1991: 214; cf. Albertí Rovira 1990; Viver i Pi-Sunyer 1990; García Morales 1993). Apart from *ad hoc* and informal bilateral bargaining, the *CCAA* have used the Constitutional Court as the major means of conflict resolution. Unlike Germany, where *Bund* and *Länder* strive to resolve intergovernmental conflicts through political agreement, Spanish territorial politics display a strong degree of judicialization.

Spain accounts for the highest level of constitutional conflict among all decentralized states in Europe (cf. Viver i Pi-Sunyer 1990). Between 1981 and 1999 the Spanish government and the *CCAA* argued over 1000 constitutional conflicts in the Spanish Constitutional Court. Two-thirds were initiated by *CCAA*. Catalonia and the Basque Country were involved in more than half of the conflicts (unpublished data of MAP, Madrid, June 2000).

The preference of the *CCAA* for solving intergovernmental conflict in the Constitutional Court rather than by political agreement is explained largely by the general distrust that the *CCAA* have against the central state. On the one hand, a ruling of the Constitutional Court provides a reliable and permanent solution for contentious issues (often relating to the distribution of competencies). On the other hand, political agreements with the central state, like intergovernmental cooperation in general, have the "stigma of betraying regional interests" (interview Gencat$_{63}$). When the Catalan government signed the formal coalition agreement with the Spanish government of José Maria Aznar in 1996, the Catalan public was deeply split over the question as to whether this agreement "betrayed the Catalan cause" (*Avui*, March 26, 1996). Official cooperation with the central state has to provide many advantages in order to be justified in the eyes of the public (interview Gencat$_{63}$). The *CCAA* share a general suspicion that the central state uses intergovernmental cooperation in order to intervene in their autonomous sphere of competencies. The *Conferencias Sectoriales* are a case in point.

Confronting centralization: The *CCAA* strategy of confrontation and cost-shifting

Confronting centralization by extending and ring-fencing regional competencies

The *CCAA* consider centralization as the major challenge to their institutional autonomy. Unlike Germany, however, the *CCAA* have not faced any transfer of their competencies to the level of the central state. On the contrary, the years following Spain's transition to democracy witnessed the subsequent devolution of state competencies to the regional level. Yet, the *CCAA* claimed that an increasing number of state policies have interfered with what they claim to be their exclusive sphere of autonomous competencies. Moreover, most *CCAA* perceived the initiatives by the central-state administration to harmonize their competencies and to introduce mechanisms of intergovernmental cooperation as another attempt by the central state to regain competencies previously devolved to the regional level.

The *CCAA* strove to consolidate and protect their newly gained sphere of institutional autonomy against perceived attempts at harmonization and centralization by a two-fold confrontational strategy. First, they tried to extend their competencies to areas that the Spanish government considered as the responsibility of the central state. And, second, the *CCAA* attempted to ring-fence their autonomous sphere of competencies by contesting in the Constitutional Court any perceived intervention of the central state into their autonomous sphere of competencies.

This two-fold strategy is reflected in the high number of constitutional conflicts between central state and the *CCAA* over the distribution and exercise of competencies (see above). The general consolidation of the territorial system has, however, made the strategy increasingly less effective. Numerous rulings of the Constitutional Court have subsequently established a delimitation of central-state and regional competencies that has not left much room for either the *CCAA* or the central state to expand their responsibilities. Many constitutional conflicts over the distribution of competencies have turned into a repetition of conflicts already fought. Moreover, the casuistic jurisdiction of the Constitutional Court has tended to bolster the position of the central state, which has drawn extensively on its competence for setting framework legislation and economic planning as a means of intervening in areas of regional competencies (Viver i Pi-Sunyer 1990; Mitjans Perelló 1993). As a result, the number of constitutional conflicts over competencies started to drop at the end of the 1980s. More than three-quarters of all constitutional conflicts originated before 1989. Yet, the number of conflicts over the constitutionality of regional law and national law has not declined. Between 1989 and 1999 the *CCAA* introduced 188 cases (compared to 215 before 1989) in which they considered central state legislation as unconstitutional because it interfered with their autonomous jurisdiction (unpublished data of MAP, Madrid, June 2000). Constitutional conflict is still more prevalent in Spanish intergovernmental relations than in other decentralized countries.

The confrontational strategy of the *CCAA* is also apparent in their refusal of systematic cooperation with the central state. The *CCAA* have by and large rejected formal, multilateral forms of intergovernmental cooperation that would coordinate the exercise of shared competencies. As a result, many central-state policies have not been implemented, or have been implemented only partially, at the regional level. While the *CCAA* recognize the problem, they requested a further devolution of state competencies, which the central state was not willing to grant, not least because of the strong socio-economic heterogeneity of the *CCAA*. On the contrary, the central state tried to recentralize some of the regional competencies in order to ensure a more effective implementation of its policies. Thus, both central state and regions tried to shift the costs of decentralization onto each other rather than sharing them. Instead of establishing viable mechanisms of intergovernmental cooperation, central state and *CCAA* competed for competencies, which resulted in serious problems of policy effectiveness.

'Cada una por su cuenta': *The refusal of regional coalition-building*

The regional strategy of confrontation and non-cooperation also shows in the relations, or so-called relations, between the 17 *CCAA*. There is strong competition among the *CCAA* for political and economic power, particularly between the *nacionalidades* and the other *CCAA*. Given this "ethnoterritorial concurrence" (Moreno 1994, 1997; cf. Linz 1973), the *CCAA* have not developed a strong sense of solidarity, which might have provided the basis for successful coalition-building of the *CCAA* vis-à-vis the central state.

There has been no forum in which the *CCAA* would discuss common issues and coordinate their interests. This is partly due to formal institutions that discourage horizontal self-coordination among the *CCAA*. Unlike the case of vertical intergovernmental coordination, the Spanish Constitution does provide explicit regulations on relationships amongst the *CCAA*. While Art. 145.1 CE prohibits the formation of any political alliance between the *CCAA*, Art. 145.2 CE offers the possibility of inter-governmental agreements between the *CCAA*. Yet, depending on their character, such agreements are subject to different levels of state control. Some need the explicit authorization of the national parliament (cf. Albertí Rovira 1993). Not surprisingly, there are less than a dozen horizontal agreements between two or more *CCAA* – compared with about 5000 vertical agreements between individual *CCAA* and the central government (Albertí Rovira 1998). If they use any mechanism at all, the *CCAA* have resorted to informal or non-public forms of cooperation.

But it is not only the rigid requirements of the constitution, often taken as the expression of a general distrust of the central state toward any kind of horizontal cooperation among the *CCAA*, which discouraged the *CCAA* from seeking mutual cooperation. The lack of a collectively shared sense of commonality and solidarity precluded the identification and pursuit of common interests. The *CCAA* have hardly sought allies among themselves in order to advance their interests vis-à-vis the central state. The economically well-off *CCAA*, such as Catalonia or the Basque Country, tend to identify themselves more with their Northern European counterparts than with the less resourceful *CCAA*, particularly in the South of Spain (interview Gencat[63]). As we see in Chapter 8, the *CCAA* have only recently started to develop a common interest in coping with the costs of Europeanization. They started this when they realized that pursuing a joint position vis-à-vis the central state was more effective in redressing the territorial balance of power than their previous approach of "*cada una por su cuenta*" (each to their own).

8 Toward a framework of joint decision-making: The impact of Europeanization on the territorial institutions of Spain

This chapter shows how the Spanish territorial institutions faced similar pressure for adaptation as the German ones but induced the Spanish regions to pursue a non-cooperative adaptational strategy, which prohibited a redressing of the territorial balance of power. In light of rising adaptational costs the *CCAA* gradually adopted a more cooperative strategy, which resulted in a profound change of Spanish competitive regionalism.

The centralization of implementation and the uneven distribution of "say and pay"

Europeanization posed a serious challenge to the still fragile territorial institutions of Spain. Similar to the former Art. 24 of the German *Grundgesetz* (GG), Art. 93 of the Spanish Constitution allows for the transfer of both national and regional competencies to the European level without requiring the consent of the *CCAA*. Unlike the *Länder*, the *CCAA* do not have any co-determination powers to lose when national competencies are transferred to the European level because they do not participate in national decision-making. Nor have the *CCAA* been so concerned about the Europeanization of their autonomous competencies *per se*, although they are considerably affected in the area of agriculture, fisheries, industry, economic planning, environment, social welfare, and consumer affairs (Borras 1990). The *CCAA* have, however, felt that the central state would use the implementation of Community Law as an "alibi" to regain competencies previously devolved to the *CCAA* (Pujol 1987: 25).

When Spain joined the European Community in 1986, the Spanish administration faced a huge implementation burden. Unlike Portugal, Spain adopted the whole *acquis communautaire* (Community legislation in force) at once, and this led to considerable policy overload. The effective implementation of European policies was more difficult because the central-state and the *CCAA* lacked effective mechanisms of

103

intergovernmental cooperation to coordinate their resources in the implementation process.

In order to speed-up the incorporation of the *acquis communautaire* into Spanish legislation, the Spanish Parliament authorized the central government to adapt national legislation to European law by *Reales Decretos* (Royal Decrees), executive regulations which have the status of a law. At the same time, the central-state administration strove to acquire the general competence for legal transposition of European policies into national law.

After a long dispute in the legal literature on whether the *CCAA* should have any role in implementing Community Law, the Constitutional Court finally ruled in 1988 that the implementation of European policies must not alter the internal distribution of competencies between central state and *CCAA*. The Court thereby denied the central state the exclusive competence to transpose Community law.[60] Nevertheless, the central state managed to "capture" the transposition of virtually all European policies – even if those policies fell under the exclusive competencies of the *CCAA*. In the first 10 years of Spain's EC membership, only one European Directive was not incorporated into the Spanish legal system by a central-state law (*Ministerio para las Administraciones Públicas* 1995). The Spanish government justified intrusion into the regional sphere of autonomy on the grounds of its foreign policy prerogative (Art. 149.1.3 CE), its competencies for external trade and commerce (Art. 1491.10 CE), and its general responsibility for economic planning (Art. 149.1.13 CE). In some policy areas, the central state also drew on its exclusive competence to set framework legislation in order to provide a "lowest common denominator" for the application of Community Law at the regional level.

As in Germany, the central state was able to access regional competencies that the Spanish Constitution removed from its reach in domestic policy-making. But this (re)centralization effect materialized at the implementation rather than the decision-making stage of European policies (Montoro Chiner 1989: 203–209; Borras 1990: 57; Tornos i Más 1991: 43; Barcelo i Serramalera 1993: 18–20; Parejo Alfonso 1993). Unlike the *Länder*, the *CCAA* fought to recapture their competencies from the central state through the Constitutional Court. The Constitutional Court initially supported the general, albeit not exclusive, competence of the central state for transposing Community Law (Casanovas y la Rosa 1989; González Ayala 1991). The Constitutional Court partly revoked its "state-friendly" jurisdiction in 1995 and decided that if an EU Directive

[60] *STC 252/1988, de 22 de diciembre, BOE n°. 11 (suplemento), de 13 de enero de 1989: 39–45; cf. STC 153/1989, de 5 de octubre, BJC 1989: 1644.*

was specific enough to provide "a lowest common denominator", then the *CCAA* could implement it directly.[61] The implementation of European policies no longer necessarily requires the legal intervention of the central state. At this point, however, the *CCAA* had already come to accept the predominance of the central state in the legal transposition of European policies, not least because the *CCAA* have different competencies in the implementation of Community law. The central state has to transpose Directives in order to provide the legal basis for those *CCAA* that are competent only to execute European policies administratively.

While the transposition of Community Law *per se* by the central state had become less of an issue, the *CCAA* and the Spanish government continued to argue over the scope and content of the transposing legislation. The *CCAA* often have the main competence to implement European Law. But it is the central state which is responsible to the EU for any implementation failure (Muñoz Machado 1985: 70). The Spanish government found itself increasingly under pressure from the European Commission for its bad implementation record. While its transposition record is relatively high, Spain is at the bottom end of the list, along with Greece and Italy, with respect to practical implementation and enforcement, for which it is mainly the *CCAA* that are responsible (Commission of the European Communities 1990, 1996, 1998). Beyond a unified and detailed transposition of Community Law, the central state has hardly any legal means to intervene in the practical application and enforcement of European policies in the *CCAA* (cf. Parejo Alfonso 1993). As a result, the central-state administration has extensively drawn on its exclusive competencies to enact and develop framework legislation, which has significantly reduced the discretion of the *CCAA* in the implementation of European policies. The Constitutional Court ruled that framework legislation provided less room than other central-state legislation for legal development at the regional level.[62] Moreover, setting framework legislation has allowed the central state to exercise executive functions otherwise entrusted to the *CCAA*.[63] The Constitutional Court itself has determined that by particularizing the transposition of European Directives, the central-state administration often "reduces their domestic legal status to the level of administrative regulations",[64] as a result of which the *CCAA* are often left without much discretion in practical application and enforcement. The centralization of regional competencies through

---

[61] *STC 102/95, de 26 de junio de 1995.*
[62] *STC 148/91, de 4 de julio de 1991; cf. STC 64/82, de 4 de noviembre de 1982.*
[63] *STC de 28 de enero de 1982; STC de 8 de julio de 1982.*
[64] *STC 149/1991, de 4 de julio de 1991*, quoted in Barcelo i Serramalera 1993: 20.

the enactment of far-reaching and detailed central-state regulations in the transposition of Community law is particularly prevalent in the areas of agriculture, fisheries, cattle-rearing, dairy production, and environment (Montoro Chiner 1990).[65]

Striving to centralize responsibilities in European policy-making, the central government was reluctant to involve the *CCAA* in the implementation of EU policies (Bengoetxea 1994). When the *CCAA* demanded a proportional participation in the management of European Structural Funds after Spain had joined the EC, the central government argued that the *CCAA* would lack the experience of "effectively managing these resources" (*Ministerio para las Administraciones Públicas* 1995: 130; my translation). Moreover, the central government claimed the main responsibility for the management of the Funds because a substantial part would be used for the restructuring of economic sectors as well as for a balanced regional development, both of which fall under the jurisdiction of the central state (*Ministerio para las Administraciones Públicas* 1995: 130). Thus, the central-state administration initially managed to resist any participation of the *CCAA* in the negotiations on the Community Support Frameworks. Between 1986 and 1988 all projects financed by the European Fund for Regional Development were central-state projects (Morata 1995: 126–129). This only started to change with the two reforms of the Structural Funds in 1988 and 1993 respectively (cf. Conejos 1993).

All in all, Europeanization led to a considerable centralization of legal and administrative competencies of the *CCAA*. The centralization of the implementation of European policies through their detailed transposition into national framework legislation seriously affected the institutional autonomy of the *CCAA*. Like Germany, the transfer of policy competencies to the European level allowed the central state to access legal and administrative competencies of the *CCAA* that the Constitution prevented it from reaching. At the same time, the *CCAA* bear the lion's share of the implementation costs because the central state left practical application and enforcement of European policies with all its costs to the *CCAA*, which neither participate in the decision-making of these policies at the EU level nor, unlike the *Länder*, in their transposition at the central-state level. As in Germany, this uneven distribution of "say and pay" in European policy-making resulted in a significant redistribution of power between central state and regions that changed the territorial balance of power to the detriment of the *CCAA*.

---

[65] For a complete list of examples, see Tornos i Más 1991: 32–33.

The *Comunidades Autónomas* fight centralization

Cooperating versus bypassing: The strategy of confronting and circumventing the state

The Spanish *CCAA* had the same strategy options as the German *Länder* in trying to redress the territorial balance of power. They could pursue a confrontational strategy of ring-fencing their autonomous sphere of responsibilities by fighting the centralization of their competencies in the Constitutional Court. Simultaneously, they could strive to bypass or circumvent the gate-keeping position of the central state in European policy-making by seeking direct contact with European institutions on an individual basis as well as through the collective representation of regional interests at the European level. Alternatively, they could follow the example of the German *Länder* and try to break the central-state monopoly in European policy-making by pushing for cooperation with the Spanish government in the decision-making as well as the implementation of European policies.

In particular, the "big four" *CCAA* (Catalonia, the Basque Country, Galicia, and Andalusia), which had attained full autonomy before the other *CCAA*, had sufficient resources to pursue either strategy. They possess the organizational capacity as well as the political self-understanding to act independently at the European level. In order to ensure the effective incorporation of Community Law into the Spanish legal system, the central state also offered the *CCAA* the opportunity to establish intergovernmental cooperation in European policy-making even before Spain joined the European Community. But unlike the *Länder*, the *CCAA* initially showed little interest in participating in European policy-making through cooperation with the central-state administration. Rather, they tried to gain direct access to the European policy arena by circumventing the central-state level. Moreover, the *CCAA* resorted to constitutional conflict to restrict intervention of the central state in their sphere of competencies.

1985–87: The failure of intergovernmental cooperation

When Spain joined the European Community in 1986, the Spanish central-state administration felt the need to establish some form of intergovernmental coordination between the central state and the *CCAA*, especially to ensure the effective implementation of Community law. Taking the German model of intrastate participation as a reference point (*Ministerio para las Administraciones Públicas* 1995: 139), the Spanish government made an initial proposal for some regional participation in

European policy-making at the end of 1985, shortly before Spain's accession to the EC.

The agreement would regulate the participation of the *CCAA* both in the decision-making and implementation of European legal acts. For the implementation stage, the Spanish government suggested a distribution of responsibilities, in which the central state, notwithstanding the internal distribution of competencies, would legally transpose European policies, and the *CCAA* would put them into practice. The *CCAA* would not be allowed to have any direct contact with European institutions. With regard to the participation of the *CCAA* in the decision-making stage, the proposal was less specific. If the central government decided that an EU proposal could affect autonomous competencies, it would inform the *CCAA*. The Spanish government would consider the concerns of the *CCAA* in the formulation of its bargaining position. The proposed agreement also foresaw the possibility of using the *Conferencias Sectoriales* to facilitate the development of common criteria for the implementation of European policies, so as to avoid contradicting implementation norms at the regional level.

The *CCAA* rejected the proposal. Several *CCAA* interpreted the clause on the transposition of European legal acts as a general competence of the central state to implement European policies. Moreover, the *CCAA* found that clear mention of mechanisms for cooperation that would facilitate their participation was lacking. The proposal mentioned the option of using the *Conferencias Sectoriales* but at the same time alluded to other mechanisms of intergovernmental coordination, such as mixed committees. Catalonia, the Basque Country, and Galicia, in particular, criticized the attempt of the central government to control fully or to gate-keep their access to the European level. First, the central government would decide which information could concern regional affairs and would be forwarded to the *CCAA*. Second, the positions of the *CCAA* would not be binding for the Spanish government. While Catalonia referred to the German model when suggesting improvements, the Basque Country insisted on a bilateral solution that would effectively allow it to voice Basque interests vis-à-vis the central government. Third, the *CCAA* would not be allowed to maintain direct official contacts with European institutions; they would not even have state-mediated access to European decision-making bodies because the agreement did not foresee the participation of their representatives in the Spanish delegation.[66]

---

[66] For documentation of the reactions of the *CCAA* to the 1985 proposal, see *Ministerio para las Administraciones Públicas* 1995: 139–143.

In early 1986 the Catalan government launched a counter proposal, which dismissed the suggestions of the government proposal for the implementation of European policies. The constitutional distribution of competencies was considered sufficient for regulating the responsibilities of central state and *CCAA* in the implementation of European policies. With regard to European decision-making, the central government would be obliged to inform the *CCAA* about all European issues concerning their competencies. The *CCAA* would have the right to make binding recommendations, if their exclusive responsibilities were affected. In order to prepare these recommendations, the *CCAA* would set up a delegation of six representatives (*Delegación de las Comunidades Autónomas para asuntos europeos*), which would include the Observer of the *CCAA* in European Affairs, his/her Deputy, and a General Secretary of the Delegation. Each of the three *CCAA* with nationality status (Catalonia, the Basque Country, and Galicia) would be entitled to nominate one of the six delegates. The Delegation would form part of the Spanish Permanent Representation in Brussels and enjoy diplomatic status. As members of the Spanish delegation, the *CCAA* Delegates would participate in all European decision-making bodies, including the Committee of Permanent Representatives (COREPER).

The majority of the *CCAA* rejected the Catalan proposal because of the privileged rights it would grant to the three historical *CCAA*. For the central government, the proposal was not only unacceptable because of the uneven representation of the *CCAA* in the regional delegation: Madrid would also not allow any direct representation of the *CCAA* at the European level (*Ministerio para las Administraciones Públicas* 1995: 141).

In April 1986 the Spanish government prepared its second proposal, which took into account some of the concerns the *CCAA* had raised against the first proposal. The first part of the proposal assured the *CCAA* that the implementation of European law would be regulated according to the distribution of responsibilities in domestic policy-making. In order to facilitate the implementation of European policies, the central-state administration and the *CCAA* would mutually inform each other of what action each was taking. With regard to the decision-making stage, the suggested procedure was "inspired" by the German *Zuleitungsverfahren* (*Ministerio para las Administraciones Públicas* 1995: 144; cf. Muñoz Machado 1986: 87). The Spanish government (*Ministerio para Administraciones Territoriales*; MAT) would provide the *CCAA* with all European documents and information concerning their competencies. The *CCAA* could formulate opinions and transmit them to MAT. The *CCAA* would create an interautonomous coordination body in order to facilitate the exchange of information, the formulation of a joint position of the *CCAA*, and the coordination of the positions of the central-state administration and the *CCAA*. However, the *CCAA* were not required to formulate joint positions. The central government would strive to give due consideration to opinions and concerns voiced by the individual *CCAA* – provided that they were compatible with "the general interest of the State and the process of integration". Finally, the interautonomous coordination body could nominate an *Observador de las Comunidades Autónomas* (Observer) and his/her deputy. The *Observador* and his/her deputy, appointed and paid by the Minister of Foreign Affairs for two years, would be members of the Spanish Permanent Representation in Brussels and, as such, enjoy diplomatic status. As members of the Spanish delegation, they could participate in the working committees of the European decision-making bodies. They would also be allowed to express opinions, as long as these opinions coincided with those of the official Spanish delegation. A representation of the *CCAA* in the COREPER and the Council of Ministers was implicitly excluded.

The general election in 1986 prevented the formal submission of this governmental proposal to the *CCAA*. After the election, fiscal issues dominated the debate between the central state and the *CCAA*. But in 1987, the Spanish government announced that it would draft a third proposal. The 1987 proposal adopted the first part of the 1986 project on the implementation of European policies. But the regulations for the participation of the *CCAA* in the decision-making phase were partly changed. The idea of an interautonomous coordination body was dropped. Instead, the *Conferencias Sectoriales* were identified as a possible forum, at which the *Ministerio para Administraciones Públicas* (MAP, formerly MAT) would provide information for the *CCAA* on European issues and where the *CCAA* could voice their opinions. Notwithstanding the *Conferencias Sectoriales*, the *CCAA* and central state could establish additional mechanisms of intergovernmental coordination. The central government would only be obliged to inform the *CCAA* on issues falling under their exclusive competencies. The same applied to the information the Autonomous Observer would pass on to the *CCAA*. The Observer would be appointed by the Minister of Public Administration for three years. As a member of the Spanish delegation, he/she would be allowed to participate not only in the decision-making bodies of Commission and Council but also in the meetings of the Council of Ministers and the COREPER. The diplomatic status of the Observer was made optional. A deputy Observer was no longer foreseen as necessary.

When the 1987 proposal was introduced to the *Comisión Mixta Congreso–Senado para las Comunidades Europeas*,[67] the *CCAA* representatives engaged in a heated debate. The representative of the Basque nationalist party voiced serious objections, especially against the specific set-up of the Observer of the *CCAA*. The nomination of only one Observer would not account for the differential status (*hecho diferencial*) of the *CCAA*. These reservations where shared by the Catalans, who also raised concerns about the *Conferencias Sectoriales* as the means for intergovernmental coordination. The presence of the Spanish government was felt inappropriate in the formulation of a joint position of the *CCAA*. Moreover, limitation to the access of information on issues concerning only exclusive competencies of the *CCAA* was criticized.[68] In light of the *CCAA*'s objections, the Spanish government withdrew its proposal.

The first three attempts of the Spanish government to establish a general framework of intergovernmental cooperation in European affairs with the *CCAA* failed. The reasons for the failure lie with the institutional culture of competitive regionalism. Due to their heterogeneity in terms of competencies, economic power and historical self-understanding, the *CCAA* did not build a uniform block vis-à-vis the central state. The different positions of the *CCAA* can be placed on a continuum reaching from "indifference" to "opposition" toward multilateral intergovernmental cooperation in European policy-making (intrastate participation).

On the one side of the continuum, there are the less resourceful *CCAA*, which lack the historical identity and/or the political and economic resources of Catalonia, the Basque Country, Galicia, Andalusia, or Valencia. Extremadura, La Rioja, Castilla-La Mancha, Castilla-León, Cantabria, or Asturias have shown little interest in systematically participating in European policy-making, either at the domestic or at the European level. They do not question the idea of multilateral intergovernmental cooperation with the central state; nor have they voiced any significant demands for extrastate participation in European decision-making. The level of their European activities is low, partly because they lack the resources to establish direct access to the European policy arena.

---

[67] The *Comisión Mixta Congreso-Senado para las Comunidades Europeas* (Joint Commission comprising nine Members of Parliament and six Senators) was established to evaluate adaptation of Spanish legislation to Community Law. It now serves as an important parliamentary committee in European policy-making. It has to be informed by the government on all Community initiatives, controls the implementation of Community Law in Spain, can make statements on Community initiatives, and maintains regular contact with the European Parliament and the EU committees of other national parliaments. Both the *Congreso* and the *Senado* delegated decision-making powers to the *Comisión Mixta* with respect to European issues.

[68] *Diario de las sesiones del Congreso, de 3 de febrero de 1987, BOE n°. 58: 227.*

On the other side of the continuum, we find the Basque Country whose strategy vis-à-vis the central state in both European and domestic politics is based on a Basque nationalism that perceives European integration as a process in which states become less and less important and in which the Basque people (comprising the Spanish and the French Basques) can advance its aspirations to become a united nation within a single Basque country. Due to its privileged taxation rights, the Basque Country has been less dependent on intergovernmental cooperation with the central-state administration. It is financially strong enough to opt out of national programs such as social services (the Basques have their own programs) and to avoid national policy standards. Following its own identification as a distinct nation rather than a region (Bengoetxea 1994), the Basque administration has insisted for a long time on strictly bilateral relations with the central state at the domestic level. It also claimed direct, diplomatic representation at the European level, be it through independent participation in the Council of Ministers or through the establishment of an official "Embassy" in Brussels.[69] Its insistence on a state-like status in European policy-making has also led to a low profile by the Basque Country in the European institutions of regional representation.

Catalonia and Galicia share the Basque aspirations for an independent and direct representation of the *CCAA* in the European decision-making bodies, especially in the Council of Ministers. The two other *CCAA* with nationality status have, however, pursued a less dogmatic, or more pragmatic, strategy than the Basque Country. Despite a clear preference for bilateral relations with the central state as well as for direct access to the European decision-making process (Albertí Rovira 1990; García Morales 1993; Dalmau i Oriol 1997), the Catalan government has never fully rejected the idea of multilateral intrastate participation in European policy-making. Yet, like the Basque Country, the Catalan nationalist party insisted on the recognition of the *hecho diferencial*. Consequently, Catalonia has requested privileged rights in any framework of intergovernmental cooperation (Morata 1995: 122).

Finally, there is a group of *CCAA* (Andalusia, Valencia, the Canaries, the Balearics, and Navarre) that have a substantial interest in participating in European policy-making; these interests vary, however, across policy sectors. They have rejected the special claims of Catalonia and the Basque Country but share their suspicion that the central state could use intergovernmental cooperation to intervene in their autonomous affairs. Thus, the idea of using the *Conferencias Sectoriales* for the formulation of joint *CCAA* positions was rejected not only by Catalonia and the Basque

---

[69] *Informe sobre la participación institucional de Euskadi en la Construcción europea, Secretaría de la Presidencia del Gobierno Vasco. Victoria-Gasteiz, 15 de noviembre 1993.*

Country but also by other *CCAA* because the central government insisted on being present at the meetings.[70]

The *CCAA*'s diverging and separate political identification have made it difficult to find a *modus operandi* of intergovernmental cooperation that would accommodate the interests and claims of all *CCAA*, especially those of Catalonia and the Basque Country. "Asymmetrical federalism" (Agranoff 1993) and "ethnoterritorial concurrence" (Moreno 1997) have precluded any effective horizontal coordination of interests among the *CCAA*, which is a prerequisite for both agreement on, and an effective functioning of, a regional intrastate participation in European decision-making. Not all *CCAA* have pursued the strategy of "confronting and circumventing the state" with the same vigor as Catalonia and the Basque Country. But any agreement on intrastate participation of the *CCAA* in European policy-making has required the consent of these two *CCAA*.

Not willing to cooperate either with the central state or amongst each other, the *CCAA* have relied on bilateral and informal contact with the central government in order to voice their interests on European issues. During negotiations on Spanish EC membership, over 200 informal and bilateral meetings took place between the central government and various *CCAA* (Bustos Gisbert 1995). In the first years after Spain's accession to the EC, some *CCAA* claimed that the Spanish government should consider their individual points of view on particular European initiatives. In the majority of cases, however, this was done on a purely bilateral and informal level. The *CCAA* have rarely voiced common claims (*Ministerio para las Administraciones Públicas* 1995: 131).

Confronting the state: Ring-fencing autonomous competencies through constitutional conflict

Not only have the *CCAA* refused to cooperate with the central-state administration in European policy-making, but they have also tried to fight central-state intervention in their sphere of competencies at the Spanish Constitutional Court. A significant number of constitutional conflicts involve Europe, especially with regard to the implementation of European policies in the area of agriculture and fisheries (cf. Pérez González 1989). Of the 237 constitutional conflicts between the Basque Country and the central state between 1981 and 1995, 36 cases (15.2%) were related to European issues. According to the Basque Country the number is even higher, at 51 (21.5%; *Ministerio para las Administraciones Públicas* 1995:

---

[70] See statements of the Galician, Valencian, and Andalusian Presidents during the first debate of the *Senado* on the State of Autonomies, *Diario de Sesiones del Senado, Comisiones, V Legislatura, 1994, núm. 128: 1–73, num. 129: 1–74.*

163). In more than 47 years of EC membership, the German *Länder*, in contrast, have filed only one constitutional conflict over competencies relating to European issues. In 1989 the Spanish Minister of Public Administration identified the "conflict over competencies generated in the application of Community law as one of the most fundamental problems to be solved between the *CCAA* and central state in European policy-making" (quoted in *Ministerio para las Administraciones Públicas* 1995: 146; my translation).

Circumventing the state: Extrastate channels of influence

The failure to agree on a participation procedure for the *CCAA* in European policy-making during the first years of Spanish EC membership does not reflect a general indifference of the *CCAA* toward European policy-making. Most *CCAA* anticipated Spain's membership of the EC by adapting their administrative institutions. Catalonia, for example, established its own European liaison office, the *Patronat Català Pro Europa*, as early as 1982. The *Patronat* is a public company of which the Catalan government holds a majority share. The company represents a whole variety of public and private interests at the European level. It was one of the first regional offices to open in Brussels. Two years later, the Catalan government created the *Dirección General de Adecuación a las Comunidades Europeas* (Directorate General for Adaptation to the European Communities) in the *Presidencia* (President's Office) which, after Spain's accession to the EC, took on the main responsibility for the development and execution of European law in Catalonia. Finally, the Catalan Parliament set up a commission in order to supervise the government's activities in adapting to Europeanization. Between 1984 and 1987 similar forms of institutional adaptation can be found in most of the *CCAA*.[71]

While the *CCAA* adjusted their administrative structures to facilitate the incorporation of European policies, they strove to break the central-state monopoly in European policy-making. They hoped to establish direct relations with European institutions in order to "outflank the central authorities" (Morata 1995: 124).

Most of the *CCAA* have been maintaining regular contact with EU institutions at an informal level. Regional politicians and delegations travel to Brussels more often than to any other foreign country (Cuerdo Pardo 1995: 77–78). In order to be regularly present at the European level, 14 of the 17 *CCAA* have opened information offices in Brussels. Like the *Länderbüros*, the offices serve the *CCAA* for collecting information, maintaining regular contact with EU institutions, and promoting their

---

[71] For an overview, see Gamero Casado 1993.

economic and cultural interests at the European level. The Basque Country, in particular, strove to turn its office into an official representation at the European level; this resulted in a constitutional conflict with the central state (see below).

The *CCAA* have also actively participated in various bodies of regional representation at the European level. When the Assembly of Regions in Europe (ARE) was created in 1989, all *CCAA* joined and provided two out of nine vice-presidents, of which one, the Catalan president Jordi Pujol, became president in 1992. The *CCAA* were also involved in the creation of the Committee of the Regions (CoR). Their joint proposal was adopted by the Spanish government, coordinated with the German government, and formed the basis for the regulations of the Maastricht Treaty that set up the CoR (Art. 198a; *Ministerio para las Administraciones Públicas* 1995: 36–40). The *CCAA* provided three out of 12 vice-presidents of the CoR, and in 1996 one of them, the Mayor of Barcelona and former president of the Council of European Municipalities, Pasqual Maragall, was elected president. Due to their identification as a nation rather than a region, the Basques have had a lower profile in the CoR as well as in other institutions of regional presentation (Bengoetxea 1994: 137). Other *CCAA* are selectively active in specific areas, such as viticulture or fisheries. Only Catalonia has pursued a more general political agenda by focusing on the institutional development of the CoR and the "third level" of the EU. During negotiations for the Maastricht Treaty, the Catalan President, Jordi Pujol, had already played an active role in coordinating the position of the "European Conference of the Regions" and the ARE (whose president he was at the time) on institutionalizing the "third level". When the CoR was established, the Catalan President became the spokesperson of the *ad hoc* committee for "Institutional Issues". Pujol also compiled a catalogue of CoR demands for the 1997 Intergovernmental Conference (Pujol Report).[72]

Catalonia has also been actively involved in initiatives of transregional and interregional cooperation, such as the "European Conference of the Regions", the "Four Motors for Europe", the "Pyrenean Working Group", and the "Transpyrenean Euro-region" (cf. Morata and Muñoz 1997). The central government only reluctantly tolerated such "foreign policy initiatives" by Catalonia.[73]

All in all, the *CCAA* have exploited European opportunities to establish several extrastate channels of access at the European level. The

---

[72] CoR 136/95.

[73] El Gobierno decide no obstacular las nuevas iniciativas de "política exterior" de Pujol, *El País*, 10.6.1990, referring to the "Four Motors for Europe" initiative. Cf. Solana: No parece que Pujol esté dispuesto a reconducir su diplomacia paralela, *El País*, 6.3.1993.

CCAA that have been critical and hostile toward the multilateral framework for intrastate participation, such as Catalonia and the Basque Country, have been the most prominent *CCAA* to make particular use of their direct contacts with European institutions in order to compensate for their domestic losses of power. Unlike the German *Länder*, however, which have deployed a similar level of European activities, the *CCAA* coordinated their activities neither among themselves nor with the central-state administration. Rather, they strove to pursue their own, often conflicting interests, on the basis of *"cada una por su cuenta"* ("each to their own") (interview Gencat₆₃).

Yet, toward the end of the 1980s the *CCAA* came to realize that their strategy of "circumventing and confronting the state" in European policy-making had little effect in opposing the centralization of their competencies.

A new strategy of cooperation and the emergence of institutional change

The pitfalls of confronting and circumventing the state

In their efforts to ring-fence their autonomous sphere of competencies by means of constitutional conflict, the *CCAA* had to realize that judicial proceedings are costly, time consuming, and not always rewarding. A ruling of the Constitutional Court could take up to five years and required considerable administrative resources (Viver i Pi-Sunyer 1990: 47). The jurisdiction of the Court indeed helped to clarify the delimitation of competencies between the central state and the *CCAA* in the implementation of European policies. But in most cases, the Constitutional Court sided with the central state. The Court adopted a broad interpretation of the central-state foreign-policy prerogative, its competencies for external trade, commerce and external health, and the setting and developing of framework legislation (Pérez Gonzalez 1989; González Ayala 1991). This broad interpretation enabled the central state to act legally in the implementation of virtually all European policies.

Initially, the Constitutional Court also supported the efforts of the Spanish government to restrict official contact between the *CCAA* and European institutions. The Court confirmed that the Spanish government was the *"interlocutor único"* (exclusive contact) with European institutions.[74] Along these lines, the Spanish government hoped to prevent

---

[74] *STC 172/1992, de 29 de octubre, BOE n°. 288, suplemento, de 1 de diciembre*: 35–37; see also *STC 80/1993, de 8 de marzo, BOE n°. 90, suplemento, de 15 de abril*: 3–13; cf. González Ayala 1991.

the establishment of an official Basque representation in Brussels, arguing that its exclusive competence for the external representation of Spain would rule out the establishment of official contact between the *CCAA* and European institutions (*Ministerio para las Administraciones Públicas* 1995: 132–133). The Constitutional Court finally decided in 1994 that the central state's foreign policy prerogative did not preclude the official representation of the *CCAA* at the European level as long as their activities did not take on any diplomatic character.[75] In this area, the *CCAA* no longer have to resort to non-official forms of representation.[76] Yet, the changing legal status of their offices in Brussels has not affected the relationship of the *CCAA* with European institutions to any great extent (interviews MAP$_{51}$; Patronat$_{64}$).

Unlike the *Länder*, the *CCAA* could not back up their lobbying efforts by formal participation in the formulation and representation of the Spanish bargaining position. Nor did they have regular access to European decision-making bodies, something which the German *Länder* had enjoyed from the very beginning. The Spanish Permanent Representation was not willing to share information with the *CCAA* in the way that the German Permanent Representation has done with the *Länder*. The central-state administration held an "almost absolute monopoly" on access to information on European affairs (Dalmau i Oriol 1997: 93). Lacking formal resources, access to European issues by the *CCAA* depended on the information and expertise that they could offer to European policy-makers as well as on their capacity to maneuver at the European level; this would involve personnel, money, etc. – resources which were scarce for almost all of the *CCAA*. Even the more powerful *CCAA* did not have sufficient resources to cover all European issues that were of regional concern (interview Gencat$_{63}$). As a result, the *CCAA* have largely concentrated their lobbying activities on particular areas, which usually involves European funding (regional policy, social policy, Cohesion Fund, agriculture, fisheries, and research and development). Attempts to influence the formulation of regulatory policies, such as environment or consumer protection, have been the exception rather than the rule (Patronat$_{64}$).

[75] *STC 165/1994, de 26 de mayo, BJC n°. 158*: 197ff. 1989, the Constitutional Court had already suspended a cooperation agreement between Denmark and the *Comunidad Autónoma de Galicia*, denying the *CCAA* any right to exert the *ius contrahendi* (treaty-making power) in foreign relations (García de Enterría 1991: 110).

[76] The new Administrative Law (*Ley de Organización y Funcionamiento de la Administración General del Estado*; LOFAGE) of 1996 recognizes the existence of regional delegations abroad and creates an obligation for the central-state administration to cooperate with them.

Direct access by the *CCAA* to European institutions has been further restricted by the cautious attitude of European policy-makers toward attempts by the regions to circumvent their central government. The European Commission, for instance, has made it clear that it would not establish official contact with regional authorities that did not involve their central government or at least had its consent.[77] Even in the area of structural funds, direct contacts between the Commission and the *CCAA* have always involved a central state representative (Morata and Muñoz 1997).

Most *CCAA* governments maintain contact with Commission officials, but only on an *ad hoc* basis. Unlike the German *Länder*, the *CCAA* administrations have hardly any regular working relations with Community officials. In Catalonia, contacts with the Commission are organized through the *Patronat Català Pro Europa*, which deals with the Directorate General of External Relations as the almost exclusive interface of the Catalan administration with the European level. The different regional departments do not maintain regular contact with the Commission.

Finally, European institutions of regional representation are of political value, especially to those *CCAA* with a strong national identity (Catalonia and the Basque Country), because they can present themselves as independent political actors in European politics (Pujol 1995). Yet, like direct contact with European policy-makers, active participation in the CoR and the ARE does not provide the *CCAA* with a systematic influence on European policies that is relevant to their interests. Moreover, like the German *Länder*, the *CCAA* have been disappointed in the high expectations that they placed on the role of the new institution of regional representation. Particularly Catalonia, the Basque Country, and Galicia have lamented the large heterogeneity of the body (mainly due to participation of the municipalities) and its low policy-making effectiveness (*El País*, March 14, 1995).

All in all, the *CCAA* increasingly realized that extrastate channels of influence neither prevent nor compensate for losses of institutional autonomy caused by Europeanization. As the long-standing Director General of the *Patronat Català Pro Europa* put it, "the aspirations of the *CCAA* to participate directly in European policy-making have experienced constant shocks of political obstacles and hostile attitudes" (Dalmau i Oriol 1997: 97; my translation). Neither direct contact with European policy-makers nor the collective representation of regional interests at the European level can ultimately compensate for the loss of formal policy-making power at the domestic level. This is not only because of limited access by the

---

[77] Statement of the Commission responding to a written request (2416/1990) of a Member of the European Parliament (*OJ C n°. 227*, 31.8.1991).

CCAA to the European policy process. The *CCAA* have mostly been concerned with the loss of their competencies that occur in the implementation of European policies because they are perceived as a loss to the central state rather than to Europe.[78] Extrastate participation in European decision-making does not prevent centralization in the implementation of European policies.

The initial strategy of the *CCAA* of confronting and circumventing the central state not only failed to redress the territorial balance of power. While the centralization of their (implementation) competencies proceeded, the non-cooperative strategy of the *CCAA* also caused additional costs on the "pay" side of the uneven distribution of "say and pay".

The lack of multilateral intergovernmental cooperation in the implementation of European policies imposed significant costs on the *CCAA*. Not only do the *CCAA* have to apply and enforce policies on a practical level without participating either in their decision-making or their transposition into national law; if the *CCAA* refuse to cooperate with the central state, they are not able to have the central state share some of the costs – e.g. by pooling resources such as expertise, information, or money, as *Bund* and *Länder* often do. More importantly, because the Spanish government controls access to European funding, the *CCAA* deprive themselves of the possibility of using European money to pay off some of their implementation costs (e.g. Cohesion Funds).

Moreover, the absence of intergovernmental cooperation has often resulted in the ineffective implementation of European policies. Implementation failure not only produces costs for the central-state administration, which is answerable to the European Union; it also imposes political costs on the *CCAA*. On the one hand, societal actors are increasingly mobilizing against the ineffective implementation of European policies. *CCAA* administrations face a growing number of complaints, administrative appeals, and referrals to both domestic courts and the European Commission for not properly applying European policies. On the other hand, failure of implementation does not fit the pro-European image, which some *CCAA* strive to convey. Thus, Catalan administrators often find it hard to reconcile a poor implementation record with Catalonia's self-image as a modern and progressive region in Europe, which claims to keep pace with its Northern European counterparts (see Part IV).

All in all, the non-cooperative strategy of "confronting and circumventing" the state, which the *CCAA* initially pursued, did not prevent the centralization of their competencies. Nor did it allow the *CCAA* to reduce implementation costs. Quite the contrary: constitutional conflict,

---

[78] See also Jordi Pujol's address to the *Senado* on September 26, 1994 (*Diario de Sesiones del Senado, Comisiones, V Legislatura, 1994, núm. 128*: 13).

circumventing, and non-cooperation tended to further promote the centralization of regional competencies and produced additional costs both for the *CCAA* and the central state due to implementation failures. As a result, the cost-shifting strategy of the *CCAA* increased rather than decreased the adaptational pressure and, hence, the costs of adaptation. Facing increasing costs, the *CCAA* became exposed to more cooperative strategies in responding to the challenges of Europeanization.

The success of the German *Länder* in redressing the territorial balance of power by obtaining formal co-decision powers in European policy-making played a crucial role in the search of the *CCAA* for a better way in dealing with the costs of Europeanization. Spanish legal and political scholars, as well as the Constitutional Court,[79] have argued that the co-operation of the *CCAA* with the central state in European policy-making is the only way to put an effective halt to the regional losses of autonomy (Albertí Rovira 1986: 208; cf. Muñoz Machado 1985: 53; Pérez Gonzalez 1989; Pueyo Losa 1989; Bustos Gisbert 1995; Rubio Llorente 1995).

1989–92: The piecemeal approach to multilateral
intergovernmental cooperation

In a resolution of February 15, 1989, the Spanish Parliament asked the Spanish government to establish a mechanism by which the *CCAA* could participate in the European policy-making process. The Parliament alluded to the various proposals of previous years and demanded the establishment of such mechanisms of intrastate participation until the end of the Spanish EC Presidency (first six months of 1989).[80] In order to overcome the political stalemate of 1986–87, the Spanish government finally abandoned the idea of a general agreement on the participation of the *CCAA* in European policy-making and adopted a more pragmatic approach of trying to settle specific issues by partial agreements. The Spanish government set up an "institutionalized dialogue" with the *CCAA* in which specific problems were to be tackled and the participation of the *CCAA* in European policy-making could be discussed.

The most important step in establishing such an institutionalized dialogue was the creation of an *ad hoc* Interministerial Conference on European Affairs (*Conferencia de Asuntos Relacionados con las Comunidades Europeas*) in December 1988. In its second meeting in March 1989, the *CCAA* and central-state representatives of the *Ministerio para Administraciones Públicas* (*MAP*) agreed on three basic principles for dealing with

---

[79] *STC 252/1988, de 22 de diciembre, BOE n°. 11 (suplemento), de 13 de enero de 1989:* 43.
[80] *Boletín Oficial de las Cortes Generales, Congreso de los Diputados, III Legislatura, Serie E, n°. 167, de 20 de febrero de 1989:* 4784.

European affairs. First, the central state has exclusive competence for foreign relations. Second, Spain's accession to the EC must not affect the internal distribution of competencies. And, third, the *CCAA* and the central state exercise their respective competencies in loyalty to the Constitution. Moreover, an agenda was set on issues to be discussed in the following months. The agenda included the exchange of information on European issues, the coordination of central-government and *CCAA* action in European infringement proceedings against Spain, the transmission of information to the European Commission in the area of public subsidies, the direct representation of the *CCAA* in Brussels through their offices, and intergovernmental coordination between central administration and *CCAA* in the management of the Structural Funds.

One of the main functions of the Conference on European Affairs, which was convened annually on a strictly informal level, consisted in the mutual exchange of information on the agenda of the European Council. Moreover, in the first four years, the conference focused on specific issues and problems arising from the implementation – as opposed to the formulation – of European policies. Two[81] important partial agreements were produced.[82] The first intergovernmental agreement was signed in 1990. It provides for the participation of the *CCAA* in infringement procedures of the European Commission against the Spanish state if the infringement was caused by one or several *CCAA*. It is an attempt to account for the shared responsibility of the central state and the *CCAA* in the implementation of Community law. If the competencies of a *Comunidad Autónoma* (*CA*) (or of several *CCAA*) are affected, then the *CA* is informed about the complaint and issues a statement, which is sent to both the central government and the European Commission. If Spain is brought before the European Court of Justice because of an implementation failure for which a *CA* is responsible, then the respective *CA* can appoint experts to participate in the legal procedure. The "flexible relations" which developed between the Secretary of State for the European Communities and the administrations of the *CCAA* in dealing with European

---

[81] A very first, but rather informal, agreement was reached in 1989, by which the *CCAA* were granted access to the database of the Secretary of State for the European Communities in the Ministry of Foreign Affairs.

[82] The *Acuerdo de la Conferencia para asuntos relacionados con las Comunidades Europeas para reglar la intervención de las Comunidades Autónomas en las actuaciones del Estado en procedimientos precontenciosos de la Comisión de las Comunidades Europeas y en los asuntos relacionados con el Tribunal de Justicia de las Comunidades Europeas que afecten sus competencias* and the *Acuerdo de la Conferencia para asuntos relacionados con las Comunidades Europeas en materia de ayudas públicas* are published in the *BOE n°. 216, de 8 de septiembre de 1992*: 30853–30854.

infringement proceedings contributed to a more effective implementation of European policies (*Ministerio para las Administraciones Públicas* 1995: 150).

In the same year, the central-state administration and the *CCAA* signed a second agreement, which regulates the obligatory announcement of public subsidies to the Commission. The central state (in the form of the *Secretaría del Estado para las Comunidades Europeas*; Secretary of State for the European Community) became the exclusive interface between the *CCAA* and the European Commission through which declarations on public subsidies of the *CCAA* as well as the reaction of the Commission are channeled. Official contact between the European and the regional level was thereby ultimately precluded.[83]

The Basque Country was the only *CA*, which refused to sign both agreements. It made its participation in any multilateral treatment of European issues conditional on a previous arrangement with the central state that would establish a bilateral relationship for dealing with these issues. In May 1990, the central-state administration and the Basque Country agreed on the creation of a Bilateral Commission for dealing with European issues that exclusively affected Basque affairs. But the Basque Country did not sign the agreement. Moreover, the convening of a meeting of the Bilateral Commission failed because the central-state administration considered the Basque Country unable to present an agenda on European issues that would not affect the interests of other *CCAA* (*Ministerio para las Administraciones Públicas* 1995: 155).

As a next step in the consolidation of the Conference on European Affairs, the *Comisión de Coordinadores de Asuntos Comunitarios Europeos* (Commission of Coordinators in European Affairs) was created. The major task of this "second order body" is to prepare the meetings of the Conference on European Affairs and to implement its decisions. At the same time, its members (one representative of each *CA* and one representative of MAP and the Secretary of State for the European Communities, respectively) serve as interlocutors between their respective *CA* and the Secretary of State for the European Communities as well as the other *CCAA*. It was this body that prepared the joint proposal of the *CCAA* for the Committee of the Regions to be included in the Maastricht Treaty,[84] and that framed the 1992 Agreement on the Institutionalization of the conference.

---

[83] In 1999 a modification of the Public Administration Act (*Ley 30/92 de Régimen Jurídico de las Administraciones Públicas y del Procedimiento Administrativo Común*) restates the monopoly of the central administration in officially dealing with European institutions (Art. 10).

[84] The Basque Country did not subscribe to the agreement reached among the other *CCAA*.

In 1992, encouraged by the success of its pragmatic approach, the Spanish government proposed the institutionalization of the Conference on European Affairs. The *CCAA* accepted. The *Acuerdos Autonómicos* of 1992 (*cap. 2, punto 12*),[85] in which the *Conferencia Sectorial sobre asuntos relacionados con las Comunidades Europeas* (Sectoral Conference of European Community Affairs) was formally included, define its major task as being the "instrument of general participation" of the *CCAA* in European policy-making. In addition, the conference is charged with exploring possible approaches for effective participation of the *CCAA* in "Europeanized" policy sectors, especially with regard to participation in the various sectoral conferences. Finally, the conference is charged with developing a "common culture" of consensus-seeking as a major prerequisite for the participation of the *CCAA* in European policy-making.

The Agreement on Institutionalization of the Conference of European Affairs, which was signed in October 1992,[86] is more specific in its various tasks. Apart from the information of the *CCAA* on the sessions of the European Council, and the joint discussion on "development of the European integration process", the conference is charged with seeking cooperative solutions to the following problems:

- technical procedures for the transmission of general information on Community issues to the *CCAA*;
- "normative techniques" for incorporating European Directives into domestic law and for complementary Regulations and Decisions;
- participation of the *CCAA* in domestic procedures in order to ensure compliance with obligations to the Community;
- implementation of Community law that affects several policy areas and hence requires horizontal coordination.

Finally, the conference is charged with further developing the framework for an intrastate participation of the *CCAA* in European policy-making through the sectoral conferences or other instruments of intergovernmental cooperation.

While the other *CCAA* accepted the multilateral framework of the conference,[87] the Basque Country refused to sign the 1992 Agreement. The Agreement on Institutionalization of the Conference on European Affairs provided for the convening of bilateral commissions, where a *CA* could discuss European issues only with the central-state administration that affected its particular concerns. Nevertheless, the Basque Country

---

[85] Art. 4, *Ley 30/1992*.

[86] *BOE n°. 241, de 8 de diciembre de 1993.*

[87] Catalonia insisted on the right to resort to bilateral commissions when linguistic issues would be affected (Cuerdo Pardo 1995: fn. 145).

continued to insist on strictly bilateral relations with the central state for dealing with European affairs. It asked for the institutionalization of a *Comisión Bilateral Euskadi–Estado para Asuntos Relacionados con las Comunidades Europeas* (Bilateral Commission of the Basque Country and the State on European Affairs) and the right to establish direct relations with European institutions as well as unmediated access to the Council of Ministers, the European Court of Justice, and all decision-making bodies of the European Commission and the Council of the EU. The Basque Country also demanded the withdrawal of the law suit that the Spanish government had filed with the Constitutional Court against the establishment of a "Basque Embassy" in Brussels and asked for the official recognition of its representation, as well as some privileged form of participation in European affairs compared with the other *CCAA*.[88]

As the participation in any form of multilateral intergovernmental cooperation in European affairs was made conditional on the existence of specific bilateral relations with the central state, the Basques refrained from officially participating in the Conference on European Affairs. Yet, the Basque Country continued to be invited, and Basque representatives regularly attended meetings without actively participating (Bustos Gisbert 1995: 155). In the meantime, negotiations between the central-state administration and the Basque Country on a bilateral framework of cooperation in European policy-making continued.

The Institutionalization of the Conference on European Affairs was the first commitment of the *CCAA* to participate in European policy-making on the basis of multilateral intergovernmental cooperation (*apartado 1* of the 1992 Agreement). They had realized that pragmatic cooperation in the conference facilitated solutions to some major problems, particularly in the implementation of European policies, and in some areas allowed them input on the position of the Spanish government, e.g. in the area of the Structural Funds. Thus, the *CCAA* perceived their cooperation with the Spanish government in European policy-making increasingly less as a threat of centralization but as a viable possibility for obtaining information, money, and political influence, which the *CCAA* previously had not had (interview Gencat$_{63}$).

Post-1993: Toward the German model?

After its institutionalization, the Conference on European Affairs focused on the elaboration of a procedural framework for the intrastate participation of the *CCAA* in European policy-making. On November 30,

---

[88] *Informe del Consejero-Secretario de la Presidencia del Gobierno Vasco*, unofficial document.

1994, after two years of intensive discussions, the central state and the *CCAA* reached a general agreement on a procedural framework to be implemented in each of the 18 *Conferencias Sectoriales* included in the Agreement.[89]

In general, the *Conferencias Sectoriales* serve for the mutual exchange of information and documents between the central-state administration and the *CCAA*; these conferences are necessary for an effective participation of the *CCAA* in European policy-making. The Spanish government briefs the *CCAA* in the Conference on European Affairs on the meetings of the European Council and the agenda of the respective Presidency of the Council. It regularly informs the *CCAA* at the various *Conferencias Sectoriales* about all European issues relevant to their competencies or interests throughout the whole decision-making process. At the beginning of each session, the *Conferencias Sectoriales* meet in order to discuss the agenda of the upcoming EU presidency. The *Conferencias Sectoriales* are also responsible for transmitting Commission proposals to the *CCAA*. If solicited by at least one *CA*, the appropriate conference deals with the proposal and the *CCAA* participate in the formulation of the Spanish position according to the extent to which their competencies are affected.

In decision-making on European policies (*fase ascendente de formación de la voluntad del Estado*), the *CCAA* may formulate joint positions on specific issues and coordinate them with the central-state administration. If an EU proposal affects the exclusive competencies of the central state, the *CCAA* can ask to be informed by the Spanish government and eventually make non-binding statements. If shared or concurrent competencies are involved or a European decision is to affect public spending, then the common position of central-state administration and the *CCAA* determine the Spanish bargaining position in the Council of Ministers. If exclusive legislative competencies of the *CCAA* are affected, the *CCAA* have the right to formulate a joint position that determines the Spanish bargaining position. In the first two cases, the *CCAA* have to be consulted on any changes in the Spanish bargaining position and, if this is not possible, the *CCAA* can ask the central state to later justify such changes. If the *CCAA* cannot agree on a joint position, the central government considers the different arguments expressed by the individual *CCAA*. In any case, intrastate participation of the *CCAA* must not impinge on the breadth of action that the Spanish government can take nor on its flexibility in European negotiations.

---

[89] *Acuerdo de la Conferencia sobre Asuntos Relacionados con las Comunidades Europeas sobre Participación Interna de las CCAA en los Asuntos Comunitarios Europeos a través de las Conferencias Sectoriales; BOE n°. 69, de 22 de marzo de 1995.*

With regard to the implementation of EU policies (*fase descendente de aplicación del derecho comunitario europeo y de los actos de las instituciones*), the central-state and regional administrations inform the appropriate conference about the legal and administrative measures taken in the transposition and practical application. The central-state administration provides the *Conferencias Sectoriales* with a complete set of the legal drafts relating to the legal incorporation of European policies in Spanish law. If the central-state administration and the *CCAA* share implementation competencies and they consider it necessary to coordinate the legal incorporation and/or the administrative execution of European policies at the regional and national level, the appropriate working group of the conference frames a respective agreement to be adopted by the plenum of the conference. The central-state administration and the *CCAA* also inform each other on the development and implementation of Community Programs (European Funds), even if only one level is involved. The *Conferencias Sectoriales* are also the forum for settling conflicts over competencies or other implementation issues.

The similarities between the 1994 Spanish and the German model of intrastate participation are striking. The procedure resembles the *Bundesratverfahren*, which was in place in Germany between 1987 and 1992. From the very start, German practice has decisively influenced the search for a Spanish model of regional participation in European policy-making. Not only is the literature full of references to German federalism and its adaptation to Europeanization,[90] but the central-state administration itself also acknowledges the importance of the German model: "*La referencia que ha sido más útil y más estudiada para la solución española ha sido el modelo alemán. Además de ser el modelo más evolucionado es el sistema con funcionamiento en la práctica más perfeccionado*" ("The German model has been the most useful and the most studied reference for the Spanish solution. Apart from being the most developed model, it is the system which functions most perfectly in practice"; *Ministerio para las Administraciones Públicas* 1995: 161).

The most striking similarity with the German model is the obligation of the central state to inform the *CCAA* and to consider their joint position according to the degree to which regional competencies are affected by

---

[90] See, for example, Albertí Rovira 1986; Montoro Chiner 1988; Pueyo Losa 1989; Fernández Farreres 1993; Parejo Alfonso 1993; *Ministerio para Administraciones Públicas* 1995; Cienfuegos Mateo 1997; see also the debate in the *Comisión General de las Comunidades Autónomas* on the law that "legalizes" the Conference on European Affairs (*Diario de Sesiones del Senado, VI Legislatura, Núm. 86, 6 de febrero de 1997*).

a European issue. Here, the Spanish regulations sometimes even borrow the German terminology.[91]

Yet, important differences remain. The *Conferencias Sectoriales* are not the *Bundesrat*; the *Conferencias*, like the *Bundesrat*, represent the regional executives, but they lack the organizational and institutional powers of a Second Chamber of territorial representation, which serves as the major instrument of intergovernmental cooperation in Germany. It is the *Bundesrat*, where the *Länder* coordinate and decide their joint position by majority vote. The *Bundesrat* lacks the sectoralized character of the sectoral conferences. The plenum of the *Bundesrat* decides on all issues, and its decisions are binding for all *Länder*. By contrast, decisions of the sectoral conferences are usually taken by consensus and are, in any case, not binding on the *CCAA* that do not consent. Unlike the *Länder*, individual *CCAA* can opt out of joint decision-making. The *Fachministerkonferenzen* – which come closest to the *Conferencias Sectoriales* because they are organized around specific policy sectors – are institutions of horizontal self-coordination of the *Länder* governments. Unlike in the *Conferencias Sectoriales*, where the central-state administration is always present and has a veto right in decision-making, the representatives of the *Bund*, if invited, have a voice but no vote. The *Fachministerkonferenzen* themselves are only one mechanism of intergovernmental cooperation, alongside the large number of *Länder* and *Bund–Länder* working committees as well as the *Bundesrat* committees. The *Conferencias Sectoriales* and their working committees, by contrast, serve as the only mechanisms of both horizontal and vertical intergovernmental coordination. So far, there are no genuine mechanisms of horizontal self-coordination among the *CCAA*, which may render the formulation of a joint position difficult. The Conference on European Affairs is the only conference where such horizontal self-coordination, albeit at an informal level, exists (interview MAP_{51}).

Another difference to the German model, is access to information on European issues, which the *CCAA* are granted, albeit restricted to specified areas. Through the *Conferencias Sectoriales*, they receive only Commission proposals and the Council agenda. The *CCAA* do not have formal access to documents, reports, and communications of the Council, the COREPER, and other European decision-making bodies. Nor are they provided with reports of the Spanish Permanent Representation on meetings of the various European institutions. Moreover, the *CCAA* do

---

[91] The 1994 Agreement contains parts which are a literal translation of German regulations; see, for instance, I.3.1.2. of the 1994 Agreement and Art. 23 n.F. Para. 5 GG; *cláusula 8* of the 1994 Agreement and Para. 5 (2) EUZBLG), or, *cláusula 3.4.* of the 1994 Agreement and III.5. of the *Bund–Länder* Agreement of October 29, 1993.

not have the option to participate formally in any of European decision-making bodies.

As in 1992, the Basque Country refused to sign the 1994 Agreement. It criticized the partial, indirect, and internal character of the participation of the *CCAA* in European policy-making as well as the mediation of individual *CCAA* positions through the horizontal and vertical coordination in the sectoral conferences (Casals 1994: 155–157). Since 1993, the Basque government had continued to negotiate with the central-state administration on a bilateral framework for its participation in European policy-making. In 1995, the Basque Country once again clarified its position on this issue. However, its statement on the Spanish EU Presidency[92] as well as the intervention of the *Secretario General de Acción Exterior del Gobierno Vasco* (Secretary General for External Activities of the Basque Government) in the *Comisión General de las Comunidades Autónomas*[93] on May 7, 1995, reflect a more moderate position (Casals 1994).

The Basque administration maintained its demand for direct participation in European policy-making and for the establishment of a Bilateral Commission. But instead of discarding the concept of a multilateral framework for intrastate participation altogether, the Basque Country proposed organizing the participation of the *CCAA* in European decision-making through a single "interautonomous body", which would exclude the central state, rather than through the various *Conferencias Sectoriales*. The joint position of the *CCAA* should then be coordinated with the central state in another body in order to arrive at a common Spanish bargaining position. Finally, the representatives of the *CCAA* should be included in the Spanish delegation and, as such, participate in the Council of Ministers as well as the different decision-making bodies of the Commission and the Council. The demands of the Basque government were not only more moderate, but many of them also referred to all of the *CCAA*, rather than just to the Basque Country.

A few months later, the Spanish government and the Basque Country finally signed an agreement on the establishment of a Bilateral Commission on European Affairs.[94] The other demands of the Basque government were either omitted (such as the creation of an interautonomous institution of horizontal self-coordination) or accommodated in the

---

[92] *Euskadi ante la Presidencia Española de la Unión Europea, Presidencia del Gobierno Vasco,* Victoria-Gasteiz, 1995.

[93] Summarized in Cienfuegos Mateo 1997: 203.

[94] *Acta de 30 de noviembre 1995, acordaba por la Administración del Estado y la Comunidad Autónoma del País Vasco, de la Comisión Bilateral de Cooperación y Administración del Estado-Administración de la Comunidad Autónoma del País Vasco para asuntos relacionados con las Comunidades Europeas.*

multilateral framework of intrastate participation (such as the creation of a Delegate of the *CCAA*; see below). The Basque Country subsequently signed all the multilateral agreements reached between the central state and the other 16 *CCAA* and officially started to participate in the multilateral framework of intrastate participation. The Basques' change of policy from strict bilateralism in European policy-making is also reflected in their more active participation in the Committee of the Regions, where they strove to initiate a follow-up of the "European Conference of the Regions" that would bring together regions with legislative competencies (Engel 1998: 163–165).

The central state and the *CCAA*, including the Basque Country, finally reached a comprehensive agreement that provides for intrastate participation of the *CCAA* in the decision-making and implementation of EU policies. The central state is no longer able to monopolize the Spanish position in European policy-making. For the first time ever, the central state shares its decision-making powers with the *CCAA*. The agreement of 1994 not only reassures the *CCAA* that Europeanization must not change the internal distribution of competencies in implementation. It also allows for a sharing of implementation costs by pooling information, expertise, and financial resources. Finally, the agreement provides an institutional framework where conflicts over competencies can be settled by political compromise rather than by constitutional conflict.

The achievement of a formal intergovernmental agreement committed to multilateral intergovernmental cooperation is the result of a change in strategy by which the *CCAA* responded to the challenges of Europeanization. In 1985, the Catalan and the Basque governments in particular rejected any participation of the *CCAA* in European policy-making mediated through the central state, because it would challenge their autonomy and result in centralization and harmonization. In 1994 the Catalan President, Jordi Pujol, declared that intrastate participation of the *CCAA* in European policy-making was essential for the preservation of the institutional autonomy of Catalonia because "*cabe temer que temas relacionados con la Unión Europea puedan ser utilizados en términos de recuperación de competencias autonómicas*" ("it is to be feared that issues relating to the European Union are used to recuperate autonomous competencies"; *Diario de Sesiones del Senado, Comisiones, V Legislatura, 1994, núm. 128*: 13). The Catalan government has finally embraced a more "pragmatic strategy... [which] combines unilateral initiatives... and collaboration with central state authorities" (Morata 1996: 110).

Not only did Catalonia accept a multilateral framework of intergovernmental cooperation, but the Catalan government also made its support for the government of José Marìa Aznar in 1996 conditional upon the fulfillment of two major demands that the *CCAA* had put forward concerning their participation in European policy-making. Both the *Consejero Autonómico* (Observer of the *CCAA*) and the participation of *CCAA* representatives in a number of committees of the European Commission entered the coalition agreement by which the conservative party of Aznar ensured the votes of the Catalan nationalists (*Convergència i Unió*; CiU) in the Spanish parliament.

The reason why Catalonia pushed for a joint position for the *CCAA* in bilateral negotiations with the Spanish government is a political paradox: While Catalonia gained power as a political ally of the Spanish government, it became increasingly difficult for Catalonia to exploit its privileged bilateral relations with the central-state administration. The coalition agreements (*pactos*) between the Catalan nationalists and the Spanish governments in 1992 and 1996 nourished the *anti-catalanismo* ("anti-Catalanism") in Spain. The other *CCAA* became even more suspicious of any privileged treatment for Catalonia. A survey of 1996 found that 85% of Spaniards believed that Catalonia received preferential treatment by the central government (*El País*, July 7, 1996). In a parliamentary debate on the State of Autonomies, the Catalan President, Jordi Pujol, complained about "*la mala imagen que Cataluña tiene en el resto del país*" where his region would be perceived as "*una comunidad ventajista, insolidaria, mercantalista, e incluso chantajista*" ("the bad image Catalonia has in the rest of the country" as a "community which only cares about its own advantage, isolates itself from the others, is market-driven and even extortionist"; *El País*, March 23, 1997). Institutionalizing regional participation in central-state decision-making within a multilateral framework not only allows Catalonia to use its political and economic resources in a less controversial way in influencing government policy, but it renders Catalan influence in Spanish policy-making less dependent on the outcome of general elections, like the 2000 election, in which the conservative government won an absolute majority and, hence, no longer requires the support of Catalan nationalists.

The importance of the new model of intergovernmental relations in European policy-making – formally established in 1994 and legally codified in 1997[95] – must not be underestimated. Given the conflicting institutional culture of Spanish territorial institutions, the 1994 Agreement has been welcomed as the expression of "*una auténtica voluntad de resolver los posibles conflictos por la vía del pacto y no del enfrentamiento*" ("an authentic willingness to resolve possible conflicts through agreement

---

[95] *Ley 7/1997, BOE n°. 64, de 15 de marzo de 1997*: 8518–8519.

instead of confrontation"; Bustos Gisbert 1995: 153). It is seen as a serious attempt by the *CCAA* and by the Spanish government to establish the mechanisms necessary for solving intergovernmental conflicts in European policy-making in a consensual and "peaceful" way (Cienfuegos Mateo 1997: 195).

These optimistic assessments of the 1994 Agreement were justified by further developments of the Agreement. Following the coalition agreement between the Catalan governing party and the Spanish governing party of 1996, the Conference on European Affairs agreed to establish a *Consejero de Asuntos Autonómicos* (counselor for *CCAA* affairs), who is one of about 50 *Consejeros* in the Spanish Permanent Representation in Brussels.[96] The Agreement of 1997 was signed for the first time by all *CCAA*, including the Basque Country. The *Consejero* follows the model of the *Länderbeobachter* (observer), although the *Länderbeobachter* is not part of the German Permanent Representation. Nor is he/she an employee of the Ministry for Foreign Affairs, like the *Consejero*. The intergovernmental agreement foresees the possibility for the *Consejero* to participate in European decision-making bodies as a member of the Spanish delegation whenever an issue affects the competencies of the *CCAA*. But the *Real Decreto*, which enacts the intergovernmental agreement, no longer mentions this point. It emphasizes the channeling of information to the *CCAA* as the only and exclusive competence of the *Consejero*. For the time being, the *Consejero* of the *CCAA* does not participate in any European decision-making body. He/she is only entitled to sit in meetings of the Conference on European Affairs. So far, his/her activities have concentrated on holding meetings with the *CCAA* to inform them on European issues (Cienfuegos Mateo 1997).

The limited role of the Autonomous Observer reflects the prevailing reluctance of the central state to allow direct participation of regional representatives in European decision-making bodies. The *Senado* passed a motion on September 28, 1994 requesting the central government to ensure that "the participation of the *CCAA* in each *Conferencia Sectorial* creates the experience necessary to articulate the inclusion of *CCAA* representatives or experts in the Spanish delegation whenever possible" (*moción n°. 9*; my translation).[97] This motion was included in the

---

[96] *Acuerdo de la Conferencia para Asuntos Relacionados con las Comunidades Europeas sobre la creación de un consejero para Asuntos Autonómicos en la Representación Permanente de España ante la Unión Europea, de 22 de julio, BOE n°. 302, de 16 de diciembre 1995:* 37314–37315. *The Agreement is enacted by Real Decreto 2105/1996 de 20 de septiembre, BOE n°. 229, de 21 de septiembre de 1996:* 28394–28395.

[97] *Boletín Oficial de las Cortes Generales, Senado, V Legislatura, serie I, núm. 171, de 6 de octubre de 1994:* 25–27.

preamble by the 1994 Agreement. In 1995, the *Congreso*, however, rejected a proposal by the *CCAA*, which foresaw the participation of the *CCAA* in the committees and working groups of European institutions if regional competencies were affected.[98] The central-state administration made it clear that the inclusion of *CCAA* representatives in the Spanish delegation was conditional upon the complementary role of such a direct representation to intrastate participation, i.e. the *CCAA* representatives had to represent positions which the *CCAA* jointly formulated in the *Conferencias Sectoriales* (*Ministerio para las Administraciones Públicas* 1995: 203).[99] Yet, the 1996 coalition agreement with Catalonia committed the incoming conservative government to regional participation in the European decision-making bodies. In 1997 the Aznar government agreed that the *CCAA* could send their representatives to 55 (out of more than 400)[100] advisory committees and working groups of the Commission (comitology) as members of the Spanish delegation. After several months of bargaining, the *CCAA* finally arrived at an agreement on how to divide up the committees among themselves. They also prepared regulations on how to determine the joint position which *CCAA* representatives were to present and on the relationship between the central-state and regional representatives in the Spanish delegation. Due to resistance from the Ministry of Foreign Affairs, the central-state administration has not yet formally approved the agreement. However, since 1998 the *CCAA* do participate informally in the various committees (interview MAP$_{51}$). In March 1998 the national Parliament passed a resolution requesting the Conference on European Affairs to establish a procedure, which allows the *CCAA* in the various sectoral conferences to send one representative to the Council of Ministers when their exclusive competencies are affected.[101] The Federal Foreign Ministry has so far successfully blocked the implementation of the procedure.[102]

One area in which the central state and the *CCAA* have reached formal agreement in the Conference on European Affairs is on the representation of the *CCAA* at the European Court of Justice (ECJ). Similar to the

[98] *Boletín Oficial de las Cortes Generales, Congreso de los Diputados, V Legislatura, serie D, núm. 298, de 27 de noviembre de 1995*: 2–4.

[99] El gobierno se enfrenta con el PNV por la presencia autonómica en la UE, *El País*, 4.3.1998; El gobierno rectifica y dejará a las autonomías participar en los Consejos de Ministros de la UE, *El País*, 5.3.1998.

[100] The 55 committees are mainly related to the sectors of environment, energy, agriculture, and regional policy.

[101] *Moción del 10 de marzo de 1998, Boletín Oficial de las Cortes Generales*.

[102] In reaction to the coalition agreement between the Catalan nationalists and the PP government, the new foreign minister, Carlos Westendorp, declared that there was no chance that the *CCAA* would participate either in the Council of Ministers or the COREPER (interviews Gencat$_{63}$; MAP$_{51}$).

German *Länder*, the *CCAA* have gained the right to request the central state to appeal to the ECJ against Community action (or non-action) that violates their competencies.[103]

Despite problems, the *CCAA* and the central-state administration have been successfully developing a framework for the domestic participation of the *CCAA* in European policy-making which is firmly based on the principle of multilateral intergovernmental cooperation. In less than 10 years, the *CCAA* have reached a level of participation in European policy-making for which the German *Länder* had to work for more than 35 years. As such, intrastate participation of the *CCAA* in European policy-making constitutes a significant domestic institutional change. It introduces a substantial element of multilateral intergovernmental cooperation and joint decision-making (both horizontal and vertical), which has so far been alien to the territorial institutions of Spain. For the first time, the central state shares its decision-making powers with the *CCAA*. The vertical coordination or power sharing is made conditional on the formulation of joint positions by the *CCAA*, which presupposes the horizontal coordination of their competencies and interests among themselves. Intrastate participation of the *CCAA* in European policy-making is also the first institution of intergovernmental cooperation which was established and has been further developed by a series of voluntary intergovernmental agreements between the central-state administration and the *CCAA*. Both the creation and the institutionalization of the sectoral conferences were imposed on the *CCAA* by national laws, which resulted from pacts between the two major national parties, the socialists and the conservatives.

Some differences aside, Spain has ultimately opted for the German model in order to adapt its territorial institutions to the challenges of Europeanization. In order to redress the territorial balance of power, regional losses are compensated for through cooperation between central state and regional governments in the formulation and representation of the national bargaining position. But with intrastate participation, Spain also took on a major deficiency of the German model: deparliamentarization and executive federalism. As in Germany, the legislatures have no role to play in the cooperation of *CCAA* and central state in European policy-making, even more so since the *Conferencias Sectoriales* – unlike the *Bundesrat* – are not part of the national parliament but are purely executive

---

[103] *Resolución de 24 de marzo de 1998, de la Subsecretaría, por la que se dispone la publicación del Acuerdo de 11 de diciembre de 1997 de la Conferencia para Asuntos Relacionados con las Comunidades Europeas, relativo a la participación de las Comunidades Autónomas en los procedimientos ante el Tribunal de Justicia de las Comunidades Europeas, BOE nº. 79, de 2 de abril de 1998.* The Basque Country did not sign the agreement because it claims a right to direct access to the ECJ.

bodies whose effectiveness largely depends on their political low-profile (interview MAP$_{51}$). Executives have always dominated the relationship between the central state and the *CCAA*. Yet, these relations used to be of a mostly informal and bilateral character and produced hardly any joint decisions. The formal introduction of joint decision-making and inter-locking politics in the area of European affairs may seriously challenge the political power of the parliaments, particularly at the regional level.

Intrastate participation of the *CCAA* in European policy-making con-stitutes a significant change to Spanish territorial institutions by intro-ducing a strong element of multilateral cooperation and joint decision-making. While the participation of the *CCAA* in European policy-making may bring Spain closer to cooperative federalism, the scope of this change is disputed. Multilateral forms of intergovernmental cooperation, such as the sectoral conferences, were largely ineffective in the past because the central state and the *CCAA* relied on informal and bilateral negotiations to coordinate their interests. More importantly, even if there was an in-crease in multilateral intergovernmental cooperation, this could simply be the result of a general consolidation of the Spanish State of Autonomies. After almost 22 years the process of decentralization is largely complete. The most recent devolution of competencies to the "slow route" *CCAA* in 1992 largely harmonized the level of autonomy among the 17 regions. In its rulings on more than 1000 constitutional conflicts, the Constitu-tional Court clarified the highly disputed distribution of competencies between the central state and the regions. Finally, between 1992 and 2000, Catalonia and the Basque Country have enjoyed privileged access to the central state because the Spanish government depended on their votes for a majority in the national parliament. These domestic devel-opments have resulted in a consolidation of intergovernmental relations that could explain the growing effectiveness of multilateral intergovern-mental cooperation better than Europeanization. Yet, the final part of this study not only shows that multilateral intergovernmental cooperation has increased in scope and output over the last years. It also demonstrates that Europeanization, rather than consolidation, is the major factor in ex-plaining the growing relevance of multilateral forms of intergovernmental cooperation over traditional forms of intergovernmental relations.

The transformation of Spanish competitive regionalism: Europeanization or institutional consolidation?

There are only two institutions of the Spanish territorial system that em-body mechanisms of multilateral intergovernmental cooperation: *El Senado* (Senate) and the *Conferencias Sectoriales* (sectoral conferences).

This section analyzes the extent to which Europeanization has had an impact on the effectiveness of these two institutions, whose performance on domestic policy-making used to be poor.

El Senado

The deficiencies of the *Senado* as a forum through which the *CCAA* could participate in central-state decision-making have already been mentioned in Chapter 7. Attempts at reforming the *Senado* constitutionally ended in deadlock. The creation of the *Comisión General de las Comunidades Autónomas* (General Commission of the *CCAA*) in 1994 has been the only outcome of the reform debate so far. The *Comisión General*, which enjoys the status of a parliamentary committee, should facilitate the representation of regional interests in national decision-making and help prepare a proposal for turning the Senate into a fully-fledged chamber of territorial representation. It has failed to produce any significant output with respect to either the Senate reform or influence over the *CCAA* on central-state decision-making at the domestic level (Cienfuegos Mateo 1997).

The *Comisión General* was also assigned some functions in European affairs, which carry the potential for the *CCAA* to exercise some influence on European policy-making. The *Comisión General* has the right to be informed by both the central government and the *Comisión Mixta Congreso-Senado* about EU issues which might be of relevance to the *CCAA*. This right to information applies specifically to the area of structural funds. Furthermore, the *Comisión General* is entitled to formulate guidelines for the participation of the *CCAA* (when such regional participation is provided) in the representation of Spain at the international and European level. Finally, their relatively strong representation in the *Comisión General* gives the *CCAA*[104] the opportunity to participate at least indirectly in the national Parliament's decision-making on EU issues, because the *Comisión General* can make recommendations and launch legal initiatives whenever competencies of the *CCAA* are involved.

Yet, the government and the *Comisión Mixta* have rarely provided information to the *Comisión General* on European issues. The *Comisión General* has not launched EU-related initiatives, nor has it made formal recommendations in this area. Moreover, since the *CCAA* do not up to this point formally participate in any of the EU decision-making bodies, no guidelines have been formulated. The only EU-related activities in which the

---

[104] Fifty percent of the members are chosen from senators designated by the *CCAA*. Moreover, the *CCAA* governments are entitled to participate in the sessions of the *Comisión General* with a voice but no vote.

Comisión General engaged was the evaluation of the 1994 Agreement on intrastate participation of the *CCAA* in European policy-making, which was criticized for being too modest.[105] The *Comisión General* also published a report on the "Role and Functions of Subnational Authorities in the Future of the European Union" which concluded with some recommendations for an improved participation of the *CCAA* in European policy-making.[106]

All in all, the *Comisión General* has not played a significant or prominent role in promoting the participation of the *CCAA* in European affairs. Without a profound reform of its composition and decision-making powers, the *Senado* appears unable to offer effective participation for the *CCAA* in either domestic or European policy-making.

Las Conferencias Sectoriales

The sectoral conferences were established in 1983 by the *Ley del Proceso Autonómico* (LPA; Law on the Antonomic Process). They resulted from one of the four *Acuerdos Autonómicos*, agreements to which the ruling conservative party (UCD) and the socialist opposition (PSOE) had agreed in the aftermath of the attempted coup of 1981 in order to bring the autonomy process under tighter central-state control. Not surprisingly the *CCAA* rejected the sectoral conferences as an attempt by the central state to intervene in their autonomous sphere of competencies. Catalonia and the Basque Country appealed to the Constitutional Court arguing that the law, which established the sectoral conferences, would violate their *estatutos de autonomía* (statutes of autonomy) by depriving them of their independent decision powers. The Court ruled that the national law was largely unconstitutional but left the sectoral conferences in place, only restricting their decision-making powers.[107] While the central administration steadily expanded the number of sectoral conferences, the *CCAA* showed little enthusiasm for participating in them. In 1992, the two major national parties, PSOE and PP, struck another *acuerdo autonómico* in order to consolidate and "dynamize" the system of sectoral conferences by providing them with a general legal basis. Grounding the conferences in a legal framework did little, however, to improve their effectiveness. Far from being "authentic arenas of collaboration", the conferences are usually held to be little more than a formal structure *"con la que se intente*

---

[105] *Diario de Sesiones del Senado, Comisiones, VI Legislatura, 1997, núm. 86:* 1–9.

[106] *Ponencia de estudio relativo al papel y funciones de los entes territoriales en el futuro de la Unión Europea, Boletín Oficial de las Cortes Generales, Senado, V Legislatura, serie I, núm. 360, de 21 de diciembre de 1995:* 18–21.

[107] *STC 76/1983, de 5 de agosto.*

atacar, pero no cumplir ... el principio de colaboración" ("meant to observe but not to put into effect the principle of collaboration"; Cienfuegos Mateo 1997: 200; cf. Dastis Quecedo 1995; Cienfuegos Mateo 1997; Dalmau i Oriol 1997). Nevertheless, a closer look at the specific functioning of each of the 23 sectoral conferences and the conference on European affairs over the last 15 years clearly shows that this negative evaluation no longer holds true. Since the introduction of the new cooperation procedure on European affairs, the effectiveness of the sectoral conferences has increased significantly.

The Conference on European Affairs does not qualify as a sectoral conference due to the cross-sectoral character of European policy, which has significantly increased the need for intergovernmental coordination. This point is important in order to understand why the Conference on European Affairs has become the "engine" of multilateral intergovernmental cooperation. It has model characteristics because it produces significant output, despite various anticipated problems such as its often politicized rather than pragmatic working style and the lack of horizontal coordination between the *CCAA*. Notwithstanding these problems, the Conference on European Affairs produced a series of intergovernmental agreements, which developed into a comprehensive framework for joint decision-making between the central-state administration and the *CCAA*.

By 1998 all sectoral conferences included in the 1994 Agreement on regional participation in European affairs had formally implemented it. None of the conferences developed the procedure further. However, an unofficial study by MAP in 1998 found that the *CCAA* participate *de facto* in the formulation and implementation of European policies in the sectoral conferences. The central-state administration regularly informs the *CCAA* about European issues that affect their competencies and interests, and the *CCAA* often make observations that are taken into account by the Spanish government. Given the pro-European leanings of all the regionalist and nationalist movements in Spain, European issues are generally non-contentious, as a result of which the *CCAA* have largely refrained from formulating joint positions to be formally considered by the Spanish government. This also explains why issues of implementation dominate the agendas of the conferences, where the regions have been most concerned about the centralization of their competencies. The central-state administration regularly consults the *CCAA* on drafts for the transposition of European policies that they have to implement. A draft that is not supported by the *CCAA* is unlikely to be submitted to the national parliament. Regional participation in the legal implementation of European policies at the national level not only prevents issues relating to the European Union being used to recuperate autonomous competencies, it also facilitates the effective implementation of European policies at the regional level. Regional support for the national transposition of legislation is ensured, thus providing the basis for a more uniform implementation of policies across the country. Moreover, central-state and regional administrations can pool their resources (e.g. information, expertise, and financial resources) in the implementation process, which helps to reduce implementation costs at the regional level. The central state and the regions increasingly develop joint plans and programs for the implementation of European policies. These programs provide the regions with a "blueprint" for legal and administrative measures for applying and enforcing the policies effectively; they also provide financial support to put them into practice (i.e. national and European funding). Working groups, which are often established to follow the process of implementation closely, facilitate the exchange of experience in implementation at the regional level and help to tackle problems that might otherwise result in implementation failure.

Apart from the implementation and development of the institutional framework for intrastate participation, the Conference on European Affairs also successfully coordinated a joint CCAA and central-government position for negotiations on the last three major Treaty revisions (Cienfuegos Mateo 1997: 197). In 1994 this coordination function of the conference was extended to all external activities of the Spanish state which affect the competencies of the CCAA, such as Spain's relationship with the Council of Europe. Finally, the Conference on European Affairs is the only intergovernmental forum where the CCAA started to establish horizontal self-coordination. In order to formulate joint positions and to negotiate the distribution of the EU committees among themselves, the CCAA held several meetings at which the central-state administration was not present. These meetings took place immediately before the conference plenum (interview Gencat$_{63}$).

While the Conference on European Affairs appears to be a success story of multilateral intergovernmental cooperation in Spain, the analysis of the 23 *Conferencias Sectoriales* results in a more differentiated picture, which, however, still challenges the overall pessimistic evaluation predominant in the literature. The analysis also presents further evidence for an independent effect of Europeanization in promoting multilateral intergovernmental cooperation. The 1994 framework for multilateral intergovernmental cooperation and joint decision-making applies exclusively to the area of European policy-making. Each of the 18 sectoral conferences listed in the 1994 Agreement was to implement and further develop the cooperation procedure for dealing with European issues that came within its remit. Hence, since 1994 there have been two parallel sets of formal rules and procedures for the sectoral conferences, one applying to decision-making on European issues and the other applying to decision-making on domestic issues. If a general consolidation of Spanish intergovernmental relations was the major factor in accounting for the emergence of multilateral intergovernmental cooperation, there should be a general proliferation of multilateral intergovernmental cooperation. The comparison of the two institutional frameworks shows, however, that multilateral intergovernmental cooperation on European issues is more effective than on domestic issues. This finding confirms the major proposition of this study that the emergence of multilateral intergovernmental cooperation is driven by Europeanization rather than by consolidation of the State of Autonomies.

This section summarizes the results of a study that analyzed and assessed the 23 sectoral conferences with respect to their level of institutionalization, degree of Europeanization, and effectiveness in dealing with domestic and European issues. The study is based mainly on the analysis of data collected by the *Ministerio para Administraciones Públicas*. In a progress report on the implementation of the 1992 *Acuerdos Autonómicos*, MAP provides an overview of the institutional framework and a summary of the outcome of each meeting as well as of the meetings of the most important working bodies for each of the 23 existing *Conferencias Sectoriales*. The data were complemented by a study of unofficial documents provided to the author by MAP and a series of interviews with participants of the *Conferencias Sectoriales* at both the central-state and the regional level.

The data set does not claim to be complete or fully reliable. The minutes of some meetings are missing, especially with regard to working groups. The official data only cover the period 1981–95. For the four years after 1995, the author had to rely on unpublished data from MAP. The summary of the minutes gives a rough overview of the outcomes of the different conferences. It does not give much information about the respective input of the different actors or about their mode of interaction. Finally, the assessments of the participants of the conferences are rather subjective. Notwithstanding an inevitable level of uncertainty, the data set provides important information on the legal basis of each conference, its rules of procedures, the structure of the working committees, the number of meetings held each year, and the outcomes produced by each meeting. Hence, the data allow inferences on the degree of institutionalization and Europeanization for each conference to be drawn, as well as inferences on each conference's effectiveness in both domestic and European policy-making as defined below.

The *Conferencias Sectoriales* are evaluated according to the extent to which they fulfill criteria laid out in the *Ley 30/1992* and in the procedural rules for each conference.

Most sectoral conferences aim to meet at least twice per annum. The national law (*Ley 30/1992*), which provides the conferences with a general legal basis, defines three main tasks for the conferences:

1. the exchange of view points;
2. the joint examination of problems in each sector; and
3. the joint examination of means to deal with or solve these problems (Art. 5.1).

As these are very broadly defined tasks, the Ministry for Public Administration, in its report on the implementation of the 1992 *Acuerdos Autonómicos*, developed three specific criteria by which it assessed the functioning of the conferences.[108] These criteria are also reflected in the rules of procedures of most conferences. The conferences are intended to provide the intergovernmental cooperation necessary for:

1. framing and implementing Joint Plans and Programs;
2. drafting and implementing national legislation that affects regional competencies or interests in order to harmonize national and regional norms and to ensure their practical application and enforcement; and
3. putting in place funding regimes (*convenios*) for joint projects such as Joint Plans or Programs.

These three criteria form the basis of the analysis of the policy-making effectiveness of the 23 conferences.

The level of institutionalization of a conference is measured by three factors:

1. the legal basis;
2. the rules of procedures; and
3. the infrastructure of second-level bodies (coordination bodies at the working level).

A high level of institutionalization results if (1) all three indicators are present or (2) the conference is equipped with a well-functioning infrastructure of second-level bodies and either a legal basis or rules of proceedings. A medium institutionalized sectoral conference (1) lacks both a legal basis and rules of procedures but is equipped with a working infrastructure of second-level bodies or (2) has either a legal basis or rules

---

[108] *Ministerio para las Administraciones Públicas* 1996.

of procedures but a less developed infrastructure of second-level bodies. A sectoral conference is classified as weakly institutionalized if all three indicators are absent.

The effectiveness of policy-making in a sectoral conference on domestic issues (not related to European policies) is determined in terms of:

1. the regularity of meetings, measured in terms of the average number of meetings a sectoral conference holds per annum; and
2. the output produced in the meetings, measured by the degree to which they fulfill the tasks defined by the MAP in its 1996 report.

A sectoral conference is considered to be effective if:

- it meets on average more than twice a year (number of annual meetings aimed for by most of the sectoral conferences);
- if it regularly deals with drafts of national and regional legislation affecting shared competencies and/or common interests of the central state and the Autonomous Communities;
- if it is actively involved in the framing of Joint Plans and Programs (JPPs); and
- if it deals with funding issues.

A medium effective sectoral conference meets on average once per annum and fulfills two of the three tasks (draft legislation, JPPs, and funding). Conferences holding few and irregular meetings combined with not fulfilling any of the three tasks are considered to be low in effectiveness.

The effectiveness of policy-making in a sectoral conference on European issues is measured by:

1. the relative number of meetings dealing with European issues; and
2. the output produced on these issues.

Effectiveness is high if a significant number (more than 30%) of the meetings deal with European issues that involve cooperation in decision-making as well as in the implementation of European policies. In medium effective sectoral conferences, European issues are regularly present on the agenda but do not involve more than information. Sectoral conferences that never deal with European issues, or only rarely and informally, are classified as low in effectiveness.

The level of Europeanization is measured by:

1. whether a sectoral conference was included in the 1994 Agreement on the participation of the Autonomous Communities in European decision-making which applies to 18 of the 23 domestic conferences;

2. whether a sectoral conference has implemented the 1994 framework of participation; and
3. whether a sectoral conference puts European issues on its agenda.

Highly Europeanized sectoral conferences are included in the 1994 Agreement, have implemented this Agreement, and put European issues on their agenda. Medium Europeanized conferences are included in the 1994 Agreement but have not implemented it; nevertheless, European issues are found on their agenda. Weakly Europeanized conferences are not included in the 1994 Agreement and/or do not deal with European issues at all.

The findings of the study are summarized in Table 4. Probably the most striking finding refers to the domestic effectiveness of the sectoral conferences. Seven of the 23 sectoral conferences (European affairs are excluded because they lack a purely domestic dimension) function in full accordance with the criteria defined by the *Ley 30/1992* and their rules of proceedings; they are firmly embedded in an institutional framework, hold regular meetings, and produce significant output with regard to the tasks assigned to them. It is interesting to note that institutionalization and effectiveness are linked to some extent. A high level of effectiveness is coupled with a high or medium level of institutionalization.

At the same time, however, three conferences do not function at all (industry and energy, infrastructure and territorial planning, and public personnel). Another seven conferences show a low level of domestic policy effectiveness. Meetings are rare and irregular and do not produce significant output. Interestingly, a low level of effectiveness does not always equal weak institutionalization. Five conferences (i.e. environment, industry and energy, telecommunication, tourism, and public personnel) lack (domestic) effectiveness but have rules of procedure and a developed infrastructure similar to that of second-level bodies.

A second interesting finding refers to the European effectiveness of the Europeanized sectoral conferences. Of the eight highly Europeanized sectoral conferences, five are highly effective and have a good institutional basis (a high to medium level of institutionalization). Of the six conferences with a medium level of Europeanization, one is also highly effective (i.e. labor), and two have a medium level of effectiveness (i.e. consumer protection, education, civilian protection, and fiscal and financial policy). The eight conferences that lack European effectiveness are also weakly Europeanized, with the exception of one (i.e. industry and energy), which shows a medium level of Europeanization. Hence, there appears to be a fairly straightforward relationship between the degree of Europeanization and the level of European effectiveness.

Table 4 *Institutionalization, Europeanization, and effectiveness in policy-making of the 24 Conferences, 1981–99*

Conference	Level of institutionalization	Level of effectiveness in policy-making on purely domestic issues	Level of effectiveness in policy-making on European issues	Level of Europeanization
European affairs	high	N/A	high	high
Agriculture	high	high	high	high
Social affairs	high	high	medium	high
Consumer protection	medium	low	medium	medium
Education	medium	high	medium	medium
Industry and energy	medium	low	low	medium
Infrastructure and territorial planning	low	low	low	low
Civilian protection	medium	medium	medium	medium
Research and development	high	medium	medium	low
Environment	high	low	high	high
Fisheries	medium	low	high	high
Health	high	high	high	high
Labor	medium	high	high	medium
Tourism	high	low	high	high
Fiscal and financial policy	high	medium	medium	medium
Transport	high	low	medium	high
Telecommunication	high	low	medium	high
Culture	low	low	medium	low
Universities	high	high	low	low
Drugs	medium	high	low	low
Water	medium	medium	low	low
Public housing	low	medium	low	low
Public personnel	medium	low	low	low
Traffic	high	medium	low	low

Source: own elaboration, after *Ministerio para las Administraciones Públicas* (1996) and unpublished data of MAP

Most striking is the disparity between the effectiveness of policy-making on European issues and the effectiveness of policy-making on domestic issues in five of the 23 cases. Of the seven conferences with low domestic effectiveness, three show a high level of effectiveness when dealing with European issues (i.e. environment, fisheries, and tourism) and two a medium level (i.e. transport, telecommunication, and culture). The difference between domestic and European policy-making with regard to effectiveness is most obvious in the cases of environment, fisheries, and tourism. These conferences constitute three out of four cases where a high level of institutionalization is coupled with low domestic effectiveness; at the same time, they show a high level of effectiveness in dealing with European issues. In culture, there is a similar finding regarding the divergence of European and domestic effectiveness; the level of institutionalization, however, is low.

Why do five of the seven domestically non-effective conferences function when it comes to dealing with European issues? The composition of the conferences cannot account for this variation because the same officials attend the conferences, irrespective of whether domestic or European issues are dealt with. Nor does the chairperson change. The level of institutionalization does not provide a satisfying explanation for this divergence either, because two of the 11 highly institutionalized conferences are European-effective but domestically ineffective. Moreover, there are good reasons to assume that in at least four cases (i.e. environment, fisheries, tourism, and telecommunication) the high/medium level of institutionalization is closely linked to the high level of Europeanization. Although they lack a legal basis, all three introduced rules of procedure in 1995 when they implemented the 1994 Agreement. In addition, four of the six second-level bodies of the conference on environment deal with the implementation of European policies. The agendas of the five "Euro-effective" conferences show that the interest of central-state and regional administrations in coordinating their activities in European policy-making is the driving force behind multilateral intergovernmental cooperation. Apart from informing the *CCAA* on European issues, the conference agendas are dominated by attempts to ensure and improve the effective implementation of European policies at the regional level. The central state and the *CCAA* discuss drafts for transposing European policies into national law, formulate joint plans and programs to facilitate their practical implementation, and establish working groups to deal with specific problems arising in the implementation process.

We can also observe an indirect effect of Europeanization on domestic effectiveness. While it is true that the domestic effectiveness of the conferences on environment, fisheries, telecommunication, transport, and culture is already low, they might not work at all if it were not for European issues. The agenda of all five conferences, in particular those on fisheries and on environment, are strongly dominated by European issues; sometimes the agenda of a meeting does not contain a single domestic issue. Fisheries started working only in 1994 and predominantly deals with the Financial Instrument for Fisheries Guidance, a sector of the EU Structural Funds that was introduced in 1993. The situation with the environment conference is similar. Since 1994 the conference has met twice a year with agendas dominated by the implementation of European environmental policies. The only issue on the agenda of the 1995 meeting of the conference on culture was the EU Council of Ministers on Cultural Affairs and the Spanish EU Presidency. Meetings that are strongly, sometimes even exclusively, dominated by European issues are also found in domestically effective and highly institutionalized conferences, such as agriculture (1992 and 1995), as well as at the second level of some conferences such as health (1993 and 1995) and consumer protection (1994).

Could it be that the disparity between European and domestic policy-making effectiveness is explained by the very Europeanization of the policy sector, with domestic issues becoming absorbed by European policy-making so that there is nothing left to be decided in the context of domestic policy-making? If this were the case, Europeanization would not only lead to an increase in European policy-making effectiveness but also to a simultaneous decrease in domestic policy-making effectiveness because of decreasing output. Yet the conferences on environment, fisheries, tourism, telecommunication, and transport have never shown a high level of effectiveness in domestic policy-making. The observation that the conferences on environment and fisheries (which unlike the other three were created after Spain had joined the EC) started functioning only when European issues appeared on their agenda strengthens rather than weakens the proposition that Europeanization promotes multilateral intergovernmental cooperation.

Moreover, even in highly Europeanized policy sectors, there are still important domestic issues to be dealt with. Given the significance of the tourist industry to Spain's economy, there are certainly more important questions to be discussed other than the regulation of travel agencies, which was about the only issue on the agenda of the conference on tourism for more than three years (1986–89). In the field of environment, the issues of deforestation and desertification – two of the most pressing environmental problems in Spain – have not been dealt with at the European level. Yet these issues only appeared on the agenda of the sectoral conference in 1996–97, 10 years after the conference had been set up. Finally, the conferences on agriculture, labor, social affairs, and education indicate that Europeanization and high European policy-making effectiveness does not necessarily take place at the expense of domestic policy-making effectiveness.

Another possible explanation for the disparity between domestic and European policy-making effectiveness could be the distribution of European funds. The provision of financial resources already serves as a major incentive for domestic intergovernmental cooperation. For the conferences on environment and fisheries, European funds are, indeed, an important agenda issue (for fisheries it accounts for almost 90%). However, the environment is a regulatory policy. The conference on environment has dealt with the transposition of many policies that do not contain distributive elements. Moreover, in the other three diverging cases (i.e. transport, telecommunication, and tourism), European financial resources are of less or of no importance. Here, the exchange of information and the implementation of European policies is the dominant issue.

The independent effect of Europeanization with respect to promoting multilateral intergovernmental cooperation is not only demonstrated by the comparison of domestic and European policy-making effectiveness of the 23 *Conferencias Sectoriales*; it is also acknowledged by the central-state administration which certifies Europeanization as a "dynamizing impact" (*Ministerio para las Administraciones Públicas* 1995: 188–189).

To conclude, the last 15 years have witnessed a significant expansion of multilateral intergovernmental cooperation in the framework of the sectoral conferences. In 1981, the *CCAA* fiercely opposed the introduction of the sectoral conferences, arguing against them as instruments of centralization and state intervention. Today, there are 24 conferences, one third of which is highly institutionalized and produces significant output, and another third of which, whilst possibly less effective, nevertheless functions. Of the remaining third, which shows poor performance on domestic issues, more than half works when dealing with European issues.

Due to the weaknesses of the data set, which have already been mentioned above, the findings should not be overstated. But they serve as an indicator for two important developments in Spanish intergovernmental relations. First, there has been a considerable extension of multilateral intergovernmental cooperation. Although the *Conferencias Sectoriales* are still far from being a working system of intergovernmental cooperation, the findings of my study should caution against a general tendency in the literature to discard the *Conferencias Sectoriales* as mere symbolic politics or "institutional courtesy" (Grau i Creus 2000).

Second, while the extension of multilateral intergovernmental cooperation may reflect a certain consolidation of Spanish intergovernmental relations, the functioning of the 16 Euro-effective conferences confirms the major proposition of this study that multilateral intergovernmental cooperation is the response to Europeanization rather than the result of the consolidation of the State of Autonomies. Not only do all but two of the conferences included in the 1994 Agreement allow for effective participation of the *CCAA* in the formulation, decision-making, and implementation of European policies; five of the seven domestically ineffective conferences also have some output when dealing with European issues. Joint Plans and Programs are framed, funds are distributed, and the transposition and practical application of EU policies are dealt with.

9   Conclusion

Part III of this book has shown that Europeanization has exerted similar pressures for adaptation on Spanish territorial institutions as it has in Germany. Due to the differences between the Spanish State of Autonomies and the German Federal State, Europeanization has resulted in partly different forms of institutional misfit, which have, however, caused a comparable degree of adaptational pressure due to an uneven distribution of "say and pay". On the "say" side, European institutions have allowed the Spanish and the German central states to access exclusive competencies of the regions. In this respect, the *CCAA* were more affected than the *Länder* because of their larger sphere of autonomous competencies. At the same time, the *CCAA* did not have any co-determination powers in central-state decision-making to lose, whereas the *Länder* did, and have consequently suffered most in this area. The *CCAA* faced the centralization of their implementation competencies, both legislative and administrative. On the "pay" side, *CCAA* and *Länder* alike are the main implementers of Community Law and, thus, have to carry the burden of implementing policies, in whose formulation and decision-making they did not participate ("pay without say"). In both countries, this uneven distribution of "say and pay" has caused a redistribution of resources, which has changed the territorial balance of power in favor of the central state.

Unlike German cooperative federalism, however, the informal institutions of Spanish competitive regionalism have prohibited rather than facilitated the adaptation of formal institutions to this shift of power. The *CCAA* have faced the same strategy options as the *Länder*. They possessed sufficient resources to either ring-fence their sphere of competencies and to establish extrastate channels of influence in European policy-making, or they could have followed the German example of requesting compensation for their losses of power through participatory rights in European policy-making. Given the lower degree of decentralization in Spain, particularly with respect to financial resources, the *CCAA* were even more likely than the *Länder* to chose the latter strategy. Initially, however, the

CCAA pursued a clear strategy of "confronting and circumventing the state". They strove to shift the adaptational costs of Europeanization onto the central state. As in case of the *Länder*, the non-cooperative response of the *CCAA* was not the result of their weighing the costs and benefits of alternative strategy options. Rather, the *CCAA* followed the "standard operating procedures" and rules of appropriateness, which they had developed in the past when dealing with similar challenges to their institutional autonomy.

Unlike the cost-sharing strategy of the *Länder*, the cost-shifting strategy of the *CCAA* proved to be ineffective in redressing the territorial balance of power and increased rather than decreased the costs of adaptation. As their strategy could neither compensate for nor prevent losses of power and implementation costs, the *CCAA* started to reconsider their strategy and to test out the effects of pragmatic cooperation with the central state. The adoption of a more cooperative approach was encouraged by successes of the German *Länder* in redressing the territorial balance of power as well as by the positive experience of the *CCAA* themselves in cooperating with the central state. Thus, the *CCAA* increasingly followed the example of the *Länder* in striving to redress the territorial balance of power by sharing and pooling their resources (competencies, expertise, information, money, etc.) with the central state. The adoption of the German model of intrastate participation resulted in new formal rules and procedures of multilateral intergovernmental cooperation and joint decision-making, which, unlike in Germany, do not correspond to the existing dominant formal and informal territorial institutions. While intrastate participation is increasingly able to redress the territorial balance of power, institutional adaptation to Europeanization has resulted in a significant transformation of formal territorial institutions, instead of a flexible adjustment and reinforcement, as was observed in Germany. But Europeanization not only transformed intergovernmental relations in Spain: It also open the door for deparliamentarization, which, unlike in Germany, had not been a dominant feature in Spanish territorial politics up to that point. As intrastate participation proceeds, so does the disempowerment of the regional parliaments.

It is too early to say whether the formal institutional changes induced by Europeanization will also transform the institutional culture of Spanish competitive regionalism. In any case, multilateral intergovernmental cooperation on European issues not only proves to be effective: As we see in Part IV, it has also started to spill over into the domestic realm of policy-making.

Sharing versus shifting the costs of adaptation: The Europeanization of environmental policy-making in Germany and Spain

Part IV of this book presents a policy study on the effects of Europeanization on environmental policy-making in Germany and Spain. The previous two empirical parts (Parts II and III) were set up to systematically test my hypotheses on Europeanization and domestic change by comparing the institutions of two member states. This final empirical part shows how my general line of argument applies to a particular policy area. The policy study allows us to explore on a more concrete level to what extent Europeanization causes an uneven distribution of "say and pay" in European policy-making, thereby producing significant costs of adaptation for the regions of decentralized member states. It demonstrates how the different strategies, which the German and the Spanish regions have chosen in order to reduce costs, have given rise to flexible adjustment and reinforcement in Germany and institutional transformation in Spain.

Environmental policy-making was chosen for this policy study because it is a highly Europeanized policy area. There is a rich and growing body of European environmental legislation which penetrates all sectors of national regulation (cf. Johnson and Corcelle 1995). Environmental policies are increasingly formulated and determined at the European level. But subordinate levels are the main implementers of these policies. In highly decentralized states, the regions not only have administrative but often also legislative implementation competencies. While the costs of policy formulation and decision-making are relatively low at the European level (particularly if compared to distributive policies such as agriculture policy; cf. Majone 1993), the implementation of European environmental policies often produces significant material and political costs at the regional level. These implementation costs are not taken into account in policy formulation and decision-making where regions are not systematically represented. Regions have to provide the administrative infrastructure for applying policies at a practical level, and they have to enforce them, often against the opposition of economic and societal actors. Moreover, compliance with European environmental regulations frequently requires regions to invest heavily in environmental infrastructure. But European environmental policies do not merely impose costs. They also entail some distributive elements. In order to help economically weaker regions in coping with implementation costs, the European Union created the Cohesion Fund, where 50% of financial resources are dedicated to the environment. European programs, such as MEDSPA, ENVIREG, or LIFE, also provide(d) funding for assisting environmental progress. All in all, the Europeanization of environmental policy-making has a significant, although somehow ambivalent, effect on the regions by providing them with considerable constraints as well as some additional opportunities.

The comparative study on the effect of Europeanization on environmental policy-making in German and Spain is not a classical policy analysis. It does not focus on a particular set of European environmental policies that it systematically follows through the different stages of the policy cycle. Rather, references to different European environmental policies are made in order to illustrate the various stages in the process of institutional adaptation that the Institution Dependency Model defines. In the Appendix, there is a brief description of the major EU environmental policies, to which the policy study refers.

10 The "blooming" of cooperative federalism: Institutional adaptation to the Europeanization of environmental policy-making in Germany

The uneven distribution of "say and pay" in European environmental policy-making

The loss of environmental co-decision powers

In Germany the responsibility for environmental policy is strongly decentralized and reflects the functional distribution of labor, which is typical for German cooperative federalism. While legislation has become increasingly centralized at the federal level, the *Länder* are mainly responsible for implementation. The German Constitution initially assigned the *Länder* the exclusive responsibility for environmental policy. But most of the *Länder* competencies became federalized in the 1970s (cf. Müller 1986). The *Länder* were compensated for the transfer of their competencies to the federal level through the participation of the *Bundesrat* in federal environmental policy-making. Apart from its co-decision powers in the formulation and decision-making of practically all federal environmental laws, the *Bundesrat* also has the right to instigate legal initiatives. Thus, the Europeanization of environmental competencies did not cause the *Länder* to lose any exclusive competencies. But the concentration of decision-making powers in the hands of the member-state governments has reduced the co-decision rights of the *Bundesrat* from legal initiatives and a veto in the decision-making to, at best, a veto that suspends the implementation of the respective environmental policy. By devaluing the co-decision powers of the *Länder*, Europeanization has seriously undermined the territorial balance of power in environmental policy-making.

Unlike in domestic policy-making, the *Länder* have no formal influence on setting the agenda, formulating, and making decisions on European environmental policies. The right to legal initiatives in European policy-making lies exclusively with the European Commission (Art. 211, 253 EC; formerly Art. 155, 190 EC Treaty). As a rule, the Commission – Directorate General (DG) for the Environment – passes a draft proposal to a working group, where Community and national officials, experts,

153

and interest groups elaborate the details and assess its political feasibility. The Commission may invite the *Länder* to participate in its advisory committees as independent experts, but they do not have systematic access. The federal government, on the contrary, not only represents Germany in the various decision-making bodies of the Council and Commission; according to Art. 208 EC (formerly Art. 152 EC Treaty), the Council can ask the Commission to present certain proposals. As the representative of one of the most powerful and environmentally leading member states, the German federal government has been the source of several Commission initiatives (Héritier *et al.* 1996).

Except for the Committee of the Regions, which may give its opinion on environmental issues (Art. 265 EC; formerly Art. 198c EC Treaty), the regions of the member states do not have any formal role in the decision-making process at the European level. The federal government, on the contrary, has a right to veto in the Council if decisions are taken unanimously, which used to be the rule until 1986. Since the Single European Act, the bulk of European environmental policies have been decided by qualified majority voting, which reduces the power advantage of the *Bund* vis-à-vis the *Länder*. Nevertheless, unlike the *Länder*, the federal government has a significant voice in European decision-making, which neither the Commission nor the other member-state governments can easily ignore. They often accommodate, at least partially, the objections of the federal government in the decision-making process.

In sum, unlike in domestic policy-making, the *Länder* used to have neither the opportunity to initiate and systematically shape European environmental policies according to their interests, nor did they have the power to veto them when they were opposed. While the *Bund* could never adopt a policy if it was opposed by the *Länder*, the *Länder* find themselves confronted by an increasing number of European environmental policies, which they either fully or partly reject, such as the Environmental Impact Assessment Directive, the Access to Information Directive, and the Integrated Pollution Prevention and Control Directive. "None of these policies would have ever passed the Bundesrat"; (interview Bay$_{32}$). The *Bund* also lost power as a consequence of Europeanization. But unlike the *Länder*, the federal government still participates in the formulation and decision-making of European environmental policies.

The centralization of administrative competencies

Europeanization has also affected the administrative autonomy of the *Länder* in implementing environmental policies, which has serious repercussions for the "pay" side (implementation costs) of the uneven distribution of "say and pay". In order to ensure uniform and effective implementation, European environmental policies are usually incorporated into the German legal system by means of federal laws. Unlike Spain, the *Länder* have never questioned the competence of the *Bund* to transpose European environmental legislation. First, the *Bundesrat* participates in the transposition process. Second, central transposition corresponds to the general preference of the *Länder* for uniform federal regulations to be implemented equally by all the *Länder* in order to avoid market distortion (Müller-Brandeck-Bocquet 1996: 123–126). The *Länder* are, however, concerned about the centralization of their competencies in the implementation (that is practical application and enforcement) of European environmental policies. On the one hand, the *Länder* see the danger of the *Bund* establishing its own administrative structures in order to implement European policies.[109] In the case of the Eco-Audit Regulation, for instance, the *Bund* implemented a European environmental policy as its own issue. While the *Länder* had initially opted for a joint *Länder* institution to accredit and supervise environmental auditors, the *Umweltgutachterausschuß* was ultimately established by federal law and acts under the tutelage of the Federal Environmental Ministry (Waskow 1997: 108–109). On the other hand, the *Länder* criticize the regulations of many European Directives, which do not leave them much discretion in practical application. Moreover, the *Länder* claim that the legalistic and formalistic approach of the Commission and the European Court of Justice (ECJ) in monitoring the implementation of European environmental law impinges seriously upon their administrative autonomy (see below).

As we see in the next section, the centralization of *Länder* competencies, both legislative and administrative, creates significant costs for the *Länder* in the implementation of European environmental policies.

Bearing the costs of implementation

The costs that the *Länder* have to bear in the implementation of European environmental policies do not arise so much from the need to bring domestic regulations up to European standards and to effectively enforce them. European environmental regulations are in many cases less stringent than German legislation demands. Rather, *Länder* administrators claim that the incorporation of European regulations into existing

---

[109] See, for instance, the declaration of the *Länder* Minister-President, Conference of December 12, 1989.

legal and administrative structures is often difficult, if not impossible (interview Bay$_{29}$). Moreover, the formalistic approach of the European Commission and the ECJ renders the incorporation of Community law even more difficult and impinges severely upon the administrative autonomy of the *Länder*.

Implementation costs as a result of policy misfit: Germany has one of the most complex and densely regulated legal systems of environmental protection in the world (Jänicke and Weidner 1997: 138). It contains more than 800 environmental laws, 2,770 environmental ordinances and around 4,690 administrative directives. There is, however, a lack of integration of the various sectoral regulations. The bulk of the environmental policies follow a command-and-control approach, which is based on the traditional police law with its focus on danger avoidance (*Gefahrenabwehr*), and a statist and legalist tradition, according to which the state hierarchically intervenes in society on the basis of the law (Dyson 1980: 9). This rather rigid approach is difficult to combine with more flexible instruments increasingly employed by European environmental law, which draw on quality standards, self-regulation, and public participation rather than stringent and detailed prescriptions and prohibitions (cf. Héritier *et al.* 1996; Knill and Lenschow 2000). European environmental policies that do not fit German administrative structures lead to considerable implementation costs. Implementation costs arise from the need to integrate these "mismatching" policies into the dense network of environmental regulation. Their effective implementation requires substantial legal and administrative changes that may impose significant material and political costs upon the *Länder* as the main implementers of environmental policy (cf. Börzel 2000a, forthcoming).

For instance, the integrated cross-media perspective of the Environmental Impact Assessment (EIA) and the Integrated Pollution Prevention and Control (IPPC) Directives as well as the Eco-Audit Regulation contradict the highly sectorized environmental regulatory structure of Germany with its medium-specific approach. In German authorization and licensing procedures, different authorities assess the potentially harmful environmental effect of a project for each medium (water, air, soil, etc.). The EIA and IPPC Directives, by contrast, demand an integrated assessment of a project with respect to the various media. Their implementation requires a high level of administrative coordination between the federal, *Länder*, and local level as well as among the different sectoral administrative divisions at each of the three levels. The vertically and horizontally fragmented administrative structure in Germany is unable to provide this coordination. Moreover, EIA, IPPC, and Eco-Audit do not contain any substantive regulations to be uniformly applied in the member states. Their procedural approach contradicts the German regulatory tradition of imposing substantive standards, which are to be reached by applying the Best Available Technology (BAT). Public administration and industry alike have criticized the fact that the three European policies do not set any substantive standards that they consider necessary to harmonize environmental protection requirements at a high level in order to prevent market distortion (Héritier *et al.* 1996: 257). Finally, German administration and industry oppose the provisions for public participation, which all three policies contain. The requirement of the EIA and IPPC Directive, as well as the Eco-Audit Regulation to publicize information and statements on the environmental performance of (planned) industrial sites, challenge the German administrative tradition and the principle of commercial and industrial confidentiality (*Betriebsgeheimnis*; cf. Héritier *et al.* 1996: 257). The Access to Information (AI) Directive is even less compatible with German provisions for public participation in administrative procedures. The comprehensive right to access environmental information, which the AI Directive grants independently of interest and procedural context (*Jedermann-Recht*), contradicts the German administrative tradition "that places the state and the law above the 'desires' of individual citizens and is reflected in a . . . structure of interest intermediation which tends to be closed to 'third parties' " (Lenschow 1997: 33). The principle of "restricted access to records" is based on the general confidentiality of information that is in the possession of the public administration. The public has access to this information only in special cases, e.g. in the context of licensing procedures and when third parties (citizens, interest groups, etc.) can claim a legitimate interest (cf. Gebers 1996).

Apart from their incompatibility with German administrative traditions, both public administration and industry complain that the implementation of AI, EIA, Eco-Audit, and IPPC imposes significant costs on them by creating a heavier workload, by leading to delays in authorization procedures, and by imposing high control costs (Héritier *et al.* 1996: 243, 296). Not only do they consider the procedural regulations of the EIA and IPPC Directives as unnecessary given the high level of substantive environmental standards in Germany, but "procedural regulation that is not tied to specific substantive standards [also] endangers the environmental *status quo* because they prevent future progress in environmental protection" (interview Bay[29]).

In sum, although an environmental leader rather than a laggard, Germany often faces significant implementation costs due to policy misfits. As the *Länder* are the main implementers of environmental policy, they have to bear the larger share of material and political implementation costs.

Implementation costs as a result of restricted administrative discretion
Not only do the *Länder* face significant adaptational costs in the implementation of mismatching European environmental policy because they have to adapt their legal and administrative structures, but they are also restricted in their discretion on how to implement European environmental policies, i.e. on which instruments they can chose. The most prominent case in which the European Union has intervened in the administrative autonomy of the *Länder* is the role of administrative directives (*Verwaltungsvorschriften*) in the implementation of European environmental policies.

Unlike ordinances, administrative directives do not have an outside effect; they only oblige the administration internally. Third parties, such as citizens or courts, are not subject to administrative directives. Hence, in principle, administrative directives do not set binding law (Kloepfer 1984: 261). While the legal effect of administrative directives is still contested both in the legal literature and the jurisdiction of German administrative courts,[110] German administration *de facto* applies administrative directives – such as the *TA-Luft* (air quality), the *TA-Lärm* (noise) or the *TA-Abfall* (waste) – as if they were laws or ordinances (Reinhardt 1992). What remains a problem, however, is that public administration does not have to publicize administrative directives, which seriously affects the ability of societal actors to participate in the monitoring and enforcement of environmental regulations. Nor are administrative directives open to litigation since they do not have legal effects on third parties.

Germany implements most European environmental policies by federal law or ordinance. But European regulations are often applied practically by means of administrative directives. This is particularly the case when substantive European regulations are incorporated into German regulations that already exist and that are presented in the form of administrative directives (such as the *TA-Luft*). The European Commission has, however, repeatedly criticized the implementation of European law by administrative directives. It argues that the implementation of European policies through legally non-binding administrative directives does not conform to the obligation of the member states to implement European law effectively (*effet utile*). Consequently, the Commission has initiated several infringement proceedings against Germany in the areas of

---

[110] Cf. Beyerlin 1987; Reinhardt 1992; Wolf 1992.

water and air pollution control. In 1991 the ECJ convicted Germany twice for the ineffective implementation of two air-pollution control Directives through the *TA-Luft*, an administrative directive under the Federal Air Pollution Control Act.[111] Administrative lawyers and practitioners perceive the two ECJ rulings against the *TA-Luft* as a "full-fledged attack of the Commission" against the German administrative practice of implementing environmental legislation by means of administrative directives (interviews Ba-Wü$_{35}$; Bay$_{27}$; Reinhardt 1992). Federal and *Länder* administrators have repeatedly emphasized that administrative directives have a crucial role in the execution of environmental law, because they specify and complement regulations in the areas of standardization, prevention, and danger avoidance. If the parliamentary legislator had to provide detailed regulations that it used to delegate to the administration, this would lead to a "legislative overkill" (interview Bay$_{27}$) in the *Bundestag*, which is already technically overwhelmed with the task of passing environmental legislation. Moreover, it is argued that Members of Parliament lack the technical expertise and administrative experience of the federal and *Länder* administrators, which are crucial in the formulation of detailed regulations. Finally, the parliamentary legislator would not be able to keep pace with rapid technological and scientific change, which has to be taken into account, for instance, in the implementation of the Best Available Technology policy. Only administrative directives are flexible enough to be effectively adapted to new developments. In fact, "legislative inflexibility" (*legislative Schwerfälligkeit*) would seriously challenge the high level of environmental protection so far achieved in Germany (interview Bay$_{29}$).

Both federal and *Länder* administrators increasingly blame the Commission and the ECJ for their formalistic and legalistic approach in the implementation of European environmental policies, which, according to them, reduces monitoring of compliance to the comparison of legal texts (Lübbe-Wolff 1991: 155). The Commission and the ECJ would embrace a conventional understanding of the parliamentary legislator as the actor that possesses the exclusive legislative competence, which does not correspond to German environmental policy-making. The "assault" of the Commission and the ECJ against major elements of German administrative culture and practice is even less acceptable to many German administrators because it would give rise to a paradox: member states, like Greece and Italy, which often only pass European directives, practically verbatim, into national laws but do not enforce them, have a better compliance record than countries like Germany, which *de facto* comply

---

[111] *EuGH Rs. C-59/89; EuGH Rs. C-361/88*; cf. Beyerlin 1987; Reinhardt 1992.

with European regulations without always explicitly transposing them (interview Bay$_{37}$).

All in all, Europeanization imposes two major types of implementation costs on the *Länder*. First, the incorporation of European policies that are not compatible with German legal and administrative structures requires costly adaptation of domestic norms, rules, and procedures. Second, the formalistic and legalistic approach of the Commission and the ECJ in the implementation of European environmental policies not only challenges administrative traditions in Germany, but it also prevents flexible adjustment of existing rules and procedures, e.g. through administrative directives.

Sharing the costs of adaptation: Joint cooperation and joint non-implementation

From the start, the *Länder* pursued a two-fold strategy in order to counterbalance the uneven distribution of "say and pay" caused by the Europeanization of environmental policy-making. First, they demanded participatory rights in the formulation and representation of the German bargaining position at the European level ("reining in"). Such co-decision rights would provide the *Länder* with compensation for the loss of their co-determination powers in the federal policy-making process by granting them access to initiative, formulation, and decision-making of European environmental policies ("say"). Moreover, intrastate participation in European policy-making would give the *Länder* the opportunity to shape European policies so as to reduce adaptational costs in the implementation process ("pay"). Direct contact between the *Länder* and European institutions became important only in the late 1980s and have always served as a complement to rather than a substitute for intrastate participation. Second, the German *Länder*, in cooperation with the *Bund*, have tried to absorb and dilute European policies that do not fit existing regulations in order to avoid or reduce adaptational costs ("joint shifting and sharing of costs"). *Bund* and *Länder* make joint efforts toward and share responsibility for incorporating European environmental law by changing domestic legal and administrative structures as little as possible, which often leads to ineffective implementation.

"Reining in" European environmental policy-making

The Europeanization of environmental policy-making started in the early 1970s and coincided with the centralization of environmental *Länder* competencies at the federal level (cf. Müller 1986). The *Länder* used the emerging environmental activities of the European Community as a further opportunity to promote their general strategy of demanding comprehensive participatory rights in European policy-making (Morawitz and Kaiser 1994: 52).

The first European environmental policies focused on water quality; in this area the *Länder* have retained important responsibilities, because the management of water resources is only a framework competence of the *Bund*. As a result, the *Bund* itself had an interest in the *Länder* (informally) participating in the negotiations on the First Environmental Action Program, which was passed in 1973 and laid out the environmental agenda of the Community for the near future. The federal government invited representatives of the *Länder* to ministerial meetings that prepared the German bargaining position. The *Länder* could also participate in the deliberations of the Council working group in Brussels as well as in the sessions of the Council of Environmental Ministers. Moreover, the federal government regularly reported on European negotiations in the different *Bund–Länder* committees.

Environmental policy was also the first policy area in which the *Länder* achieved an element of formal co-decision rights in European decision-making. On November 22, 1976 the Federal Minister of the Interior signed a formal agreement with the *Länder* concerning European decisions on issues relating to the River Rhine, which come under the responsibility of the *Deutsche Rheinschutz-Kommission* (German Commission for the Protection of the Rhine). In cases affecting the competencies of the *Internationale Rheinschutz-Kommission*, the unanimous decision of the *Deutsche Rheinschutz-Kommission*, in which the *Länder* bordering the Rhine are represented, would determine the German position in European decision-making. If the *Länder* dissented, the Federal Republic of Germany would vote against any European proposal that would affect the domestic competencies of the *Länder* in this area (Morawitz 1981: 11–12). In other words, the *Länder* received the formal power to determine the German bargaining position on all issues that affected the activities of the International Commission for the protection of the Rhine.

Untill the mid-1980s the *Länder* were regularly, albeit largely informally, involved in the formulation of the German bargaining position at the domestic level when European proposals affected their legislative or administrative competencies. Not only did the federal government formally notify the *Bundesrat*, it also consulted the *Länder* at the informal level. The *Länder* were often permitted to attend the ministerial meetings, which prepared the German bargaining position, as well as the negotiations in the competent European Council working group. But the federal government kept any *Länder* participation that went beyond the provisions of the *Zuleitungsverfahren* strictly informal in order not to set a formal precedent for *Länder* participation in European policy-making (Bulmer 1986: 282).

The Single European Act of 1986 made environmental policy a formal competence of the European Community (Art. 174, 175, 176 EC; formerly Art. 130 r-t EC Treaty). The expanding environmental activities of the European Community in the 1970s and early 1980s (at that time based on Arts. 100 and 235 ECT), had become a major concern of the *Länder*. In fact, environmental policy was an area in which the *Länder* mostly felt the losses of their competencies as a consequence of Europeanization (Merten 1990). The *Länder* welcomed the opportunity to participate informally in the European decision-making process, but considered it inadequate compensation for their loss of formal co-decision powers in federal policy-making. They continued to push for comprehensive and legally binding participatory rights.

The *Bundesratverfahren* of 1987 formalized the participation of the *Länder* in European policy-making. In 1992 the *Länder* finally achieved constitutional and legally binding co-decision rights in the formulation and representation of the German bargaining position. Art. 23 n.F. GG grants the *Länder* comprehensive formal access to the formulation of decision-making on European environmental policies. It largely compensated the *Länder* for their losses of competencies and redressed the territorial balance of power.

Shifting and sharing implementation costs together with the central state

Influencing the form and content of European environmental policy has been an important part of the *Länder* strategy as a means of reducing implementation costs. The "upgrading" of German policies to the European level not only prevents competitive disadvantage for German industry, but also spares the *Länder* adaptational costs. Particularly in the area of water, waste, and control of air-pollution, Germany has succeeded in harmonizing national regulations at the European level along the lines of German standards (cf. Aguilar Fernández 1997: 96–100).

In many cases, however, Germany had ultimately not been able to prevent the adoption of European environmental policies that seriously challenged its regulatory structures, such as the Environmental Impact Assessment Directive of 1985 and its revision of 1997, the Access to

Information Directive of 1990, the Integrated Pollution Prevention and Control Directive of 1996, and the Eco-Audit Regulation of 1993 (see above). In these cases, *Bund* and *Länder* pursued a joint strategy of reducing adaptational costs by "absorbing" European policies and avoiding substantial changes to existing regulatory structures.

Absorbing mismatching policies into existing regulatory structures: By absorbing mismatching policies into existing regulatory structures, *Bund* and *Länder* strive to integrate European legislation into regulations that already exist without substantially changing or replacing them. This strategy has often led to delays in legal implementation. The full incorporation of the Drinking Water Directive into the German legal system took 10 years; the EIA and the AI Directives were transposed with a delay of 1.5 years, and Germany has missed the 1999 transposition deadline for the IPPC Directive and the revision of the EIA Directive.

The *Länder* are often the source of such delays because the *Bundesrat* blocks transposition. Yet, in many cases incomplete or delayed implementation is the result of a joint unwillingness of both *Bund* and *Länder* to transpose a Directive because they oppose substantial changes in legal or administrative structures. Sometimes, German administrators claim that existing legislation already fulfills the requirements of a Directive. Thus, parts of the German administration (at all levels) contested the necessity of a proper law to transpose the Environmental Impact Assessment Directive, arguing that German authorization and licensing procedures *de facto* complied with the EIA requirements. In a similar vein, *Bund* and *Länder* rejected the Access to Information Directive as superfluous in German environmental law and consequently opted for a very restrictive implementation (see below).

Bund and *Länder* often managed to absorb European policies into existing regulatory structures by resorting to administrative directives. Existing legislation is subsumed under, or "reinterpreted" in light of, a European policy which, according to the German administration, simply requires a change in the administrative practice, or, at best, the issuing of new administrative directives. Yet, mere absorption has become increasingly difficult. Making legal changes in order to implement European policies is often unavoidable. German administrators cannot always ignore the fact that existing regulations do not comply with the objectives of some European policies, particularly after a ruling by the European Court of Justice (e.g. Drinking Water, EIA, AI). But even if Germany enacts new legislation to implement a European environmental policy, the effect of European regulations is often minimized in practical application and enforcement.

Diffusing the pressure for adaptation by watering down European regulations: If *Bund* and *Länder* enact new rules and procedures to implement a mismatching European policy (often only after an EU infringement proceeding), they tend to reduce the effect of such legal and administrative changes as far as possible. The EIA Directive is a case in point. Following the recommendations of the *Rat der Sachverständigen für Umweltfragen* (Scientific Council on Environmental Issues), Germany finally opted for the implementation of the Directive through a proper EIA law (*Umweltverträglichkeitsprüfungsgesetz*; *UVPG*).[112] But instead of establishing a separate EIA procedure, which would have been the most effective solution given the highly sectorized, medium-specific approach of German environmental policy, the *UVPG* integrated the EIA into existing authorization and licensing procedures and thus minimized the effects of the EIA Directive on German authorization practice. Even after the enactment of the *UVPG* (with a two-year delay), implementation of the EIA Directive remained incomplete. The *UVPG* exempts 35 of a total of 90 projects listed in Appendix 2 from any EIA requirement. German administrators justified this omission by the fact that these projects were already subject to an EIA under German sectoral authorization procedures, like the Air Pollution Control Act (interview BMU₇). A further attempt to diffuse the pressure for adaptation was the administrative directive, which is charged with formalizing the rather general provisions of the *UVPG*. The directive was issued in 1995[113] and gives little guidance for the practical application of the EIA procedure. Some administrative lawyers argue that the German implementation of the EIA Directive reduces its impact to compliance with existing environmental standards (Erbguth 1991; Schwanenflügel 1993).

The implementation of the AI Directive serves as another example of the joint diffusion strategy of *Bund* and *Länder*. First, transposition was delayed by 1.5 years. The Federal Environmental Ministry prepared several drafts, which did not gain either the support of the federal government or of the *Länder*. Both the *Länder* as well as some federal ministries insisted on a narrower interpretation of the public authorities that are subject, by the requirements of the AI Directive, to provide access to environmental information. Moreover, the *Länder* requested ample

---

[112] *Gesetz über die Umweltverträglichkeitsprüfung vom 12. Februar 1990, BGBl. I: 205.*

[113] *Allgemeinen Verwaltungsvorschrift zur Ausführung des Gesetzes über die Umweltverträglichkeitsprüfung (UVPVwV) vom 18. September, Gemeinsames Ministerialblatt Nr. 32: 671–694.*

administrative discretion in deciding when and how to grant access to environmental information.[114] Although the federal government rejected the *Länder* claims, the formulation of the German Environmental Information Act (*Umweltinformationsgesetz; UIG*)[115] is still very vague and ambiguous on this point. This vagueness is rather unusual given the German tradition of the rule of law, which strives to avoid legal uncertainty. Because the German AI regulations are not specific enough, they can be easily interpreted against the spirit or even the wording of the Directive and significantly dilute the effect of the AI Directive on administrative practice (Schwanenflügel 1993; Scherzberg 1994). Environmental organizations and citizen groups have filed a number of complaints with the Commission about ineffective implementation of the AI Directive (cf. Gebers 1993). The Commission opened an infringement proceeding against Germany in March 1995, which resulted in a judgement against Germany in October 1999. The ECJ ruling forces Germany to revise the Environmental Information Act (*UIG*). So far, however, *Bund* and *Länder* have largely avoided any significant adaptation of their administrative practices by diluting the "mismatching" regulations of the AI Directive in their legal transposition and practical application.

In sum, mismatching European environmental policies tend to be absorbed into existing regulatory structures and subsequently diluted in their effect. The *Länder* appear to be responsible mainly for these cases of ineffective implementation of the European environmental Directives. Yet, *Bund* and *Länder* jointly formulate and decide on the laws, ordinances, and administrative directives by which they legally transpose EU policies. Even those *Länder* that are governed by a coalition of Social Democrats and the Green Party have by and large joined the conservative *Länder* in attempting to diffuse European pressure for adaptation rather than using it for advancing environmental innovation. The 16 *Länder* usually refrain from enacting full regulations that would complement or correct federal legislation (ineffectively) implementing European Directives.

The joint absorption and diffusion strategy of *Bund* and *Länder* corresponds to an attitude that many German administrators share: "*verlorene Schlachten noch einmal schlagen*" ("fight lost battles all over again"; interview BMU₇). The reluctance toward effectively implementing European policies that do not fit the German approach is promoted by a

---

[114] *Stellungnahme des Bundesrates vom 17.12.1993, zum Gesetzesentwurf der Bundesregierung, Nr. 10 zu Art. 1, §7 II UIG-Vorschlag, BT-Drs. 12/7138 vom 23.3.1994.*

[115] *Gesetz zur Umsetzung der Richtlinie 90/313/EWG des Rates vom 7. Juni 1990 über den freien Zugang zu Informationen über die Umwelt vom 8. Juli 1994, BGBl. I 1994: 1490.*

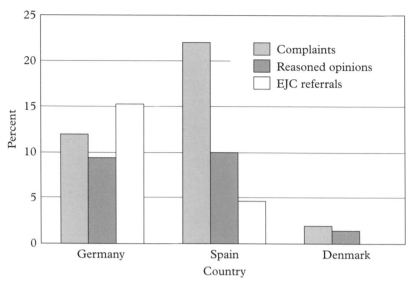

Sources: Own elaboration based on data drawn from Commission (1993b; 1996) and a database on member state infringements constructed by the author, accessible on the internet via www.iue.it/RSC/Research.html. The complaints refer to the time period 1988–95. They also entail questions and petitions made to the European Parliament as well as cases detected by the Commission. European infringement proceedings are regulated in Article 226 EC (formerly Article 169 EC Treaty). They comprise three stages. If the Commission suspects a member state of an infringement (mostly on the basis of complaints and petitions that societal actors submitted), then it sends the member state government a so-called "Warning letter" stating the suspected infringement. The member state government responds to this letter and tries to reach agreement with the Commission on how to remedy the situation. If, however, compliance does not improve, then the Commission sends a so-called "Reasoned opinion", which it refers to the European Court of Justice (ECJ), if the member state still does not clarify the issue. Finally, if a member state does not comply with an ECJ judgement, the Commission can ask the ECJ to impose fines.

Figure 4 Average share of Germany, Spain, and Denmark in the total number of infringements of European environmental law, 1988–97

certain arrogance rooted in the belief that Germany is "top of the class" in environmental policy and does not need to be told by the European Union how to improve environmental protection (Héritier *et al.* 1996: 176–177). Its implementation record does not, in any case, reflect Germany's understanding of itself as a pace-setter on European environmental policy (see Figure 4). The distinction that German bureaucrats used to make between "'*die Germanen*' ... who play it straight on detailed implementation, and '*die Romanen*' ... whose bureaucracies often frustrate the goals of European policy at the stage of detailed implementation" (Bulmer and Paterson 1987: 183) no longer holds (cf. Börzel 2000a, forthcoming).

Pulling all possible strings: Extrastate channels of influence

The cost-sharing strategy of the *Länder* in environmental policy-making –
in order to counterbalance their loss of competencies and to reduce implementation costs – formed part of their general "rein in" strategy to
gain ample intrastate participation in European policy-making. Likewise,
the "roll back" strategy has played only a subordinate role.

Unlike in areas of their exclusive competencies, such as culture and
media, the *Länder* have never really aspired to "ring-fencing" their environmental competencies against Europeanization. Like the *Bund*, the
Länder have an inherent interest in upgrading German environmental
regulations to the European level in order to avoid competitive disadvantages for their industry and to reduce adaptational costs in implementing European environmental legislation. Acknowledging the crossbound-
ary nature of environmental pollution, the *Länder* have never questioned
the need for European environmental regulations (Bulmer and Paterson
1987: 281). Rather, the *Länder* have criticized the formalistic approach
and the detailed regulations of EU environmental policies, which leave
little discretion in implementation (see above). Thus, the *Länder* have
repeatedly called for stricter application of the principle of subsidiarity as
it was included in Art. 130 r (4) EC Treaty (now Art. 174 EC) for environmental policy and generalized by Art. B (now Art. 2 EU) and Art.
3b (now Art. 5 EU) EU Treaty for all areas which do not fall within the
exclusive competence of the European Community.[116] However, "subsidiarity does not mean that the Community must not regulate at all. It is
the way in which it regulates that we often do not agree with" (interview
Bay₃₃). Thus, the *Länder* invoked the principle of subsidiarity to criticize the EU for setting purely procedural regulations, such as the EIA
or the IPPC Directive, without linking them to any uniform, substantial
standards. Rather than fending off Community interventions in environmental policy, the *Länder* opted to exercise as much influence as possible
on the form of Community environmental regulations.

The "rein in" strategy is not restricted to intrastate participation in European policy-making at the domestic level. The *Länder* have also tried
to become directly involved with European environmental policy initiatives. Direct access to the European policy arena is of vital interest to
most of the *Länder* because it allows them to participate in the policy
process at an early stage. When the *Bundesrat* becomes involved in the
decision-making phase, modifications of a proposal are more difficult to
achieve (interview Ba-Wü₃₅). While many of their channels of influence
at the European level are mediated by the central state (see Chapter 2

[116] See, for example, *BR-Drs. 779/94 vom 4.11.1994.*

of Part II), the *Länder* have established independent relationships with European institutions. The most important channels of such extrastate access to the European policy arena are direct contact with the European Commission and the European Parliament, organized mainly through the *Länder* offices in Brussels, on the one hand, and representation in the Committee of the Regions and the Assembly of the Regions in Europe, on the other hand.

Networking with the Commission and the European Parliament: Since the mid-1980s the *Länder* have had offices in Brussels, and these fulfill two important functions in European environmental policy-making. First, they serve as a major source of information, particularly with respect to what is in "the pipe-line" of the Commission. Regular informal contacts between DG (Environment Directorate General) and the *Umweltreferenten* (officials charged with European environmental policy) of the *Länder* offices as well as the *EG-Referenten* of the *Länder* Environmental Ministries provide important information on what kind of initiatives the Commission is likely to present in the near future. The *Länder* consider such information as vital for an effective lobbying strategy at the European level. Since about 80% of official Commission proposals become European law, the *Länder* believe that the injection of their interests is most effective in the initiative stage, although they do not have formal access to Commission advisory bodies.

Second, the *Länder* offices are the basis for lobbying European institutions in the policy-formulation and decision-making process. The *Länder* have invested considerable resources in the establishment of informal links with the Commission and the European Parliament. Such links are largely based on the expertise and information they can offer. The co-decision powers of the *Länder* in the formulation and representation of the German bargaining position provide them with an additional resource to draw on in dealing with European decision-makers. Due to its limited personnel resources, the Commission also encourages the delegation of experts from the national and subnational levels (Héritier *et al.* 1996: 152–153), and the *Länder* have made ample use of this opportunity.

While the more resourceful *Länder* in particular pursue a general networking strategy – by, for example, organizing social events or discussion circles in their Brussels offices, to which representatives of the various European institutions as well as other member states and regions are invited – the focus of attention is the Commission as the "policy-making engine of the EU" (interview Bay[22]). Contacts with the Commission may be facilitated by the fact that *Länder* officials working on European environmental policy had spent some years in the Environment DG as national experts and afterwards returned to the *Länder* office in Brussels or to their home ministries. Not only can these officials rely on their old networks and informal contact with former colleagues in the Commission and member-state administration; they also have a certain understanding and knowledge of "how the Commission ticks" (interview Bay$_{22}$).

Contact with Members of the European Parliament (MEPs) can also provide an important venue for the *Länder* to channel their interests into the European policy process. Bavaria and North Rhine–Westphalia, for instance, enjoyed privileged access to the European Parliament when their regional deputies served as the spokesperson for the Environment Committee of the European Parliament. On several occasions, Bavaria used these contacts to "channel" its position into the European Parliament by "lending" its experts to members of the Environment Committee, who prepare discussion papers and write final reports (cf. Käppler 1996).

Most *Länder* governments also keep direct political contact with European policy-makers, especially in the Commission. *Länder* Ministers travel to Brussels in order to present their positions to the Environmental Commissioner, the Director General, and other members of the Commission. Moreover, the *Länder* strive to establish contact with other member-state governments – such as the Danish, Swedish, and the British – hoping to have an indirect influence not only on decision-making in the Council but also in the Commission. The Environmental Commissioner is a Swede; the position used to be held by a Dane, while the British hold several key positions in the Environment DG (interview Bay$_{24}$).

Gaining regional allies: The only institutionalized extrastate access which the *Länder* enjoy to European policy-making are the Committee of the Regions (CoR) and the Assembly of the Regions in Europe (ARE). *Länder* administrators consider these institutionalized channels of influence as less effective than informal and direct contact with the Commission and the European Parliament. Yet, particularly Bavaria repeatedly and successfully tried to present its positions on CoR decisions, as in the case of the IPPC Directive, the revision of the EIA Directive, or the Water-framework Directive. Bavaria is the *Land* that most successfully pursues a strategy of "pulling all the possible strings", striving to use any opportunity available to represent its interests in the European policy-making process. "A position supported by several hundred other regions is far more powerful than an individual Bavarian position" (interview Bay$_{28}$). Other *Länder*, however, tend to focus their lobbying activities on channels of influence that they consider as more effective (interviews Ba-Wü$_{14}$; NRW$_{36}$).

The brief overview of the extrastate channels of influence, which the *Länder* have at their disposal to influence European environmental policy-making, shows that particularly Bavaria actively exploits opportunities to access the European policy arena directly. The Bavarian level of European activity is certainly unusual, if not unique, among the *Länder*. As such, Bavaria presents a critical case for the assumption that regions circumvent the central state by directly interacting with European institutions; although Bavaria exploits these opportunities more than most other regions, it does not (ab)use them to bypass the interests of the federal government or the other *Länder*.

First, Bavaria usually does not promote interests that contradict the official German bargaining position (interview BMU$_5$). Rather, the Bavarian government strives to turn its interests into a joint *Bund–Länder* position, which is normally coordinated in one of the joint-decision-making committees and later also officially adopted by the *Bundesrat*. Even in informal consultations and expert hearings organized by the Commission or the European Parliament, the *Länder* representatives tend to act as national rather than regional experts, which distinguishes them from other subnational actors and facilitates their contact particularly with the Commission "which is more likely to listen if Germany speaks with one voice rather than with 17" (interviews Bay$_{32}$; NRW$_{36}$).

Second, Bavaria usually coordinates its activities both with the other *Länder* and the federal government or, at least, keeps them informed. Regular meetings of the *Arbeitskreis der Umweltreferenten der Ländervertretungen* (officials in charge of the environment in the Brussels offices), which Bavaria has chaired since 1997 and in which members of the German Permanent Representation also participate, ensure a general exchange of information and often avoid duplicating work in lobbying the Commission, the Parliament, or the Committee of the Regions. In some cases, the *Länder* and the *Bund* join forces to pursue a common position. Even if the *Länder* act independently at the EU level, "we [the federal government and the *Länder*] often pursue a strategy of *getrennt marschieren und gemeinsam schlagen*" ("march separately but beat them jointly"; interview BMU$_7$).

The Water-framework Directive provides a good illustration of the interplay between *Bund* and *Länder*, i.e. intrastate and extrastate channels of influence in European environmental policy-making. Bavaria praises itself for having brought about a "paradigm shift" in the Commission, which finally adopted an emission-based approach in its formal proposal, as opposed to the exclusively quality-based approach it had initially endorsed in a first, unofficial Directive proposal.[117] The Bavarian administration used all of the extrastate channels of influence mentioned above in order to promote this shift (cf. Käppler 1996). Yet, the demand for an emission-based approach was not a specific Bavarian position; nor was it presented as such. An *ad hoc Arbeitsgruppe* (working group) of the *Länderarbeitsgemeinschaft Wasser* (*LAWA*), the joint decision-making body in which *Bund* and *Länder* coordinate their interests in water policy, prepared a joint position under the lead of Bavaria and Baden-Württemberg, which strongly influenced the work of the Environmental Committee of the *Bundesrat*. The official stance that the *Bundesrat* adopted in response to the Commission's communication for the Water-framework Directive corresponded to the joint position of the *LAWA*.[118] It formed the basis for the German position in consultations with the Commission in which Bavaria represented the *Länder*. The *LAWA ad hoc Arbeitsgruppe* also coordinated the German position for the expert hearing of the Environment Committee of the EP, which was decisive in persuading the Committee and, hence, the European Parliament, of the necessity to combine the quality-based approach with an emission-based approach.

It was hence a German position, rather than a particularly Bavarian opinion, for which the Bavarian environmental administration lobbied. The environmental working group of the 16 *Länder* offices provided the coordination of the European activities of the *Länder*. Most of the meetings with the Commission as well as with the representatives of other member states on the Water-framework Directive were organized within the *ad hoc* working group of *LAWA*. When the Bavarian Minister of the Environment, Thomas Goppel, went to see the Danish Environmental Minister Auken to discuss the issue of the Water-framework Directive, he was accompanied by the State Secretary of the Federal Ministry for the Environment, Eberhard Jauk and the spokesman of the Environment Committee of the European Parliament, Karl-Heinz Florenz.

Most observers would agree – and the Bavarians do too – that the Water-framework Directive is an extraordinary case of regional lobbying which is not necessarily representative with respect to both scope and effect (interview Bay$_{28}$). Yet, it shows that in cases of intense lobbying, the *Länder* still tend to coordinate their interests and activities rather than engage in unilateral initiatives.

All in all, Bavaria often has a strong viewpoint with respect to European environmental policies, which it actively pursues at the European

---

[117] *Information des Bayerischen Staatsministerium für Landesentwicklung und Umweltfragen, "Umweltschutz und Landesentwicklung in Bayern", 2/98*: 38.
[118] *BR-Drs. 779/94 vom 4.11.1994.*

level. Sometimes such European activities are accompanied by a lot of political rhetoric about "the right of the Bavarian *Freistaat* [free state] to defend its interests independent of domestic constraints" (interview Bay$_{24}$). Yet, such rhetoric is of symbolic rather than practical relevance. Important Bavarian initiatives at the EU level have never undermined the German bargaining position and are often coordinated with the federal government and the other *Länder*. Intergovernmental coordination between *Bund* and *Länder* is facilitated by a common interest in up-loading German environmental policies to the European level. Moreover, due to its superior administrative resources – and its privileged bilateral relations with the federal government as a formal coalition partner (until September 1998) – Bavaria is often able to turn its preferences into a joint *Bund–Länder* position, which has far more political weight at the European level than an individual Bavarian position. A Bavarian position which is coordinated with the federal governmental and the other *Länder* has not only the "political blessings" of the federal government but is also likely to determine the German bargaining position in the Council due to the co-decision powers of the *Länder* at the domestic level.

Flexible adjustment through the joint shifting and joint sharing of adaptational costs: "Fertilizing" cooperative federalism

The two-fold strategy of joint shifting and joint sharing has effectively reduced the costs of Europeanization. The transfer of domestic institutions to the realm of European policy-making allowed the territorial balance of power in the area of environmental policy-making to be redressed. As a result, Europeanization has ultimately reinforced rather than altered existing institutions.

With respect to the "say" side (centralization of *Länder* competencies), intrastate participation in European policy-making provides the *Länder* with formal access to most stages of the European environmental policy-making process. The *Länder* participate in about 20 working groups of the Commission and Council dealing with environmental issues. The *Bundesrat* issues official statements on about 80% of EU environmental proposals. Ten out of 12 issues on the agenda of the *Bundesrat* Environmental Committee are related to European issues (interview Bay$_{31}$). Where intrastate participation is limited – as in the stage of policy initiative – or less effective – because the *Bundesrat* intervenes too late or is not flexible enough to adapt its position to the dynamics of European negotiations – the *Länder* can draw on their extrastate channels of access to the European policy arena. In order to coordinate their interests and activities in European environmental policy-making effectively, *Bund* and *Länder* rely on the existing institutions of joint decision-making and interlocking politics.

The Bundesrat *and the* Umweltministerkonferenz *as the major axes of* Bund–Länder *cooperation*

The two major institutions of intergovernmental cooperation in German policy-making are the Sectoral Ministerial Conferences of the *Länder* (*Fachministerkonferenzen*) with their *Länder* working groups (*Länderarbeitsgemeinschaften*), and the *Bundesrat*, with its several hundreds of committees and commissions. The participation of the *Länder* in European policy-making in general – and in European environmental policy-making in particular – is organized through these two institutions, whereby we can observe a certain division of labor between the two.

The *Umweltministerkonferenz* (*UMK*; Standing Conference of the federal and the *Länder* Environmental Ministers) with its committees and working groups mainly serves to coordinate a joint position for the *Länder* (and the *Bund*) at the stage of the policy initiative. This position often provides the basis for both European lobbying activities of the *Länder* and their joint position, later adopted in the *Bundesrat*. The major strength of a position coordinated in the framework of the *Umweltministerkonferenz* is that *Bund* and *Länder* representatives can make decisions without requiring a mandate from their respective government, and this facilitates consensus-building.[119] Moreover, as all decisions must be unanimous, they constitute a strong political mandate of the *Länder* that neither the federal government nor the European Commission can easily ignore.

The *Bundesrat* usually deals only with formal (draft) proposals or official communications of the Commission, which are discussed in the Environmental Committee as well as other committees of the *Bundesrat*. The official opinion of the *Bundesrat* is coordinated by the EU Committee and is subsequently adopted by the plenum of the *Bundesrat*. The Environment Committee often cooperates closely with the competent *Länderarbeitsgemeinschaften*. Thus, European proposals affecting water policy are usually dealt with in the *Länderarbeitsgemeinschaft Wasser* (*LAWA*), a working group of the *UMK*, which prepares reports for the Environmental Committee of the *Bundesrat*. The informal interlocking of the two institutions is facilitated by the overlap of personnel to a certain

---

[119] In the *Bundesrat*, the *Länder* representatives may only act upon the decision of their governments as a result of which the interests of other ministries such as industry or agriculture often mediate *Länder* positions.

degree. Due the principle of functional specialization of the *Länder*,[120] the representative of the *Land* that is *federführend* (in charge of) in the Environment Committee of the *Bundesrat* also often takes the lead in the corresponding *Länderarbeitsgemeinschaft* and *Bund–Länder Arbeitskreis* as well as in the European decision-making bodies.

This dual structure of intergovernmental coordination and cooperation channels the participation of the *Länder* in both domestic and European environmental policy-making. In fact, Community proposals undergo the same treatment as federal draft legislation (cf. Müller-Brandeck-Bocquet 1996). The process of intergovernmental coordination in domestic and European environmental policy-making is interchangeable. Unlike Spain, Europeanization has not given rise to any new institutions. The formal and informal rules and procedures apply to European issues in the same way as they apply to domestic issues (cf. Bulmer 1986: 255–285; Müller-Brandeck-Bocquet 1996: 122–145). The same is true for the implementation of European and domestic environmental policies. "As regards federal law or law of the *Länder* implementing EC directives, no distinction is made between that and 'normal' German law" (Streinz and Pechstein 1995: 143). European environmental policy is transposed by federal law, ordinance, and/or administrative directives, which are subject to the same decision-making rules and procedures as those applying to domestic issues. There are no special procedures for implementing European law (cf. Bulmer and Paterson 1987: 177–179; Streinz and Pechstein 1995).

The formal and informal institutions of German federalism facilitate the effective participation of the *Länder* in European environmental policy-making. Whether the *Länder* do, in fact, have a significant impact on European policy outcomes is beyond the scope of this study. Most of the time *Bund* and *Länder* pursue a joint position as a result of which the success and failure of *Länder* positions is closely linked to the success and failure of the German bargaining position. Nor is the question of the independent impact of *Länder* interests on European policy outcomes relevant to the institutional balance of power between *Bund* and *Länder*. By sharing decision powers with the federal government the *Länder* have a similar relationship with the *Bund* in European policy-making as they do in domestic policy-making. The crucial point for redressing the territorial balance of power is that formal participation of the *Länder* in European policy-making is no longer reduced to implementation but comprises all

---

[120] Each *Land* specializes on certain policy areas that are of particular interest and for which it takes the lead in the corresponding *Bundesrat* and *Länder* committees. It also represents the *Länder* in the European decision-making bodies on these issues.

stages of the policy process (initiative, formulation, decision-making, and implementation).

Sectorization and deparliamentarization: Two sides of the same coin

The reinforcing effect of Europeanization on German territorial institutions does not only show in the transfer of territorial institutions from the domestic to the European area of environmental policy-making: it is also manifest in the increasing sectorization of *Länder* participation in European policy-making. Domestic conflicts on European environmental policies run between different sectors of the administration rather than between levels of government. Furthermore, V*ertikale Ressortkumpanei* (sectoral fraternities across different levels of government) and *Fachbruderschaften* (sectoral particularism) (Morass 1994: 64), which are prevalent in German federalism, increasingly rein in European policy-making. The effect of sectorization becomes most obvious with respect to "new policy instruments". Environmental Impact Assessment, Integrated Pollution Prevention and Control, and Access to Information, with their integrated, cross-media approach and their emphasis on transparency and public participation, pitch the "generalists" – usually lawyers working in the EU division (*Europareferat*) of their ministry – against the "specialists" – natural scientists and engineers in the sectoral divisions (*Fachverwaltungen*), who are experts in particular areas, such as water, air, soil, etc.

The differences between the two fractions run deep. The "generalists" have a more integrated and political view on European issues. As they are often directly involved in the European negotiations, their perspective is political, that is oriented toward the need for accommodating the interests of different parties. The "specialists" have a more sectorized view and are guided by technical considerations. Often they are not so atuned to the "rules of the game" at the European level. "Generalists" also note that "specialists" may be too missionary and inflexible in their positions on European policies. While "generalists" tend to adopt a more progressive view on European Directives, such as AI and IPPC, which they believe bring about necessary policy innovations, "specialists" are more conservative and perceive "new" policies as a threat to proven German regulatory structures. The view of a member of the air-quality control division in the Bavarian Environmental Ministry illustrates this point well: "Europe does not have to teach us environmental policy. We had enacted our first environmental regulations when nobody had even thought about the existence of the European Community" (interview Bay[29]).

As "generalists" are usually those who work in the *Länder* representations at the federal and EU level and in the EU divisions of the different *Länder* ministries, they have privileged access to information. And they strive to "keep the sectoral experts out of business for as long as possible" (BMU$_4$). At the same time, however, the "specialists" are those who participate in the *Länderarbeitsgemeinschaften* and *Bund–Länder* committees, and hence coordinate the joint positions of the *Länder* (and the *Bund*). The political leadership of *Bund* and *Länder* alike complains about the "*Eigenleben*" (autonomy) which "specialists" develop in the *Länderarbeitsgemeinschaften* and *Bund–Länder* committees. Long-term personal contact, a shared professional background, and a common view on the world render them "largely immune to external control" (interview SH$_{48}$). The *Land* government ultimately decides the position that a *Land* represents in the *Bundesrat* or at the EU level. Hence, the concerns of other ministries as well as the general political line of the *Land* often mediate the positions of the environmental specialists. Yet, "it is very difficult for our [the Bavarian] government to ignore a position that enjoys the support of 17 environmental administrations" (interview Bay$_{28}$).

As in domestic policy-making, *Ressortpartikularismus* facilitates the coordination of a joint (*Bund* and) *Länder* position on European issues. Thus, sectorization is an important element in redressing the balance of power between *Bund* and *Länder*. At the same time, however, interadministrative networks, which are difficult to control even by their own political leadership, reinforce the lack of transparency and non-accountability, and thus complement deparliamentarization as a major problem in the Europeanization of environmental policy-making.

The *Länder* participate in European policy-making through the *Bundesrat*, and the *Länder* coordinate their interests in the institutions of horizontal and vertical intergovernmental cooperation. The role of the *Länder* parliaments, the *Landtage*, at the stage of EU policy initiative and decision-making is reduced to a passive right to control the activities of their respective governments. Most *Landtage* are informed about major EU proposals on environmental policy. But the *Landtage* have no direct influence on the formulation and representation of the German bargaining position. Even in the implementation of European environmental law, the *Landtage* usually only ratify decisions that were agreed upon in intergovernmental negotiations. Many policies are implemented at the *Länder* level by ordinances or administrative directives, authorized by federal law, instead of a specific *Land* law, as a result of which the involvement of the *Landtage* is even further reduced.

The *Landtage* have been surprisingly passive in their reaction toward subsequent loss of their power caused by Europeanization. Apart from some general initiatives calling for more information and broader consultation (see Chapter 5), the *Landtage* have started to seek new functions in the area of controlling implementation (*Vollzugskontrolle*). As their role in legislation and even legal implementation decreases, the *Länder* parliaments have started to focus on practical application and enforcement of domestic as well as European environmental policies (Ritter 1999). The Members of Parliament must increasingly deal with petitions and questions that citizens (and citizen groups) in their respective constituencies raise with respect to ineffective practical application and enforcement of environmental regulations, be they national or European. As a result, the Environmental Ministries of the *Länder* face a growing number of questions and petitions from their parliaments that refer to implementation issues at the local level. Whether or not this reflects a general transformation in the functions of *Länder* legislatures in terms of a shift from legislation to implementation is beyond the scope of this study.

11 The "greening" of competitive regionalism: Institutional adaptation to the Europeanization of environmental policy-making in Spain

The uneven distribution of "say and pay" in European environmental policy-making

The centralization of environmental competencies at the national level

As in Germany, the central state and the *CCAA* share responsibility for environmental policy-making. Sharing competencies, however, does not result in joint decision-making. Rather, the central state sets *legislación básica* (framework legislation) in order to provide a "lowest common denominator" of environmental standards throughout the country. The *CCAA* have the responsibility of implementing framework legislation. They may also enact additional norms, which complete or reinforce the regulations of national framework legislation, e.g. by setting stricter standards (Art. 149.23; 148.9 CE).[121] The problem is that the *CCAA* do not always equally invoke their competence to develop central-state legislation. Some *CCAA* enact additional regulations, which go beyond the central-state legislation, while others simply apply the national laws. This tends to result in an uneven implementation at the regional level, which is reinforced by the lack of intergovernmental cooperation. Unlike Germany, where the *Länder* participate in central-state decision-making, intergovernmental coordination and cooperation used to be weak to non-existing in Spain. Consequently, the *CCAA* had no co-decision powers to lose as a result of Europeanization. Rather, centralization proceeded through the central state "capturing" legal and administrative competencies of the *CCAA* in the implementation of European environmental policies. The Spanish government managed to intervene in the transposition

---

[121] Before 1992, the 10 *CCAA* that had to take the slow route to autonomy had, strictly speaking, lacked the legal competence to develop environmental framework legislation; they were allowed only to execute it. However, as a result of the jurisdiction of the Constitutional Court, which followed a uniform interpretation of Art. 149.1.23 CE, all *CCAA* have always been able legally to develop central-state framework legislation (*STC 64/1982, de 4 de noviembre de 1982* and *170/1989, de 19 de octubre 1989*).

of virtually all European environmental policies by drawing on its exclusive competence to set and develop framework legislation. Either the central state enacts new framework legislation, or European environmental policies are incorporated into existing national legislation that enjoys the status of framework legislation. In the case of the former, central-state intervention is explicitly justified by the necessity to provide a uniform legal framework for the implementation of the policies. Due to the "state-friendly" jurisdiction of the Constitutional Court, enacting or developing framework legislation to transpose European policies severely limits the discretion of the *CCAA* in legal implementation (see Chapter 8).

The requirement of an effective and uniform implementation of European environmental policies may justify the centralization of legal transposition through enacting or developing framework legislation – particularly given the heterogeneity of the *CCAA* and the lack of inter-governmental coordination. Like the *Länder*, the *CCAA* came to accept the general competence of the central state to transpose European environmental policies. But they criticize the central state for using the implementation of European environmental policies to recapture regional competencies by enacting framework legislation that goes far beyond a "lowest common denominator." Thus, the central state frequently sets framework legislation for the application of EU policies in order to regulate issues that fall in the sphere of exclusive competencies of the *CCAA*. In the implementation of the Eco-Audit Regulation, for example, the central state interfered with the executive competencies of the *CCAA* by establishing a central supervision of regional institutions for the accreditation of environmental verifiers.[122]

Another area where the *CCAA* accuse the central-state administration of recapturing regional competencies in the Europeanization of environmental policy concerns the management of the Cohesion Fund. Up to 2000 Spain had received 1.5 billion pesetas (55% of the total funds), of which almost half – 700,000 million pesetas – was to be earmarked for the environment. The central-state administration decides on the distribution of European funds. Upto 1994 the *CCAA* benefited from the European money only indirectly when the central-state administration carried out projects in their territory or allocated money to them through *convenios* (agreements) for specific regional projects. In 1993 100% of the projects that received funding from the Cohesion Fund were central-state projects. The Catalan government, in particular, perceived

---

[122] For further examples of where the central state used the implementation of EU environmental policies to intervene in legal and executive competencies of the *CCAA*, see Pérez Sola 1996.

this central state "gate-keeping" of European funds as a clear attempt to "recuperate" or "subjugate" regional competencies "in an area where the central state is practically left without any competencies".[123] In early 1994 the Catalan Minister of the Environment, Albert Vilalta, publicly demanded the regionalization of the Cohesion Fund so that the *CCAA* would have the main competencies for managing the Fund in the sector of environment. He proposed that the money should be distributed among the *CCAA* in proportion to the ratio of environmental problems that each *CA* faced. The State Secretary of the Environment, Christina Narbona, rejected Catalan allegations of "a conspiracy of the MOPTMA [Ministry of Public Works, Transport and Environment] – inspired by its Minister Borrell – to recapture environmental competencies" (my translation).[124] She referred to the central-state competence for setting environmental framework legislation, on the one hand, and its foreign prerogative in dealing with European institutions, on the other. The situation started to change only in 1996, when the Spanish government and the *CCAA* developed a procedure for cooperation (see below).

Bearing the costs of implementation at the regional level

The adaptation to European environmental policies imposes higher costs on Spain than on Germany. Spain is an environmental latecomer, which started to develop a comprehensive regulatory structure only after its transition to democracy and under the strong pressure of implementing the European environmental *acquis* after having joined the European Community in 1986 (cf. Font and Morata 1998). Spain is a "policy-taker" rather than a "policy-maker" in European environmental policy-making (Aguilar Fernández 1997). Lacking policies to upgrade to the European level, Spain has to build up a regulatory structure in order to adapt to European standards and procedures, which tend to be tailored toward the problems and levels of socio-economic development of the northern environmental leaders. Thus, Spain often faces high adaptational costs for implementing European environmental policies that do not necessarily address its most pressing problems and are often considered as impairing its socio-economic development (Börzel 2000a, forthcoming).

Like the German *Länder*, the *CCAA* are left with the lion's share of the implementation costs, both material and political. First, the *CCAA* have to provide the administrative infrastructure for practical application and

---

[123] The Catalan Minister of the Environment, Albert Vilalta, in an article in *La Vanguardia*, February 15, 1994; my translation.

[124] The Spanish State Secretary of the Environment, Christina Narbona, in her response to Albert Vilalta; *La Vanguardia*; February 28, 1994.

monitoring of policies. Unlike the *Länder*, the *CCAA* face problems of mobilizing additional resources to build up the necessary legal and administrative structures for implementing EU policies. In this regard, effective monitoring is one of the most important cost factors in Spain. Spanish public authorities have traditionally given little priority to monitoring compliance with environmental standards (Aguilar Fernández 1994b). Environmental monitoring in Spain suffers from an uneven geographical distribution of measurement stations and a measurement technology that is often not up to standard (*Instituto para la Política Ambiental Europea* 1997; OECD 1997). The measurement of some parameters set by the Drinking Water Directive, for instance, requires sophisticated technological equipment, which is not only expensive but also demands personnel and expertise that are often lacking at the subnational level (cf. Börzel 2000a). Another problem of monitoring environmental quality is related to the different measurement methods that the *CCAA* apply. The lack of uniform measurement methods does not allow for comparison of data from different regions in Spain and makes compliance assessment for Spain as a whole almost impossible. While the Spanish administration has managed to centralize the legal implementation of European environmental policies, it has not been able to set up a unified monitoring system to control practical application and enforcement.

Second, the regional governments have to invest considerable financial resources in environmental infrastructure to ensure compliance with European environmental regulations. One of the most costly European environmental policies to be implemented in Spain is the Urban Waste Water Treatment Directive of 1994 (UWWT). The UWWT Directive obliges member states to provide conurbations with systems collecting and treating urban waste water. In 1995, only 40.7% of Spanish urban conurbations had waste-water treatment facilities that complied with the requirements of the Directive. The National Water Treatment Plan envisages public investments of 1.9 trillion pesetas (ca. US$ 9.9 billion) in order to bring Spain into full compliance with the Directive by 2005 (total waste-water investment between 1985 and 1993 equaled only 329 billion pesetas). The Catalan government calculated that it would need 312 billion pesetas (the equivalent of 28.3% of the 1997 Catalan budget) in order to bring Catalonia into compliance with the Directive (creation of new, and the extension and improvement of existing, waste-water treatment systems as well as the expansion and improvement of the monitoring system).

Third, in order to enforce the policies, regional authorities must ultimately impose sanctions on actors on whose political support they rely. Regional authorities often experience the enforcement of environmental standards, which are oriented toward the level of industrial development and environmental technology of northern European countries, as contradicting their political priorities of promoting economic growth and employment. While larger firms, mostly multinationals, usually comply with environmental laws, small- and medium-sized enterprises, which account for 90% of the total number in Spain, show a low level of compliance.[125] The consequent enforcement of air, water, and waste regulations would require many enterprises to introduce significant technological changes. Such technological changes are not only prohibitive for most small- and medium-sized enterprises. Even larger companies indicate that modernization measures are often too expensive, as a result of which many plants would have to close down (interviews BUS$_{94}$; BUS$_{92}$). Regional authorities are rarely able to provide sufficient public subsidies for technological changes. Nor are they willing to risk jobs, or future economic investments by strictly enforcing environmental legislation. Environmental Impact Assessment requirements, for example, can increase the costs of a project by 5–10% due to the imposition of corrective measures. Moreover, the EIA procedure often results in delays of several months in the authorization process (Commission 1993a). Particularly when it comes to industrial projects, environmental authorities frequently find themselves under considerable pressure – from economic factors as well as from political leadership and municipalities – because a negative EIA declaration, which prevents authorization, or corrective measures that are too stringent may put at risk badly needed economic investment (interviews DMA$_{80}$; CON$_{98}$).

Shifting the costs of adaptation: Confrontation, non-implementation, and non-cooperation

Unlike the German *Länder*, the *CCAA* did not initially cooperate with the central state to share adaptational costs that the Europeanization of environmental policy-making imposed on them. Rather, the *CCAA* responded to the uneven distribution of "say and pay" in European environmental policy-making by confrontation, non-implementation, and non-cooperation. First, the *CCAA* induced, or provoked, constitutional conflict in order to fight the centralization of their competencies. Second, regional authorities often resorted to reducing implementation costs through deficient practical application and non-enforcement of environmental policies. And, third, the *CCAA* refused to coordinate the

---

[125] An estimated 83% of Spanish enterprises do not comply with environmental laws (OECD 1997: 129).

implementation of European policies with the central state. In contrast to the area of structural policy for instance, circumventing the state has been a less prevalent strategy. Unlike the German *Länder*, the *CCAA* feel that they lack the necessary resources to influence directly the formulation of regulatory policies at the EU level (interview $Gencat_{64}$; DMA_{66}).

The threefold strategy of confrontation, non-implementation, and non-cooperation corresponds to the general strategy by which the *CCAA* initially responded to the challenges of Europeanization. As we see below, a cooperative strategy of cost-sharing was not only an option, given the efforts of the Spanish government to achieve some intergovernmental coordination in the implementation of European environmental policies, but it would also have offered significant benefits to the *CCAA*. However, the latter came to acknowledge these benefits only when their cost-shifting strategy turned out to increase rather than decrease adaptational costs. The institutional culture of bilateralism, confrontation, and competition had initially induced the *CCAA* to pursue a strategy that aimed to ring-fence their competencies through constitutional conflict and to reduce implementation costs by shifting them to the central-state level.

Ring-fencing regional competencies by constitutional conflict

The *legislación básica* is one of the major objects of constitutional conflicts over competencies between the central state and the *CCAA* in the area of environmental policy (*Ministerio para las Administraciones Públicas* 1995). Since the central state usually resorts to framework legislation in order to transpose European environmental policies, the *CCAA* mostly brought cases to the Constitutional Court in which they rejected an application of framework legislation that interfered with their competencies. Many conflicts arose because national transposing legislation designated certain (central-state) institutions for the practical application and enforcement of EU policies at the subnational level.[126] The *CCAA* not only initiated a series of constitutional conflicts to stop the intervention of the central state in the sphere of their competencies but, in order to gain more discretion in the practical application of European policies, some *CCAA* enacted subsequent legislation that "complemented" central-state transposing regulations in such a way that the central-state administration considered this an infringement of its exclusive competence for international relations and framework legislation (cf. Martín 1997).

---

[126] For an overview of the various conflicts over environmental competencies in the area of European policy-making, see Martín 1997.

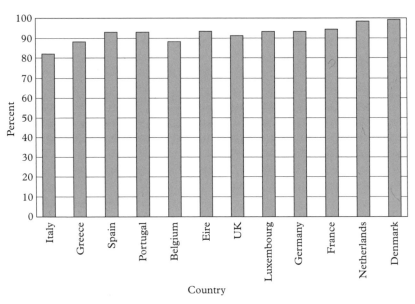

Sources: Own elaboration on the basis of data provided by Commission (1993b, 1996, 1999, 2000).

Figure 5 Average transposition rate in 12 member states, 1990–99

Reducing and shifting implementation costs by lax application and enforcement

With respect to the "pay" side of the Europeanization of environmental policy-making, the *CCAA* tried to reduce the costs of implementation by shifting them to the central-state level. In many cases, Spanish regional authorities simply do not fully apply and enforce European environmental regulations due to the high costs involved, both material and political. While Spain's average transposition in environmental policy (93%) compares well against northern European countries, such as Germany (93%) and France (94%), practical application often looks rather poor (cf. Börzel 2000a). See Figures 5 and 6.

Difficulties in detecting implementation failure at the level of practical application and enforcement favor the cost-avoiding and cost-shifting strategy of the *CCAA* in the implementation of European environmental policies (Börzel 1998b). Insufficient monitoring, for instance, does not provide reliable data to assess whether Spain is complying with air or water quality standards (interviews ENV_{88}; $IPAE_{96}$). Regional authorities do not deny this problem. However, they maintain that they want

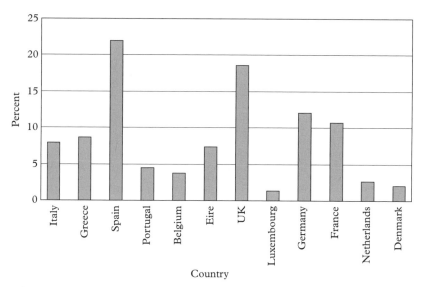

Sources: Own elaboration on the basis of data provided by Commission (1993b, 1996).

Note: Suspected infr ingements refer to complaints to the Commission, questions and petitions made to the European Parliament, as well as to cases detected by the Commission.

Figure 6 Average percentage of suspected infringements by member states, 1988–95

the necessary resources to remedy the situation and blame the central state for not providing the municipalities with sufficient financial means to exercise their monitoring competencies properly (interviews DMA_{76}; FMC_{84}). The *CCAA* themselves are not willing to support the local authorities in fulfilling tasks that the central state delegated to the local and not to the regional level (Börzel 1998b, forthcoming).

Moreover, because of economic and employment concerns (OECD 1997: 80–82), regional authorities make considerable concessions when it comes to enforcing European regulations. Compliance with air-quality standards, for instance, is low. Best Available Technology (BAT) is rarely applied in Spain because many companies lack the financial resources necessary to upgrade their production technologies. Few authorities are willing to sacrifice jobs in order to fight environmental pollution. While the *CCAA* admit that they do not systematically enforce the BAT concept, they point to the exclusive responsibility of the central state to define some common standards for operationalizing the BAT concept. Such standards are still lacking. The Spanish Environmental Ministry only recently established six to seven working groups, in which representatives of the central-state administration, the *CCAA*, as well as industry and universities, participate in order to define what constitutes the BAT standard for the various industrial sectors in Spain.

Procedural regulations – such as the Environmental Impact Assessment or the Access to Information Directives – are consequently not applied and enforced either. Only one quarter of the Environmental Impact Studies, which promoters submit to regional environmental authorities, meet the requirements of the Directive (Commission 1993a). Environmental authorities do not insist that alternatives to proposed projects are discussed seriously. Nor are substantial corrective measures consequently imposed (Escobar Gómez 1994). Many projects proceed without the necessary EIA. And of those submitted, authorities turn down very few industrial and public projects (cf. Börzel 2000a, 2000b). Even more resourceful *CCAA*, like Catalonia, complain that they lack the necessary personnel to monitor and enforce the requirements of the EIA Directive effectively (interview DMA$_{80}$). Nor are the *CCAA* necessarily willing to correct and complete central-state transposing legislation. Thus, as in Germany, the Access to Information Directive does not specify procedures to be applied practically at the regional level. Central-state transposition of the EU Directive is not only incomplete, but it is also very general and does not give any guidelines to administrators for deciding when and how to provide the requested information. Murcia is the only *CA* that has so far enacted some full legislation. The *CCAA* leave it to the central state to remedy deficient transposing legislation and to develop more detailed procedures for applying the AI Directive (interview MIMA$_{58}$).

The often ineffective and heterogeneous application of European environmental policies at the regional level, on the one hand, and the increasing number of conflicts over competencies with the *CCAA*, on the other hand, have resulted in significant implementation failure. More than half of the environmental complaints that Spanish societal actors submitted to the Commission, were motivated by ineffective implementation at the regional level (*Medio Ambiente en España* 1996). About 50% of the infringement proceedings that the Commission initiates against Spain originate at the *CCAA* level. Since the development and execution of environmental legislation, be it domestic or European, falls under the exclusive competence of the *CCAA*, the central state has no power to intervene in the practical application, monitoring, and enforcement of European environmental policies. At the same time, however, it is the Spanish central state that bears the costs of implementation failures, because it is liable to the European Union.

All in all, the *CCAA* have tried to avoid and reduce implementation costs by lax application and enforcement, for which the central state has to take responsibility. On the one hand, the Spanish government faces many infringement proceedings provoked by implementation failures that originate in the *CCAA*. On the other hand, the *CCAA* blame the central state for not providing the necessary means (legal regulations, financial resources) for an effective implementation of EU environmental policies at the regional and local level; even if this reproach seems to contradict *CCAA* complaints about the centralization of their implementation competencies!

Intergovernmental cooperation: Cost-sharing versus cost-shifting

Conflicts over the distribution of competencies and the lack of coordination and cooperation between the different levels of government are a major source of implementation problems in Spain (Commission 1991, 1993b; cf. *Instituto para la Política Ambiental Europea* 1997; OECD 1997). The huge implementation load, which Spain faced after having adopted the whole environmental *acquis* at once, resulted in an increasing implementation gap and rendered intergovernmental coordination for the central-state administration a political priority (interview MIMA$_{59}$). Initially, however, the *CCAA* showed little interest in engaging in any cooperation with respect to the practical application, monitoring, and enforcement of environmental policies.

The refusal of the *CCAA* to cooperate with the central state in the implementation of EU environmental policies presents a certain paradox. As we saw, the *CCAA* face considerable implementation costs with respect to the provision of legal and administrative rules and procedures, administrative capacity, and financial investment. Intergovernmental cooperation could help to reduce these costs by sharing them with the central state and the other *CCAA*. It is not just financial resources (access to national as well as EU funds) that the Spanish government can provide. The legal implementation of EU policies at the central-state level, in which the *CCAA* could participate through the Sectoral Conference on Environment, as well as a coordinated practical application at the regional level, would allow the *CCAA* to economize on resources, such as information, expertise, and personnel. Moreover, a more uniform implementation of EU environmental policies across the *CCAA* could prevent competitive disadvantages for regional industry, particularly in the economically more advanced *CCAA*, like Catalonia and the Basque Country.

The institutional culture of bilateralism, confrontation, and competition has, however, led the *CCAA* to ignore or discard the potential benefits of multilateral intergovernmental cooperation. The Sectoral Conference on Environment – which the central-state administration established in 1988, not least of all to improve intergovernmental coordination in the implementation of EU policies, accounting for more than 80% of Spanish environmental legislation ($MIMA_{60}$) – remained ineffective for six years (see below).

The increasing failure of cost-shifting in reducing adaptational costs

The *CCAA* had to realize that constitutional conflict was ineffective in preventing the centralization of regional environmental competencies at the central-state level. It even turned out to be counterproductive because the jurisdiction of the Constitutional Court tended to support the Spanish central state in setting and developing framework legislation to legally transpose European environmental policies (cf. Martín 1997).

The *CCAA* were initially more successful in reducing implementation costs by not, or by only partially, implementing European environmental legislation. But the subsequent tightening-up of European environmental regulations as well as the increasing mobilization of domestic actors putting pressure on public authorities to implement European environmental policies effectively rendered such a cost-avoidance strategy more and more expensive. Rather than reducing costs, the strategy of non-cooperation and cost-shifting appeared to increase them.

The rising costs of non-implementation

The reluctance of regional environmental authorities subsequently to ensure compliance with European regulations in order to avoid costs led to a widening implementation gap, which has been further enhanced through the revision of existing European legislation. Spain, for instance, has never effectively implemented the Large Combustion Plant of 1988 and its mother directive of 1984. In the absence of any serious attempts to reduce air pollution, Spain's large combustion plants are hardly able to comply with the new Directive on Integrated Pollution Prevention and Control and the recently revised Large Combustion Plant Directive. Both policies require the strict application of the "Best available Technology". Most of the Spanish plants were constructed in the late 1960s – early 1970s and, hence, do not reach modern technical standards. Moreover, given the lack enforcement of European and domestic air pollution control regulations (cf. Börzel 2000a. 2000b), plants have made little effort to reduce emissions. Industry is increasingly aware of this problem. The two companies that run the seven large combustion plants in Catalonia are currently negotiating voluntary agreements with the *Departament de Medi Ambient* (Department of the Environment) so as to facilitate a gradual modernization of their plants. They also seek public subsidies both from the Commission and Spanish authorities for implementing ISO 14001, an international environmental management system, which is to be a first step toward the European Eco-Audit Management System.

Increasingly, more stringent European environmental regulations not only raise the interest of economic actors in a more effective adaptation to European environmental policies, but societal groups also become more and more active in pressuring public administration to apply and enforce certain policies. Societal mobilization is particularly visible in the implementation of the EIA and the AI Directive. The two European environmental policies aim at strengthening public participation in the policy-making process. In Spain, the overall effectiveness of implementation in both cases is rather low. But environmental groups have been mobilizing increasingly in order to pull the policies down to the domestic level (cf. Börzel 2000a, 2000b).

The widening implementation gap and growing domestic societal pressure render cost avoidance by non-implementation more and more expensive. At the same time, some *CCAA* started to employ a "pace-setting strategy" in implementing European environmental policies. In particular, the Basque Country and Catalonia sometimes go ahead with the implementation of European Directives before the central state does. In the case of the Directive on the Incineration of Hazardous Waste, the Eco-Audit Regulation, the revision of the EIA Directive, and the IPPC Directive, Catalonia had enacted transposing legislation long before the central state legally intervened in its implementation. In these cases, regional implementation is usually more ambitious than central-state legislation. For example, Catalonia decided to accelerate compliance with parts of the Urban Waste Water Treatment Directive by seven years. This pace-setting strategy is connected less to a special environmental vocation of the individual *CA*: on the one hand, the economically more developed *CCAA* increasingly recognize that an advanced environmental infrastructure can be a competitive advantage to attract foreign investments. Thus, the Catalan administration perceives the implementation of some European environmental policies as a window of opportunity to modernize domestic environmental regulations and to push through environmental initiatives (interview DMA[78]). On the other hand, an early and ambitious transposition of European environmental policies is of high political and symbolic value to some *CCAA*. By preempting central-state legislation, the *CCAA* deploy competencies which they consider as their autonomous responsibilities and can, thus, counteract legal centralization. Moreover, early transposition may grant them a first-mover advantage by setting the agenda for the central-state transposition. Finally, the prompt and ambitious transposition of European environmental policies is also part of the image of a "model" region in Spain, which the Catalan government in particular strives to promote.[127]

However, the exemplary role of some *CCAA* is often confined to the legal implementation of European environmental policies. Catalan incineration plants, for instance, have great difficulties in complying with the stringent limit value for NO_x that the Catalan law imposes on the incineration of hazardous waste. Although the implementation of the Catalan Water Treatment Plan proceeds, Catalonia was not able to meet its self-imposed deadline of 1998. The practical application of the IPPC Directive, which Catalonia transposed before any other member state in the EU, appears to be even more problematic. Most industrial sites are a long way from applying the "Best Available Technology" in the production process. While the Catalan environmental administration hopes to confront such problems by a strategy of "*mejorar sin trauma*" (improvement without provoking a trauma), the gap between exemplary legal implementation, on the one hand, and ineffective practical application and enforcement, on the other hand, tends to undermine the image of Catalonia as a model region in Spain and Europe (interviews DMA_{71}; COM_{102}). The Catalan government also became aware that a pace-setting strategy may incur additional costs, particularly if other *CCAA* respond by "environmental free-riding" rather than by adapting similar environmental regulations. The success of pace-setting depends very much on whether the central state is willing to use regional laws as a base line for its own legislation.

The *CCAA* have increasingly realized that the implementation gap in European environmental policy-making might produce costs that eventually supersede the costs of adaptation in order to comply with European regulations. As a result, the *CCAA* have started to seek closer cooperation with the respective industry, especially by striking voluntary agreements and providing subsidies (cf. Aguilar Fernández 1997: 208–12; OECD 1997). The *CCAA* have also turned to Madrid for assistance for covering with implementation costs.

---

[127] See, for example, the Catalan EMAS brochure *El sistema d'ecogestió i ecoauditoria de la Unió Europea a Catalunya* (DMA, Barcelona, 1995), the *Plan de saneamiento de Catalunya* (Junta de Sanejament, Barcelona, 1995) and the homepage of the DMA (http://www.gencat.es/mediamb).

From cost-shifting to cost-sharing

Apart from rising costs of non-implementation, restricted access to European funds has played an important role in inducing a strategy change in the *CCAA*. The central-state administration gate-keeps access to European funds and programs. Despite pressure from the Commission, it has successfully resisted the "regionalization" of European funds for which Spain is eligible (Morata and Muñoz 1997). Given the centralized structure of the Spanish fiscal system and the gate-keeping position of the central state in the management of European funds, on the one hand, and the absence of horizontal coordination among the *CCAA*, on the other hand, access of the *CCAA* to both domestic and European financial resources strongly depends on the coordinating role of the central state. The central-state administration has to integrate regional programs that are eligible for European funding into a national plan or program. It also coordinates the distribution of funds among the *CCAA*. When in 1992 the Spanish government became dependent on the votes of the Catalan nationalists in the Spanish Parliament, the Catalan government pushed an agreement that provided for a sharing of European funding on environmental projects. Since 1994, the central state and the *CCAA* coordinate the distribution of Cohesion Fund money in the *Consejo de Política Fiscal y Financiera* (Council of Fiscal and Financial Policy) and the Sectoral Conference on Environment. While in 1993 100% of the Cohesion Fund money went into central-state projects, in 1998 50% are regional and 20% local projects. The rest are joint projects of the central state and the *CCAA*. By cooperating with the central state and among each other, the *CCAA* gained access to central-state and European funds, which may help to reduce the implementation costs of European environmental policies significantly.

Cooperation with the central state in European policy-making not only provides the *CCAA* with access to European funding, but it also lowers information costs. Almost all *CCAA* opened an information office in Brussels. But these offices do not enjoy the same systematic and comprehensive access to information as the central-state administration. Besides, they concentrate their limited resources on policy areas of specific interest to the *CCAA*, such as structural policy. Finally, unlike the German *Länder*, the *CCAA* did not participate in the EU decision-making bodies until 1998. Thus, the central state is the most reliable source for early and comprehensive information about ongoing developments at the European level. The central-state administration cannot only provide the *CCAA* with all the documentation, but the Environmental Ministry also often prepares a dossier with an assessment of the policy implications of specific Community initiatives for Spain.

Early and comprehensive information about (planned) European policies is of particular importance to those *CCAA* that pursue a "pace-setting" strategy. Thus, the Catalan government used the Incineration of Hazardous Waste (IHW) and the Integrated Pollution Prevention and Control Directives to enact and modernize regional legislation, respectively. For the implementation of the IHW Directive of 1993, the Catalan administration had received the relevant information through transregional channels within the working group on waste of the Assembly of the Regions in Europe (interview DMA$_{78}$). For the implementation of the IPPC Directive of 1996, by contrast, the Spanish Environmental Ministry provided the *CCAA* with all the documentation about the IPPC through the information procedure established by the 1994 Agreement on the internal participation of the *CCAA* in European policy-making.

But environmental pace-setting not only requires early and comprehensive information about European developments: the economic development of the different *CCAA* is also strongly interlinked with the modernization of the overall Spanish economy. Even the economically strong regions, like Catalonia and the Basque Country, are firmly integrated into the Spanish market (Held 1993). In order to avoid domestic competitive disadvantages by environmental free-riding on other *CCAA*, a pace-setting strategy very much relies on a certain harmonization of environmental regulations in other *CCAA* (OECD 1997). The Catalan administration has come to realize that such harmonization can be best provided by policy coordination at the central-state level (interview DMA$_{68}$).

Making implementation work: mutual consultation and pragmatic collaboration

As we saw in the previous section, constitutional conflict, non-implementation, and non-cooperation with the central-state administration increased rather than decreased the costs of Europeanization. While the centralization of regional competencies proceeded, implementation costs rose, not least because of the tightening-up of European regulations and the emerging domestic mobilization of domestic actors in favor of a more effective implementation of European environmental policies. The cost and benefits of intergovernmental cooperation had not changed much. But continuing centralization and growing implementation costs made the *CCAA* reconsider their strategy of cost avoidance and cost-shifting.

A first result of the emerging strategy change of the *CCAA* was their engagement in a multilateral dialogue with each other and the central-state administration in order to tackle specific problems of European policy-making on an *ad hoc* basis. One of the major issues in this dialogue, which was initiated in 1988, was the growing implementation deficit in environmental policy (interview MAP$_{51}$). The European Commission had repeatedly pointed to the lack of intergovernmental coordination between the central state and the *CCAA* as a major cause of implementation failure (Commission 1991, 1993b). As mentioned earlier, Spain has been facing a number of infringement proceedings where the responsibility for implementation failure lies – fully or in part – with (one of) the *CCAA*. In order to deal with such problems, the central-state administration and the *CCAA* agreed in 1990 on the participation of regional representatives in the so-called "package reunions" (*reuniones paquetes*). Representatives of the Commission (DG Environment), the central state, and regional environmental authorities meet twice a year in order to deal with implementation issues that are subject to complaints or infringement proceedings. Over the years, the package reunions have developed a "culture of cooperation and interadministrative understanding", which has often allowed pragmatic solutions to be found for problems in the implementation of European environmental policies (interview MAP$_{51}$).

Another manifestation of the emerging strategy change by the *CCAA* has been their increasing willingness to coordinate the implementation of European environmental policies with the central state. First, the *CCAA* started to engage actively in consultations with the central-state administration on the transposition of certain European environmental policies. Initially, such consultations used to be on an informal and often bilateral basis. Over the last five years, however, the Sectoral Conference on Environment has increasingly dealt with these issues. Since the implementation of the 1994 Agreement in 1995, the competent working groups of the conference discuss national draft legislation on the transposition of European environmental policies, which is finally approved by the plenum of the conference. The central-state administration sends the *CCAA* the documentation before the meetings so that they can prepare observations, which are then discussed in the meetings. After the meeting, the Spanish Environmental Ministry revises the draft proposal in light of the debate, indicating in the final version which observations of the *CCAA* were included and stating reasons for discarding others (interview DMA$_{66}$). While active participation varies across the *CCAA* – depending on the issue at stake and their administrative capacity to deal with the issue – the bigger *CCAA* in particular make extensive use of the opportunity to give their input (interviews MIMA$_{55}$, DMA$_{66}$). Since 1995, the central state has not passed transposing legislation without prior approval of the sectoral conference.

Second, the *CCAA* has started to participate in structuring Joint Plans and Programs in order to implement some European environmental policies. Joint Plans and Programs identify common objectives and formulate guidelines on how to implement them at the regional level. They also set the framework for the distribution of funding. When the JPPs are related to the implementation of European environmental policies, part of the money is provided by the Cohesion Fund. As these are Community programs, the *CCAA* actively participate in their formulation, which requires substantial intergovernmental coordination both with the central-state administration and the other *CCAA*. The most prominent example of such intergovernmental coordination is the implementation of the Urban Waste Water Treatment Directive (UWWT). As already indicated, the implementation of the UWWT Directive requires immense effort on the part of the public administration, both at national and regional levels, to build new purification plants as well as to bring existing ones up to European standards. None of the *CCAA* was able to finance the necessary construction and extension of water treatment facilities. In order to share the burden, the central-state administration and the *CCAA* agreed to co-ordinate their efforts in the implementation of the UWWT Directive in the multilateral framework of the Sectoral Conference on Environment. The UWWT Directive was one of the first major European issues on the agenda of the sectoral conference. The central-state administration proposed that the *CCAA* develop a National Plan for the Treatment and Purification of Waste Water.

When, in 1992, the sectoral conference established an *ad hoc* working group to prepare the plan, the central-state administration initially faced great difficulties in convincing the *CCAA* that the plan was not meant to recapture regional competencies. But in the subsequent years, the Ministry of Public Works, Transport, and Environment managed to establish a good working relationship with the *CCAA*, based on personal contacts and a shared technical approach to the issue; this helped to overcome the initial distrust (interview MIMA$_{56}$). In September 1994 the sectoral conference approved the National Plan unanimously. In February 1995 the Spanish government adopted the Plan, six months before the transposition of the UWWT Directive. With the National Plan the central state committed itself to provide 25% of the 1.9 trillion pesetas (ca. US$ 9.9 billion) to be invested at the regional level between 1995 and 2005. The money is drawn in part from the Cohesion Fund. The central-state administration subsequently signed bilateral *convenios* with each *CA* in order to allocate money at the regional level. For 12 *CCAA* (including Catalonia) these bilateral *convenios* also entail an intergovernmental agreement on interadministrative cooperation in the implementation of the National Plan. Although negotiations with the *CCAA* for the National Water Treatment Plan were often difficult and had to be backed by a strong element of bilateral bargaining, it made a major attempt to implement European environmental policies by means of multilateral intergovernmental cooperation rather than bilateral or unilateral initiatives.

The National Water Treatment Plan is not a unique case. The *CCAA* and the central-state administration subsequently negotiated similar plans to implement other Directives. Two prominent examples are the National Plan of Hazardous Waste, which previews the investment of 180 billion pesetas (US$ 944 million) for 1995–2000, including a 25% contribution from the Cohesion Fund, and the National Plan for the Redemption of Contaminated Soil, envisioning an investment of 132 billion pesetas (US$ 692 million) for 1995–2000, including a 50% contribution from the Cohesion Fund. In all three cases, the provision of national and European funds provided a major incentive for the *CCAA* to refrain from the strategy of confrontation, non-cooperation, and non-implementation.

But intergovernmental cooperation helps not only to reduce implementation costs of European environmental policies; the *CCAA* also increasingly acknowledge that their consultation in the implementation of the policies may provide a certain remedy against the centralization of their competencies (interview DMA$_{66}$). The co-financing of regional projects through Joint Plans and Programs is a compromise in the conflict between the central-state administration and the *CCAA* on regional participation in the management of the Cohesion Fund. While the *CCAA* are not independent in spending European funds, the coordination of Joint Plans and Programs, which identify regional projects to be financed by European funding, allows for a significant input from the *CCAA* on the management of European funds. Multilateral intergovernmental cooperation in the sectoral conference also allows the *CCAA* to have significant influence on the transposition of European environmental policies by the central state.

The "big four" (Catalonia, the Basque Country, Andalusia, and, to a lesser extent, also Galicia) have begun to identify another advantage of multilateral intergovernmental cooperation. While all 17 *CCAA* gain access to funds, information, and influence on central-state legislation, the environmentally more progressive *CCAA* can also exploit their "first mover strategy". Catalonia has been particularly successful in setting environmental legislation by transposing European policies, which later became a model for central-state transposition. Such a pace-setting effect can be found for the Urban Waste Water Treatment, the Incineration of Hazardous Waste, and the Integrated Pollution Prevention and Control Directive as well as the Framework Directive for Waste. In all these cases, Catalan legislation served as a "reference and potential model" for the national draft legislation (interview MIMA$_{61}$). As in Germany, the more powerful *CCAA* dominate the multilateral cooperation: "*Son las voces de Catalunya, el Pais Vasco, Andalucia y Galicia que cantan*" ("It is always Catalonia, the Basque Country, Andalusia and Galicia which set the tone"; interview MIMA$_{55}$). Not only do these *CCAA* often have more intense preferences than the others, they are also better prepared due to their superior administrative resources. From 1992 to 2000 the Catalan administration had an additional card to play because of its privileged bilateral relationship with the central government, which depended on the Catalan administration's support in the national parliament.

Europeanization and the emergence of multilateral intergovernmental cooperation

The Europeanization of environmental policy-making in Spain had a visible effect on both the degree of institutionalization and the effectiveness of multilateral intergovernmental cooperation. The general low-profile of the *Senado* in European policy-making, which we saw in Chapter 8, is equally manifest in the area of environmental policy. The policy study also confirms the positive effect of Europeanization on the other major institution of multilateral intergovernmental cooperation in environmental policy-making: the *Conferencia Sectorial de Medio Ambiente* (the Sectoral Conference on Environment).

The following study on the policy-making effectiveness of the Sectoral Conference on Environment is based on an analysis of the minutes of the meetings that the conference held between its creation in 1988 and the end of the study in summer 2000, as well as the minutes of its working groups and committees. The Ministry of Public Administration published parts of the minutes (*Ministerio para las Administraciones Públicas* 1996). I completed the missing data by a study of unofficial documents, which the Ministry of Public Administration and the Environment Ministry kindly provided to me. For details on the operationalization of policy-making effectiveness on European versus domestic issues, see Chapter 8.

The Spanish government established the Sectoral Conference on Environment in 1988 in order to provide some intergovernmental coordination that was felt necessary to deal with problems in the environmental sector. Initially, the conference had a very low level of institutionalization. The conference lacked a proper legal basis. Rules of procedures were only introduced in 1995, seven years after its creation. Working groups were not established before 1991 and started functioning only in 1993. The policy-making effectiveness of the conference in the first six years was low. After the constitutive meeting in November 1988, the conference convened only three times before the end of 1993, with no meetings held in 1989 and 1993. The conference did not produce any significant output on domestic issues. In the few meetings which took place, the *CCAA* and the central-state administration discussed almost exclusively European issues, such as the application of the Environmental Impact Assessment

Directive in 1988, 1990 and 1991, and the Urban Waste Water Treatment Directive in 1990 and 1991. The first substantial output that the conference produced was the *Plan Nacional de Residuos Industriales* (National Plan on Industrial Waste), which the *CCAA* and central-state administration approved in 1989 in order to implement the Directive on Toxic and Hazardous Waste.

As a consequence of its ineffective working, the conference passed a resolution in May 1990, which aimed at its "revival" by

1. meeting at least twice per year;
2. having meetings prepared by coordination bodies at the working level; and
3. setting common objectives to be achieved by the conference.

Yet, the conference started functioning only in 1994 when European issues began to dominate the agenda. Since then, the conference has held regular meetings. Additionally, coordination bodies at the working level did not start working properly before 1994. Programs on areas of joint objectives and cooperation, which the conference had defined in a meeting in 1991, centered on European issues (waste, water treatment, and environmental impact assessment) and resulted in the first significant output that the conference produced. For summary details of the Sectoral Conference on Environment, see Table 5.

The Sectoral Conference on Environment is one of those conferences where the discrepancy between domestic and European policy-making effectiveness is striking. From its very beginning, the conference has produced little output with respect to domestic issues. There were no national environmental laws at all on the agenda before 1996. Until recently, the conference did not provide any input on central-state decision-making on domestic environmental legislation. Nor did the conference have much coordination in its application. No national plan or program has been adopted by the conference to implement a domestic policy. The second "revival" of the conference in 1994 – after two years of functioning ineffectively – is marked by three National Plans – on Waste Water Treatment, on Hazardous Waste, and on Contaminated Soil – which the sectoral conference elaborated and adopted in order to implement three European environmental policies. Subsequently, the conference has almost exclusively dealt with issues relating to the participation of the *CCAA* in the formulation and, above all, the implementation of European environmental policies.

The *Conferencia Sectorial de Medio Ambiente* was the first sectoral conference to formally implement the 1994 Agreement in 1995. While the conference still did not deal with central-state legislation on purely domestic issues, the transposition of European policies increasingly

Table 5 *Degree of institutionalization and number of meetings of the Sectoral Conference on Environment, 1988–99*

Legal basis	Rules of procedure	Coordination bodies at the working level	Number of meetings 1988–99
No proper legal basis, integrated in *Ley 30/92*	Decided in February 1995 and revised in 1999	Reunion of the Directors General (1986) Working groups	• 1988: 1 • 1989: 0 • 1990: 1 • 1991: 1
Included in the 1994 Agreement on the intrastate participation of the *CCAA* in European policy-making in 1995		*1990–96* • water* • air* • environmental impact* • environmental education • waste and used oil* • Eco-Label* • normative issues* • information and statistics*	• 1992: 1 • 1993: 0 • 1994: 2 • 1995: 2 • 1996: 2 • 1997: 1 • 1998: 2 • 1999: 2
		1997 • continental water* • marine environment* • environmental quality (air pollution)* • environmental impact assessment and sectoral activities* • Eco-label* • nature conservation and biodiversity* • waste* • environmental education • information and statistics* • law-making and international relations • Community affairs*	
		Governing Council of the National Plan on Industrial Waste (1989)*	
		Commission for the implementation and coordination of the National Plan on Industrial Waste (1989)*	

Table 5 (*cont.*)

Legal basis	Rules of procedure	Coordination bodies at the working level	Number of meetings 1988–99
		National Commission for Nature Protection (1997) • nature reserves • swamps • prevention of forest fires	
		Council for National Parks (1997)	
		Thematic Commission for Environmental Education (1998)	

Note: *directly related to European issues

dominated the agenda. The Europeanization of the *Conferencia Sectorial de Medio Ambiente* also strengthened its institutional framework. The majority of the working groups owe their existence to the implementation of a specific European policy, such as EIA or Eco-Label (see below). Moreover, in order to implement the 1994 Agreement on the intrastate participation of the *CCAA* in European policy-making, the conference finally adopted some rules of procedures. For summary details of the effectiveness of policy-making on domestic and European environmental issues, see Tables 6 and 7.

All in all, the sectoral conference began as a forum of intergovernmental cooperation in both the formulation and the implementation of environmental policies in 1994, when European policies systematically "captured" the agenda and the 1994 Agreement on the intrastate participation of the *CCAA* in European policy-making began to be implemented.

The effect of Europeanization on multilateral intergovernmental cooperation is even more visible at the working level of the conference. The three meetings, which the coordination body of the Directors General held between 1992 and 1994, dealt mostly with European issues, such as the three National Plans mentioned above, the implementation of the Eco-Label Regulation, or the preparation of the Council of Ministers of the Environment. Since the implementation of the 1994 Agreement on the internal participation of the *CCAA* in European policy-making, the meetings of the Directors General have dealt regularly with Community proposals and issues that concern the Cohesion Fund. Moreover, the

Table 6 *Policy-making effectiveness on domestic and European issues related to the environment, 1988–93*

	1988	1989	1990	1991	1992	1993
Output relating to domestic issues		No meeting	• resolution on the revival of the conference • discussion on procedures of joint decision-making in environmental emergency situations • systematization of statistical information • minimal requirements for depositing environmental equipment	• approval of a set of joint objectives in order to revive the sectoral conference: waste management, waste water treatment, establishment of EIA procedures to be integrated in urban planning (all objectives relate to EU policies)	• discussion of environmental problems and activities in Spain	No meeting
Output relating to European issues	• development of the National Plan on Industrial Waste • application of EIA • Spanish EU presidency and the environment	No meeting	• development of the National Plan on Industrial Waste • discussion of the procedures for the implementation of Community Law • harmonization of the application of EIA • analysis of the situation on the quality of waste water treatment	• report on application of National Plan on Industrial Waste • development of the Community program ENVIREG • development of a Program of Cooperation on waste water treatment and the establishment of a procedure for the application of the EIA and its integration in urban planning	• information on the Maastricht Treaty with respect to environmental policy • discussion of access to financial Community programs • discussion of the establishment of a "contact network" which would consist of a coordinator in each *CA* responsible for complaints and infringement procedures	No meeting

Source: Own elaboration based on data published in Ministerio para las Administraciones Públicas (1996) and unofficial documents.

Table 7 *Policy-making effectiveness on domestic and European issues related to the environment, 1994–99*

	1994	1995	1996	1997	1998	1999
Output relating to domestic issues	• presentation and discussion of the new environmental agenda for the new legislature and the development of National Environmental Strategy (*CCAA* asked to give input) • information on the establishment of the *Consejo Asesor de Medio Ambiente*	• presentation of the guidelines for an industrial policy in Spain by the Ministry of Industry and Energy • information on environmental legal projects (European and domestic)	• report of the Minister on past achievements and future projects such as the reform of the National Water Act, a Law of Civil Liability for Environmental Damage, a National Plan on the Struggle Against Forest Fires • creation of the *Comisión Nacional de Protección de la Naturaleza*	• debate on the revision of the internal rules of procedure • information on the planned reform of the National Water Act • information on the planned Law of Civil Liability for Environmental Damage • debate on the National Plan on the Struggle Against Forest Fires • debate on the National Plan of Environmental Cartography	• debate on the National Water Plan • approval of the *Consejo Nacional del Clima* (National Climate Council) which will develop a national strategy to respond to climate change • debate on the actions to be taken by each level of government to implement the results of the Kyoto Summit The last two issues are neither strictly domestic nor directly related to Europe.	• debate on the National Water Plan • debate on the National Water Law • debate on the National Forest Strategy and on actions to be taken by each level of government to implement it

Table 7 (cont.)

	1994	1995	1996	1997	1998	1999
Output relating to European issues	• discussion of the central-state framework legislation on the National Plan on Industrial Waste • approval of procedural regulation of the conference which implements the 1994 Agreement on the application of the Cohesion Fund in the sector of environmental policy • debate on how to facilitate intergovernmental cooperation in the transposition of EU policies, access to Community programs and preparation of the	• discussion of the agenda for the Spanish EU Presidency related to environmental issues • debate on the National Strategy for Nature Conservation and Biodiversity • debate on the transposition of the UWWT Directive • debate on the legal draft for the transposition of the Packaging Waste Directive • debate on the legal draft for a revision of the transposition legislation on the EIA	• debate on the strengthening of the participation of the CCAA in EU policy-making (reorganization of working groups, informal participation in EU decision-making committees) • information on the agenda of the EU presidencies • debate on the draft legislation for transposing the Directive on the Incineration of Hazardous Waste, the Packaging Waste Directive, and the revision of the EIA Directive	• information on the agenda of the EU presidencies • information about the changes in environmental policy in the Amsterdam Treaty • information about the progress in transposing EU environmental Directives and about the calendar for future legal projects • information about the execution of the National Plans for Hazardous Waste, Contaminated Soils and Waste Water Treatment • debate on the National Plan for Solid Urban Waste • information about	• information on the agenda of the EU presidencies • information about the Climate Change Summit in Buenos Aires • approval of the draft for the regulation on the application of the Packaging Waste Law • agreement on the establishment of a Commission for intergovernmental cooperation in the application of the Packaging Waste Regulation • rejection of the latest draft for the revision of the national legislation transposing the AI	• information on the agenda of the EU presidencies • debate on the actions to be taken by each level of government to implement the Spanish Strategy on Biodiversity • Approval of the National Plan on solid Urban Waste

Table 7 (cont.)

	1994	1995	1996	1997	1998	1999
Output relating to European issues	meetings of the Council of Ministers on the Environment • discussion on draft law for implementation of the Eco-Label Regulation • formulation of base lines for the National Plans to implement European policies on hazardous waste, waste water treatment and contaminated soil	• debate on the draft legislation for *Ley 38/1995* transposing the AI Directive • information on the evaluation on the implementation of the three National Plans • information on current infringement procedures against Spain		the progress in the implementation of the Habitat Directive and debate about the necessity to coordinate the Network *Natura 2000* with the *CCAA*, especially with respect to Community funding • information on different programs funded by the Structural Funds and LIFE • presentation of the Director of the European Environmental Agency on the European Environmental Information Network	Directive by the *CCAA* • debate on the Spanish Strategy on Biodiversity • debate on the demand of Catalonia to formally include a representative of the *CCAA* in the Spanish delegation for international environmental summits	

Source: Own elaboration based on data published in Ministerio para las Administraciones Públicas (1996) and unofficial documents.

activities of the working groups have always been centered on European issues. The majority of the working groups, which have been established since 1990, are directly related to the implementation of European policies. The participation of the *CCAA* in the EU decision-making committees further advances intergovernmental cooperation in European environmental policy-making. While the formal participation of the *CCAA* in EU decision-making bodies is still a pending issue, the Spanish Environmental Ministry informally agreed in 1997 that the *CCAA* could send one representative to each of the Commission committees dealing with the implementation of EU environmental law.

The relatively high effectiveness of the sectoral conference on policy-making when dealing with European issues is closely related to elaboration of Joint Plans and Programs (JPPs). Unlike other policy areas, all environmental JPPs, which the *CCAA* and the central-state administration have approved, are Community-funded programs for the implementation of different European environmental policies. The formulation and implementation of these JPPs were coordinated in the sectoral conference. The Community JPPs owe their success as a means of implementing European environmental policies to their ability to deal with several issues at a time in the uneven distribution of "say and pay" in European environmental policy-making. First, the JPPs help the *CCAA* in reducing implementation costs (by up to 85%). They also allow for a more consensual distribution of European funding among the *CCAA* because the JPPs are negotiated and approved by all *CCAA*. Second, Community-related JPPs entail a strong element of joint decision-making and thereby provide a formal participation for the *CCAA* in managing Cohesion Fund money. Third, the joint formulation of policy objectives and their operationalization in the implementation of the JPPs offer the opportunity to overcome potential conflicts over competencies.

Both the central state and the *CCAA* agree that multilateral cooperation helps to improve the implementation of European environmental policies in Spain (*Información de Medio Ambiente, n°. 35,* June 1995; interview DMA_{66}). Multilateral intergovernmental cooperation is not, of course, able to overcome all implementation problems. The functioning of the sectoral conference tends to be hampered by its high degree of politicization, which could be taken as another indicator for its growing importance. The plenum of the conference is sometimes instrumentalized by the socialist-governed *CCAA* to oppose the incumbent conservative government politically (interviews $MIMA_{55}$; DMA_{66}). At the same time, however, the working-level bodies of the conference are becoming more and more effective. While agreement at the political level depends very much on the overall political climate, cooperation at a more technical level (e.g. cooperation amongst engineers and lawyers, etc.) in the working groups is effective. The working groups meet every three months on average. Most of the conference output is negotiated and agreed upon at the working level and is ultimately approved by ministers, often despite political disagreement within the plenum of the conference (interview MIMA$_{55}$).

Another problem for the effectiveness of intergovernmental cooperation in general – and the participation of the *CCAA* in European policy-making in particular – is the lack of sufficiently qualified regional experts who have the time and knowledge to deal with often highly technical and complex European environmental regulations. As in the city states in Germany (e.g. Berlin, Hamburg), the small *CCAA* have environmental departments that often employ not more than 15–20 people. But even the larger *CCAA*, such as Catalonia, the Basque Country, or Andalusia, as well as the central-state administration itself, often suffer from the lack of a supporting group of experts and technicians (Aguilar Fernández and Jiménez Sánchez 1998).

Insufficient personnel and expertise might be also a reason why the activities of the conference with respect to the internal participation of the *CCAA* in European policy-making reflect a strong bias toward the descending phase, i.e. the transposition and practical application of European environmental policies. So far, the *CCAA* have not confronted the central government with joint positions, which it should take into consideration for the formulation of the Spanish bargaining position. This is not necessarily related to a lack of interest or consensus among the *CCAA*. The limited capacity of most *CCAA* to process all the relevant information in time and to formulate a clear position that could be co-ordinated with the others might be part of the explanation. But, so far, the *CCAA* have also not felt the need to make their voices formally heard in the formulation of European policies. They make observations at the informal level when the Spanish Minister informs them about Community initiatives. In many cases, their interests coincide with the position of the central state (interview DMA$_{66}$). If one or several *CCAA* have a particular interest in a specific initiative, this is usually dealt with between the central-state administration and the *CCAA* that are affected (cf. Aguilar Fernández and Jiménez Sánchez 1998).

The focus on the implementation rather than the formulation of European environmental policies also reflects the predominant concern of the *CCAA* in the Europeanization of environmental policy-making, which centers on the protection of their competencies to legally develop and execute central-state policies. The centralization of regional competencies occurs with respect to implementation rather than policy formulation. While the participation of the *CCAA* in the formulation and decision-making of European policies is highly symbolic, up to now it has attracted less attention from the *CCAA*. In their perception, EU policies often simple replace central-state framework legislation, in whose formulation the *CCAA* do not formally participate (interview DMA$_{66}$). It is the intervention of the central state in the implementation of European environmental policies that the *CCAA* are concerned about.

All in all, the effect of Europeanization on multilateral intergovernmental cooperation in the area of environmental policy is quite striking. The rise of European policies to be the dominant issues on the agenda of the sectoral conference, together with the implementation of the 1994 Agreement on the intrastate participation of the *CCAA* in European policy-making, have had a significant impact upon both the level of institutionalization and the policy-making effectiveness of the conference. The Sectoral Conference on Environment has turned from an ill-functioning body into a forum of intergovernmental cooperation, which meets regularly and produces significant output, particularly with respect to the implementation of European environmental policies. The *CCAA* are kept informed about Community initiatives and they participate in the transposition of European policies at the central-state level. The sectoral conference has produced various National Plans to finance the implementation of important European policies. Since 1994 there has not been a transposition law or Community-related program that has not been examined and approved by the sectoral conference.

The emergence of multilateral intergovernmental cooperation in European environmental policy-making does not mean that bilateral intergovernmental cooperation is no longer important. As already mentioned, some *CCAA* strive to coordinate their interests with the central state on an informal level before the meetings of the sectoral conference. Very important issues are usually first subject to bilateral exchanges at the top-level. Negotiations in the sectoral conference are often preempted by bilateral consultations so as to facilitate agreement (MIMA$_{55}$). In many cases, the practical application of multilaterally agreed policies, plans, and programs is still dealt with bilaterally. Yet, bilateral contacts increasingly appear to be a complement to rather than a substitute for multilateral intergovernmental cooperation. Bilateral Commissions in European policy-making exist only for the Basque Country and Catalonia. They deal with very broad issues and do not allow for the treatment of specific problems (interviews DMA$_{66}$). Informal contact between high-ranking officials (Subdirectors and Directors General) are frequent. But since European issues have systematically been introduced to the agenda of the sectoral conference, the *CCAA* cannot simply circumvent this forum, particularly not Catalonia that strives to avoid the impression of special treatment by the Spanish government. All in all, bilateral contact is still important. But such contact increasingly serves as a resource in controlling multilateral intergovernmental cooperation rather than as a real alternative.

The case study on the Europeanization of environmental policy provides a more detailed illustration of the constraints and opportunities that Europeanization provides to the *CCAA* and which induced them to endorse a more cooperative approach in their relationship with the central state as well as among each other. Multilateral intergovernmental cooperation can counterbalance the centralization of regional competencies. It helps to reduce implementation costs and grants additional access to information. Finally, European infringement proceedings often exert additional pressure for effective implementation, both from below and from above.

This European "incentive structure" for intergovernmental cooperation is not specific to environmental policy. The uneven distribution of "say and pay" applies to all policy areas in which the *CCAA* hold exclusive competencies in the implementation of European policies, such as transport, fisheries, health, tourism, regional development, culture, or education, with the "pay" side being more pronounced for regulatory policies. While access to financial resources might be less relevant in policy areas that lack significant European funding, the argument about information costs and political influence on central-state decision-making still holds. The most significant variation appears to be between domestic and European policy-making within one policy area rather than between different policy areas. This is because the incentive structure for multilateral cooperation primarily contains factors that are specific to European policy-making. Europeanization gave rise to significant institutional change as a result of which environmental policy-making on European issues is subject to a new and different set of formal rules and procedures to environmental policy-making on purely domestic issues. Nevertheless, there are some indications of a spill-over effect.

Toward a spill-over from European to domestic policy-making?

While the sectoral conference used to play a minor role in domestic environmental policy-making, the central-state administration is increasingly pushing domestic issues onto the agenda (interview MIMA[54]). As in the area of European policy-making, the *CCAA* slowly become involved in the formulation and implementation of national environmental policies by participating in the drafting of legislation as well as the elaboration of national plans and programs. In 1997, for instance, the sectoral conference extensively discussed, and finally rejected, the draft for a reform of the National Water Act of 1985 (*Ley de Aguas*), which the central-state administration had prepared.

In 1997 the Minister of Environment announced her intention to strengthen the sectoral conference as the "*eje básico de la política ambiental*" ("basic axis of environmental policy-making"; *Información de Medio Ambiente, n°. 47*, December/January 1997) by enhancing the participation of the *CCAA* in environmental policy-making. The announcement resulted in a reform of the internal rules of procedures of the conference adopted in 1999. The reform broadens the composition of the conference, allowing for the participation of ministers from other sectors if the plenum debates issues that concern their competencies. The new rules also foresee the position of a vice-president of the conference to be elected among the representatives of the *CCAA*. The working level of the conference is strengthened by the reorganization of existing working groups and the creation of eight new ones. A systematic distinction between the commissions and the working groups of the conference is introduced by restricting the participation in the commissions to the level of Directors General, while the working groups are open to experts from all levels as well as from non-public bodies. The attempt to separate the political (Director Generals, who are political civil servants) from the technical level shall help to depoliticize intergovernmental cooperation. To what extent this reform will be successful in strengthening the participation of the *CCAA* in both domestic and European policy-making remains to be seen.

The emergence of domestic issue on the agenda of the sectoral conference is quite a recent phenomenon. Yet, the fact that domestic issues are gaining ground and start receiving the same treatment as European issues, i.e. are made subject to the same policy-making rules, might serve as a first indicator for a spill-over effect by which domestic issues are increasingly dealt with in the framework of multilateral intergovernmental cooperation. In any case, the *CCAA* coordinate the implementation of policies with the central state as they participate in the formulation of these policies at the central-state level. And this coordination and participation is no longer limited to the realm of European policy-making.

12   Conclusion

The policy study on the Europeanization of environmental policy-making in Germany and Spain confirms the major findings of the institutional analysis presented in Parts II and III of this book. In both countries, Europeanization caused an uneven distribution of "say and pay" in favor of the central state. The *Länder* lost their formal co-decision powers in policy initiative and decision-making, while the *CCAA* faced the centralization of their legislative and administrative competencies on the implementation level. With respect to the "pay" side, the *Länder* have to bear significant implementation costs by incorporating European policies, which do not fit German regulatory structures. The *CCAA*, in turn, carry the major burden of building up regulatory structures and capacities that are required for the effective implementation of European environmental policies in the first place.

The uneven distribution of "say and pay" in EU environmental policy-making has changed the territorial balance of power to the detriment of the *Länder* and the *CCAA*. The regions of the two countries have, however, resorted to very different strategies in responding to this pressure for adaptation. The *Länder* have tried to share the costs of adaptation with the central state. Co-decision powers in the formulation and representation of the German bargaining position compensated the *Länder* for their loss of competencies. The joint shifting and sharing of implementation costs by upgrading German regulations to the European level, on the one hand, and absorbing and watering down of mismatching European policies, on the other hand, have so far helped to reduce implementation costs. The strategy of joint sharing and joint shifting of the costs of adaptation has by and large allowed the territorial balance of power to be redressed and has resulted in a transfer of formal institutions from the domestic to the European realm of policy-making; this has ultimately reinforced rather than changed them.

The *CCAA*, on the contrary, initially tried to shift the costs of adaptation onto the central state. Despite the huge implementation load that Spain faced after joining the EC, the *CCAA* rejected the offer of the central state to join forces and coordinate implementation at the national and regional level. Instead, the *CCAA* strove to ring-fence their competencies by constitutional conflict and often refrained from implementing costly EU policies effectively. However, this non-cooperative strategy increased rather than decreased the costs of adaptation. The *CCAA* more and more realized that cooperation with the central state not only allowed them to pay off some of their implementation costs by gaining access to national and European funding; it also halted the centralization of their implementation competencies because the *CCAA* could participate in the legal transposition of EU policies at the central-state level.

The strategy change of the *CCAA* resulted in a significant shift toward multilateral intergovernmental cooperation in environmental policy-making. The Sectoral Conference on Environment, the major formal institution for intergovernmental cooperation, became increasingly effective and produced some real joint decision-making within the newly established rules and procedures for intrastate participation of the *CCAA* in European policy-making. In recent years, these new forms of joint decision-making appear to have spilled over gradually to the area of domestic policy-making.

Finally, the Europeanization of environmental policy-making illustrates the problem of de-parliamentarization, which is reinforced in Germany and increasingly pronounced in Spain. The participation of both *Länder* and *CCAA* in European policy-making is exclusively organized through cooperation between regional and central-state administration. Like the *Landtage*, the role of the *CCAA* parliaments in ratifying decisions and agreements that their governments reached with the central state in the sectoral conference may be increasingly reduced.

Conclusions: Toward convergence in Europe?

The concluding chapter summarizes the empirical comparative study in light of the theoretical propositions generated by my Institution Dependency Model. I argue that the findings challenge dominant approaches in the field of European studies, which cannot explain the differential effect of Europeanization on the territorial institutions of Germany and Spain. I then discuss the scope of my model. Drawing on other empirical studies, I maintain that the Institution Dependency Model is generalizable enough to analyze the domestic impact of Europe across different policy areas, member states, and institutions. I also propose areas for future research where the model could provide new insights. I conclude by considering implications of my theoretical argument and empirical findings for the European system of governance. The Institution Dependency Model should lead us to expect some "clustered convergence" among member states that face similar pressure for adaptation. If these expectations hold, the prospects of a "Europe of the regions" are rather gloomy. Moreover, the participation of the regions in European policy-making will increase rather than decrease the democratic deficit of the European Union.

The domestic impact of Europe: Transformation versus reinforcement

The book started with an empirical puzzle. Europeanization has caused some considerable changes in the territorial institutions of Germany and Spain. These changes converge around the participation of the Spanish *Comunidades Autónomas* and the German *Länder* in European policy-making through cooperation with the central state rather than through direct relations with European institutions. The regions of both countries predominantly rely on their co-decision rights in the formulation and representation of the national bargaining position to channel their interests into the European policy-making process. Moreover, the formal rules and procedures through which this intrastate participation

211

of the regions is organized are similar. Spain subsequently adopted the German model (cf. Table 8). However, while regional participation in central-state decision-making on European issues constitutes a major change in the Spanish system of intergovernmental relations, it has resulted in flexible adjustment and ultimate reinforcement of existing territorial institutions in Germany. None of the dominant approaches to Europeanization can explain the similarity in outcome and the variation in the degree of territorial institutional change in Germany and Spain.

Most studies on the domestic impact of Europe embrace some sort of resource dependency approach. They conceive of the European Union as a structure with new political opportunity that provides some domestic actors with new resources while depriving others. Liberal intergovernmentalists suggest that the redistribution of resources among domestic actors enhances the political autonomy of central-state actors. Neofunctionalist or supranationalist approaches come to the opposite conclusion: that Europeanization shifts the domestic balance of power in favor of non-state actors (domestic and European). Proponents of multilevel governance approaches argue that Europeanization does not favor one particular group of domestic actors over others but increases their mutual interdependence, giving rise to greater cooperation.

The German and the Spanish cases challenge both the liberal intergovernmentalist and the neofunctionalist/supranationalist propositions. Europeanization initially changed the domestic distribution of power in favor of the central state in both countries. However, the *Länder* and the *Comunidades Autónomas* subsequently succeeded in redressing the territorial balance of power. Neither the German nor the Spanish central state was strengthened or weakened. Central state and regions share their resources in European policy-making, as a result of which both win, or both lose.

The outcome of institutional adaptation to Europeanization in Germany and Spain appears to be more consistent with the expectations of multilevel governance approaches. Yet, the cooperation of central state and regions in European policy-making follows the logic of a two-level game. Contrary to what is suggested by multilevel governance approaches, the central state is the major channel of influence in European policy-making for both the *Länder* and the *Comunidades Autónomas*. Direct relations with European institutions are also important but they serve as a complement to rather than a substitute for cooperation with the central state. The national governments do not monopolize access to the European policy arena, but they remain central gate-keepers.

Table 8 *Convergence in the participation of the German and Spanish regions in European policy-making*

	Germany	Spain
Information of the regions on European issues	The Federal government comprehensively informs the *Länder* in the *Bundesrat* as early as possible on all issues that are relevant to their competencies or interests.	The Spanish government informs the *CCAA* in the competent sectoral conferences about all issues that are relevant to their competencies or interests.
Co-decision rights of the regions in the formulation of central-state position on European policy initiatives	The *Bundesrat* formulates an opinion, which determines the German bargaining position if an issue mainly affects the legislative or administrative competencies of the *Länder*. Otherwise, the Federal government gives the *Bundesrat* positions due consideration.	The *CCAA* formulate a joint opinion in the competent sectoral conference, which determines the Spanish bargaining position if an issue affects their exclusive legislative competencies. Otherwise, the Spanish government gives the *CCAA* positions due consideration.
Regional participation in the implementation of European policies at the central-state level	The *Bundesrat* has a co-decision right in the legal implementation of EU policies at the national level.	The central-state administration and the *CCAA* inform each other in the competent sectoral conference about the legal and administrative measures taken in the transposition and application of European policies. They can coordinate their implementation activities (through, for example, Joint Plans and Programs).
Participation of regional representatives in the national delegation		
a) Observer of the regions	a) The *Länderbeobachter* has access to all EU decision-making bodies as a member of the German delegation, except COREPER.	a) The *Consejero Autonómico* is a member of the Spanish Permanent Representation and may participate in the EU decision-making bodies as a member of the Spanish delegation.
b) Access to decision-making committees of the Commission and the Council	b) The *Bundesrat* can delegate one or two representatives to the working groups of the Council and the Commission (comitology) if the competencies of the *Länder* are affected.	b) The *CCAA* can delegate two representatives to 55 working groups of the Commission (comitology).
c) Access to the Council of Ministers (Art. 146)	c) A *Länder* minister represents Germany in the Council of Ministers if exclusive competencies of the *Länder* are affected.	c) The *CCAA* may have access to the Council as members of the Spanish delegation (to be formally approved).
Access of the regions to the European Court of Justice on behalf of the central state	The Federal government takes legal action before the ECJ on behalf of the *Länder* if EU (non)activities affect their competencies.	The Spanish government takes legal action before the ECJ on behalf of the *CCAA* if EU (non)activities affect their competencies.

Therefore, intergovernmental cooperation between central state and regions in European policy-making does not necessarily transform the "state" as multilevel governance approaches often propose. In Germany, existing state institutions have been reinforced. And while one might argue about whether the emergence of multilateral intergovernmental cooperation and joint decision-making transforms the Spanish "state", multilevel governance – like the other two approaches – cannot explain the variation in the degree of institutional change in Germany and Spain. In sum, resource dependency wrongly predicts or, at best, is indeterminate with regard to outcome and degree of domestic institutional change triggered by Europeanization.

Rather than discarding resource dependency altogether, I argue that it needs to be embedded in an institutionalist approach in order to explain the differential effect of Europeanization on the domestic institutions of the member states. Institutions mediate the domestic impact of Europe in two fundamental ways: First, the "goodness of fit" between European and domestic institutions impacts upon the degree of pressure for adaptation that domestic institutions face and, hence, the likelihood of domestic institutional change. Second, the adaptability of domestic institutions, that is, their ability to accommodate pressure for adaptation, influences whether institutional mismatch gives rise to profound change or only flexible adjustments that reinforce rather than change existing institutions (degree of change).

The historical institutionalist approach, adopted in this book, combines assumptions of both rational choice and sociological institutionalism to specify conditions under which Europeanization has what kind of effect on the institutions of the member states. The combination of (some elements) of the two institutionalisms allows two important dimensions of institutions that mediate the effect of Europeanization to be accounted for:

• formal institutions, which influence the distribution of resources among actors (power constellation) defining actors' capabilities; and
• informal institutions (institutional culture) which entail collectively shared rules of appropriateness shaping actors' understandings of socially accepted behavior.

While formal institutions delimit the range of strategy options that actors face in pursuing a given interest, informal institutions impact upon their ultimate strategy choice.

The Institution Dependency Model, which I develop in Part I, uses the distinction between formal and informal institutions to conceptualize and operationalize its two major variables in explaining the domestic impact of Europeanization:

- pressure for adaptation; and
- adaptability.

Pressure for adaptation is the result of a mismatch or misfit between European and domestic formal institutions which leads to a redistribution of resources among domestic actors and changes the balance of power within a domestic institution. A significant change in the balance of power itself already constitutes formal institutional change. Yet, those domestic actors who lose power will strive to redress the balance of power by adapting their institutions to the challenges of Europeanization. The adaptational strategy, which the losers will choose, not only depends on their (remaining) resources (formal institutions), but the strategy choice is also influenced by the institutional culture, in which actors are embedded (informal institutions). The particular strategy that actors choose is decisive for the adaptability of domestic institutions.

The Institution Dependency Model distinguishes two major strategies between which domestic actors can choose in order to redress the balance of power:

- a cooperative strategy of sharing the adaptational costs with other domestic actors; and
- a non-cooperative strategy of shifting the costs of adaptation onto others.

While the former strategy aims at the compensation of the losers by the winners which share their resources with the losers, the latter attempts to prevent losses and regain resources from others (inside and outside the institution). I argue that a cooperative strategy of cost-sharing facilitates institutional adaptation and allows the institutional balance of power to be redressed by flexible adjustment. Conversely, a non-cooperative strategy of cost-shifting prevents institutional adaptation, that is, it does not allow the balance of power to be redressed in the first place. Yet, actors who suffer loss of power can be expected to reconsider their initial strategy choice, particularly if their strategy tends to further increase rather than decrease their losses. If domestic actors change the strategy by which they respond to the challenges of Europeanization, then this strategy change may result in domestic institutional changes which not only affect formal but also informal institutions.

The theoretical assumptions of my Institution Dependency Model generate the following hypotheses with respect to the domestic impact of

Europe. I use these hypotheses to summarize the empirical findings of my comparative study on the effect of Europeanization on the territorial institutions of Germany and Spain.

1. The more that formal norms, rules, and procedures at the European level challenge those at the domestic level (misfit), the greater changes in the distribution of resources among domestic actors (pressure for adaptation) will be and the more likely domestic institutional change will occur.

Europeanization entails a shift of policy competencies from the domestic to the European level, where member-state governments enjoy privileged institutional access. European institutions largely exclude the regions of the member states from decision-making. At the same time, given the lack of a European administration, the regions have to bear the costs of implementing European policies. The concentration of decision-making powers in the hands of national executives and the shifting of implementation costs to the regional level challenges the territorial institutions of both Germany and Spain.

In German federalism, the *Länder* share both decision-making powers and implementation costs with the central state. In Spanish regionalism, the *Comunidades Autónomas* enjoy considerable autonomy both in decision-making and implementation. Despite the institutional differences, Europeanization has led to an uneven distribution of "say and pay" in Germany and Spain, which has changed the territorial balance of power in favor of the central state. In both countries, the shift of policy competencies from the domestic level to the European level allows the central state to access exclusive competencies of the regions that the respective constitutions placed out of its reach in domestic policy-making. Due to their larger sphere of autonomous competencies, the *Comunidades Autónomas* have been more affected in this area than the *Länder*, which have suffered most from losses of their co-decision powers in federal policy-making. Yet, in both cases, Europeanization has led to a significant centralization of regional competencies. Moreover, *Comunidades Autónomas* and *Länder* alike have to bear the costs of implementing policies in whose decision-making they do not participate.

The redistribution of resources resulted in similar pressure for adaptation in Spain and Germany as the uneven distribution of "say and pay" considerably changed the territorial balance of power in favor of the central state. The shift toward centralization has resulted in some formal institutional changes in both countries. Yet, the regions have hit back. They have striven to redress the balance of power, albeit by resorting to very different strategies facilitating institutional adaptation in the one case, while prohibiting it in the other. In other words, pressure for adaptation is a necessary but not a sufficient cause of domestic institutional change.

2. The more cooperative the institutional culture is, the easier a redressing of the balance of power between domestic actors (institutional adaptability) and the lower the degree of domestic institutional change will be.

In principle, the *Länder* and the *Comunidades Autónomas* faced the same strategy options in trying to redress the territorial balance of power. Due to a similar degree of decentralization, the territorial institutions of both countries provided their regions with sufficient resources to pursue a non-cooperative strategy of cost-shifting, or a cooperative strategy of cost-sharing. The *Länder* and *Comunidades Autónomas* could opt either to confront and circumvent the central state in European policy-making by ring-fencing their competencies and establishing direct relations with European institutions, or to use their resources to push for compensation of their losses by participating in the formulation and representation of the national bargaining position at the European level. While the *Länder* opted for the latter strategy, the *Comunidades Autónomas* initially relied on the former, non-cooperative strategy.

The explanation for the different strategy choices of the *Länder* and the *Comunidades Autónomas* lies in the different institutional cultures in which they are embedded. An approach that looks solely at the distribution of resources and the self-interests of the actors wrongly predicts the strategy choices of the regions or, at least, is indeterminate. More than the regions of any other member state, the *Länder* had the necessary resources to circumvent the central state in European policy-making. Nevertheless, the *Länder* have employed their substantial direct contact with European institutions as a complement to rather than a supplement for their cooperation with the central state on European affairs. The informal institutions of cooperative federalism prevented the *Länder* from using their extrastate channels of influence to undermine the power of the central state.

Rather, the culture of multilateral bargaining and consensus-seeking induced the *Länder* to pursue a cooperative strategy of "compensation-through-participation", which they had already employed in dealing with similar challenges to their institutional autonomy in the past. By cooperating with the central state the *Länder* have increasingly participated in the formulation and representation of the German bargaining position at the European level, which has also allowed a sharing of implementation costs in some instances. The sharing of decision-making powers and implementation costs between *Bund* and *Länder* in European policy-making redressed the territorial balance of power by adjusting the institutions of cooperative federalism in a flexible way. The transfer of joint decision-making and interlocking politics from the domestic to the European realm of policy-making reinforced rather than altered German territorial institutions.

3. The greater the changes in the distribution of power at the domestic level (pressure for adaptation) and the less cooperative the institutional culture (non-adaptability), the greater the formal changes in domestic institutions (centralization/decentralization).

Although the *Comunidades Autónomas* faced similar pressure for adaptation as the *Länder* and had similar resources, the *Comunidades Autónomas* opted for a different strategy. The informal institutions of competitive regionalism prevented the *Comunidades Autónomas* from engaging in any significant form of intergovernmental cooperation with the central state in European policy-making. Rather, the culture of bilateralism, confrontation, and competition induced them to bring any perceived intervention of the central state into their sphere of competencies before the Constitutional Court and to circumvent the Spanish government in European decision-making by establishing direct links with European institutions. Like the *Länder*, the *Comunidades Autónomas* did not consciously calculate the costs and benefits of the alternative strategies. They simply followed standard operating procedures and rules of appropriateness that had evolved in the past from dealing with similar challenges to their institutional autonomy.

The effect of the institutional culture on the initial strategy choice of the *Comunidades Autónomas* is most striking in the area of environmental policy, on which the policy study of Part IV focused. When Spain joined the European Community, it was faced with a huge implementation load since it had agreed to adopt the whole *acquis communautaire* at once. Spain did not have a developed regulatory structure in environmental policy. As a result, the *Comunidades Autónomas*, which have the exclusive competence for practical application and enforcement of most environmental policies, faced the challenge of building up the necessary legal and administrative infrastructure in order to ensure compliance with European environmental regulations. But instead of accepting the offer of the central-state administration to pool resources (competencies, expertise, funding) in order to cope with the challenge, the *Comunidades Autónomas* refused to cooperate with the Spanish government as well as with each other. Instead, they engaged in a series of constitutional conflicts trying to fight off the attempt of the central state to centralize the implementation of European environmental policies.

The confrontational strategy of the *Comunidades Autónomas* prevented the territorial balance of power from being redressed. Constitutional conflict and non-cooperation promoted rather than prevented the centralization of regional competencies. Nor did it reduce implementation costs. Changes in the territorial balance of power in favor of the central state were increasingly sustained (formal institutional change).

4. The greater the changes in formal institutions (as a result of adaptational pressure and lacking adaptability), the more likely there will be changes in adaptational strategies and the changes in institutional culture.

As the cost-shifting strategy of the *Comunidades Autónomas* prohibited institutional adaptation, adaptational pressure increased. The *Comunidades Autónomas* realized that their confrontational strategy did not allow the territorial balance of power to be redressed. On the contrary, it increased centralization and implementation costs alike. In light of rising adaptational costs, the *Comunidades Autónomas* started to reconsider their initial strategy and subsequently adopted a more cooperative approach. The cooperative strategy was encouraged by Spain's recognition of its success in the case of the German *Länder*, as well as the positive experience that the *CCAA* and the central state had on adopting this approach. The gradual adoption of a more cooperative strategy through a process of experiential learning led to a fundamental change in the formal territorial institutions of Spain, which is also likely to affect its institutional culture. For the first time, central state and regions formally share decision-making power in a multilateral framework of intergovernmental cooperation.

The analysis of the 23 sectoral conferences in Chapter 5 demonstrated that the newly established framework of multilateral intergovernmental cooperation is more than "institutional window-dressing". Unlike in domestic policy-making, a third of the sectoral conferences produce significant policy output when dealing with European issues. The more detailed study of the Sectoral Conference on Environment in Chapter 11 not only confirmed these findings, but it also presented some evidence on an emerging spill-over of multilateral intergovernmental cooperation from European to domestic policy-making.

It is too early to tell whether the fundamental changes in formal territorial institutions will bring Spanish competitive regionalism closer to German cooperative federalism with respect to the underlying institutional culture. Yet, the Institution Dependency Model would lead us to expect that the positive experience with the new formal institutions of joint decision-making render multilateral cooperation and consensus-seeking – as opposed to traditional bilateralism, confrontation, and competition – increasingly acceptable for the *Comunidades Autónomas*. There are good reasons to believe that, in the long run, the process of experiential learning in which the *Comunidades Autónomas* have engaged, may give rise to a new collectively shared understanding of appropriate behavior in Spanish intergovernmental relations; see Figure 7.

Cooperative regionalism on the rise?

This book presents empirical evidence as well as a theoretical explanation for the differential impact of Europe on the institutions of the member states. Before discussing the theoretical and empirical implications of my findings, I would like to evaluate their generalizability.

The Institution Dependency Model identifies two major variables in explaining the degree and outcome of domestic institutional change triggered by Europeanization: pressure for adaptation and adaptability. The structured, focused comparison of the effect of Europeanization on the territorial institutions of Germany and Spain allowed me to test systematically only for adaptability. I controlled for the second explanatory factor by keeping the variable "pressure for adaptation" constant. As I claim that pressure for adaptation is only a necessary cause of domestic institutional change, this "omission" does not seriously affect the validity of my findings. However, to test for the relevance of pressure for adaptation as a necessary cause of domestic institutional change properly, I should have included a third country. On the basis of the issues in this study, the domestic institutions of this hypothetical third country would not face pressure for adaptation, nor would they entail a cooperative institutional culture, as a result of which they should not undergo any significant institutional changes. Before a limited amount of devolution at the end of the 1990s, the United Kingdom could have provided such a case. Its territorial institutions used to be highly centralized. Subnational authorities had hardly any decision-making powers to lose by Europeanization. And while the counties and the local authorities have a role to play in the implementation of European policies, at least in some areas, the central-state administration bears a large share of implementation costs given the limited financial resources of local authorities. Thus, Europeanization did not result in an uneven distribution of "say and pay", which would have changed the territorial balance of power. While not imposing any significant constraints on subnational actors or the United Kingdom, European institutions do provide them with some new opportunities. The rather tense and at times conflicting relationship between the local and the central level (Rhodes 1997: Chapter 6) creates a strong incentive for exploiting European resources to circumvent the UK government. Yet, most UK counties lack the necessary resources to exploit these new

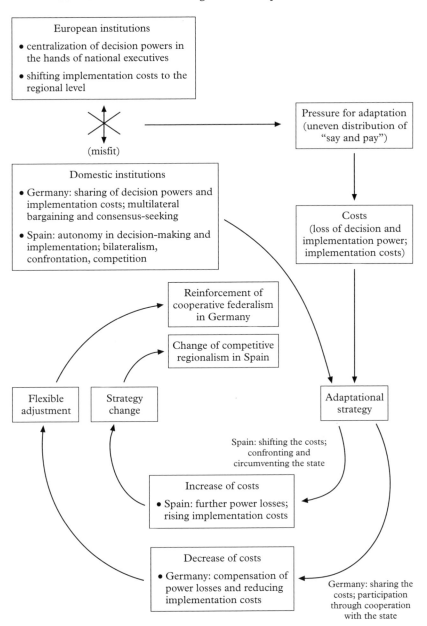

Figure 7 Europeanization and territorial institutional change in Germany and Spain

opportunities systematically. While the first-tier authorities (regional councils in Scotland, and county councils in England and Wales) and the big cities tried to circumvent the central level, especially in the area of structural funds (Tofarides 1997; Martin and Pearce 1999), the UK government successfully defended its gate-keeping position. Moreover, in response to the circumventing strategy of some local authorities, the UK government strove to centralize the management of the structural funds even further (Bache *et al.* 1996). Not surprisingly then, the existing literature on the effect of Europeanization on the territorial institutions of the United Kingdom presents little evidence for significant changes (Anderson 1990; Bache *et al.* 1996; John 1997; Bache 1998; Martin and Pearce 1999). Devolution certainly constitutes a substantial change in British territorial politics, particularly in the case of Scotland. Like the Basques, Scottish nationalists perceive the structure of the European Union as offering an opportunity to push their claims for independence (Keating 1996). But devolution in the UK has been driven by more general dynamics than a Europe-induced redistribution of domestic resources (Keating and Elcock 1998).

France is another case where Europeanization has not exerted any significant pressure for adaptation on territorial institutions. Lacking substantive political powers the *régions* and the *départements* have had little to lose to Europe. They do, however, play an important role in the implementation of European policies. But the French State bears the cost to a large extent. The Europeanization of regional policy has strengthened the regional level in France and, hence, reinforced the regionalization process initiated in 1982 (Le Galès 1994). But representatives of the central state at the regional level (*préfets*) and their field services were much more apt to exploit these new opportunities than the *régions* and *départements* (Benz 1998). State representatives, not autonomous regional actors, have the necessary resources to influence European policy-making. With the *préfets* serving as the major interface (*relais*) between the different levels of government, the central state maintains its gate-keeping position in European policy-making (Balme 1995; Smyrl 1997). While French subnational authorities have too few resources to develop direct relations systematically with European institutions, they also lack incentives for circumventing their central government. Unlike in the UK, French territorial institutions embody a culture of consultation and cooperation, which provides subnational actors with substantial influence on central-state policy-making despite their lack of formal powers. This *"centralisme coopératif"* (Yves Mény) manifests itself in various institutions such as the *Contrat de Plan État-Régions* (planning contracts between state and regions), the *cumul de mandats* (accumulation of electoral mandates) and innumerous informal networks coordinating local, regional, and central-state interests in French policy-making (Mény 1987, 1989; Balme 1995). Rather than circumventing the central state, regional and local actors rely on these institutions for channeling their interests into the European policy process (Smyrl 1997; Benz 1998). Thus, Europeanization fosters the regionalization of the central-state administration rather than the emergence of a level of regional self-government. One could, indeed, argue that French territorial institutions are reinforced rather than substantially changed.

The brief reference to the United Kingdom and France indicates that the convergence of formal territorial institutions which I found in Germany and Spain is not representative of a general shift toward co-operative regionalism or "interactive governance" (Kohler-Koch 1998) in Europe. The empirical findings of my comparative study on Germany and Spain do not apply to countries like the UK, France, Greece, or Portugal. These are unitary or decentralized states and, therefore, their territorial institutions do not face the same pressure for adaptation as the German Federal State or the Spanish State of Autonomies. This is not to say that Europeanization has no impact on the domestic institutions of unitary or decentralized member states. There are other causal mechanisms than institutional mismatch and redistribution of resources through which the domestic impact of Europe may materialize (see below). In any case, my findings should hold for the other three federal and regionalized member states, that is, Belgium, Austria and, to some extent, Italy. The three countries show a high degree of territorial decentralization. Their regions are not only responsible for the implementation of most European policies, but they also have a significant amount of legislative competencies, be it autonomous or shared with the central state. Thus, the territorial institutions of all three member states should have faced similar pressure for adaptation as the result of an uneven distribution of "say and pay" to the detriment of the regions. They differ, however, with respect to their adaptability.

Austrian federalism shares the cooperative institutional culture of German federalism. My Institution Dependency Model would therefore expect Austrian territorial institutions to adjust flexibly to the challenges of Europeanization and for these to be reinforced rather than significantly changed. Intergovernmental relations in Belgium and Italy, on the contrary, are characterized by a similar degree of confrontation and competition as Spanish competitive regionalism. Consequently, Belgian and Italian territorial institutions should induce their regions to pursue a strategy which prohibits rather than facilitates institutional adaptation. The lack of adaptability may result either in a formal change in the form of increasing centralization or, if the regions reconsider their strategy, in the emergence of cooperative formal institutions, which could also eventually affect the institutional culture. A brief review of the literature by and large confirms the expectations generated by my model.

The Austrian *Länder* have not experienced Europeanization gradually because Austria joined the European Union only in 1995. But they have learned from the experience of the German *Länder* and demanded compensation for their anticipated losses of power through similar co-decision rights in European policy-making, as the German *Länder* have enjoyed since 1993 (Morass 1994). Even before Austria's accession to the EU, the federal government and the *Länder* agreed on a procedure for intrastate participation that imitates the German model, although the co-determination powers of the Austrian *Länder* are weaker. The federal government is obliged to inform the *Länder* on all EU-related projects that affect their competencies or interests. The *Länder* are entitled to state their viewpoint, which is binding in the area of their exclusive competencies (if their position is unanimous). Yet, the government may deviate from the *Länder* position for compelling reasons of foreign or integration policy. The *Länder* can also directly participate in the Council of the European Union. Like their German counterparts, the Austrian *Länder* and the central state could draw on their comprehensive albeit largely informal networks of intergovernmental cooperation, which were formalized partly through the introduction of intrastate participation of the *Länder* in European policy-making. Unlike Germany, the second chamber of the national parliament, the *Bundesrat*, is composed of representatives of the *Länder* parliaments. As the European participatory rights of the *Länder* are exercised by their governments, some formal institutions were needed. In order to coordinate their positions, the *Länder* set up an "Integration Conference of the *Länder*", which consists of the *Länder* governors and the presidents of the *Länder* parliaments (cf. Morass 1997; Falkner 2000). Thus, Europeanization introduced a significant element of executive federalism. It reinforced existing structures of interadministrative networks and informal interlocking politics. If there is a significant change in domestic institutions, it affects the relationship between executive and legislature rather than between central state and regions.

Belgian territorial institutions are similar to those of Spanish competitive regionalism since they also display a high degree of competition and conflict between the different regions, different communities, and the central state (Hooghe 1995). In order to accommodate the strong cultural heterogeneity within the Belgian State, in 1993 the federal system granted the regional level of government considerable autonomy. Inter-governmental cooperation is more difficult to achieve than in Spain because the Belgian government is not empowered to offer the regions and communities cooperation incentives, such as grants, nor is it able to threaten to centralize legislation: the revenue of the Belgian central state is rather limited and Belgian law does not automatically override regional law. Given their considerable resources and the highly conflicting nature of intergovernmental relations, the Belgian regions and communities initially adopted a non-cooperative strategy of confronting and circumventing the central state in order to compensate Europe-induced loss of power. The Belgian regions had sufficient resources to establish direct relations with European institutions. In contrast to other federal states, they even enjoy the right to conduct their own external relations in the area of their competencies. This has, however, proved of little value when dealing with European institutions, because the institutions require member states to speak with one voice in the European policy process. If the Belgian regions and communities wanted roles greater than being lobby groups, albeit powerful ones, and wanted to have formal influence at the European level, then they would have to reach a common position among themselves as well as with the central government. The same is true for gaining access to European financial resources in order to pay for some of the implementation costs, because member-state governments control the management of European funds (Hooghe 1995). Like the *Comunidades Autónomas*, the Belgian regions and communities realized that circumventing and non-cooperation did not counterbalance the uneven distribution of "say and pay" in European policy-making. They gradually adopted a more cooperative approach to Europeanization that led to a co-determination procedure in European affairs, in which the Belgian regions and communities enjoy stronger powers than the German *Länder*. In the area of shared competencies, the Belgian government has to reach a common position with the regions and communities from which it must not deviate under any circumstances. If exclusive regional competencies are affected, the Belgian government has no say in the formulation of the Belgian bargaining position. Moreover, the regions and communities can claim the leadership of the Belgian delegation in European decision bodies, not only when their exclusive competencies are affected but also in the area of competencies shared with the central state. These powerful co-decision rights of the regions and communities have created a strong need for intergovernmental and interadministrative coordination between the region, communities, and the central-state administration. Unlike in domestic policy-making, neither level is able to act without the consent of the other. The resulting structures of joint decision-making and interlocking politics bring Belgian territorial institutions close to a form of cooperative federalism (Kerremans and Beyers 1997).

The Italian regions, finally, have far fewer legislative decision-making powers to lose than their German, Austrian, Belgian, and Spanish counterparts. Nevertheless, they hold important competencies in the implementation of many European policies. Because Italian intergovernmental relations are in as much conflict and competition as the Spanish ones, Europeanization has given rise to serious implementation problems. Like Spain, the Italian central state tried to centralize regional competencies in the implementation of EU policies. At the same time, the Northern Italian regions in particular strove to use Europe as a political arena in which they could strengthen their autonomy vis-à-vis the central state (Desideri and Santantonio 1997). Yet, the Italian central state successfully constrained the circumventing capacity of its regions by, for example, legally prohibiting the establishment of regional offices in Brussels (Desideri 1995). Moreover, most Italian regions do not have sufficient resources to maintain regular contact with European institutions. Finally, the Italian regions have little fiscal autonomy and, hence, strongly depend on the central state for funding. In the second half of the 1980s, the Italian regions therefore took the opportunity to participate in European policy-making at the domestic level, which the Italian government had offered them in order to deal with the growing implementation deficit. Since 1987 the Italian government has provided the regions with information on all EU proposals that concern them, to which the regions can respond (recommendations are, however, non-binding). Additionally, the regions can express their opinions on the Italian government's European policy at the *Conferenza Permanente Stato-Regioni* (Standing Conference of the State and the Regions), which also provides an element of coordination in the implementation of EU policies. In 1994 the Italian government not only authorised the regions to open up information offices in Brussels, but also allowed them to delegate representatives to the Italian Permanent Representation. Although the new institutions of intergovernmental co-operation in European affairs are far less effective than in Spain and Belgium (Desideri and Santantonio 1997), their introduction may be considered as an important step toward a more cooperative form of regionalism in Italy.

This brief overview of the other three highly decentralized member states of the European Union is, of course, no substitute for a systematical testing of my model. However, it indicates that member-state institutions that face similar pressure for adaptation are likely to converge around a certain outcome, with some institutions undergoing more significant adaptation than others.

The empirical findings on the effect of Europeanization on the territorial institutions apply to all highly decentralized member states and are largely independent of particular policy areas. The policy study on the Europeanization of environmental policy-making in Part IV was intended to show how the general line of argument, developed in Parts II and III, works in a particular policy area. I do not deny that different types of policy areas may be subject to different policy-making patterns (Lowi 1972). The effect of Europeanization on the resources of the regions certainly varies across policy areas, depending on the amount of competency that both the regions and the European Union hold in a particular area. Thus, the regions lose more power in areas of their exclusive or shared competencies (culture, education, media, regional development, justice and home affairs, environment) than in areas where they have little or no competency (customs, currency, foreign policy, defense policy). Moreover, some policy areas are more Europeanized than others. The European Union intervenes more in environmental policy of member states than in their cultural policy. The accessibility of the European policy-making process for the regions, as well as their lobbying activities at the European level, also vary, not only across policy areas but also with respect to the different stages in the policy cycle. Regions have been more successful in establishing direct relations with the Commission in the area of structural policy than media policy, for instance, although the central states still monopolize the decision-making on the Community Support Frameworks (Hooghe 1996). Finally, regulatory policies tend to have a greater affect on regional competencies and impose greater implementation costs on the regions than distributive policies.

Due to these differences, the uneven distribution of "say and pay" may vary to a certain extent across policy areas, with the "say without pay" being more pronounced in the area of highly Europeanized regulatory policy. But even in structural policy, where regions not only enjoy the broadest access to European policy-making, both at the domestic and the European level, but also obtain considerable benefits, the *Comunidades Autónomas* and the *Länder* have suffered loss of autonomy. An example of this is a conflict between the German *Land* of Saxony (*Sachsen*) and the European Commission over regional subsidies for Volkswagen.[128] While the *Länder* have been largely compensated for losses through their intrastate participation in the European policy-making

---

[128] The Commission insisted on repayment of US$ 45 million in what it considered to be state aid paid illegally by Saxony to Volkswagen. The Commission argued that the aid payments did not qualify as aid for restructuring moribund industrial plants in the former German Democratic Republic and, hence, was subject to normal rules for regional aid in the Common Market (Commission of the European Communities 1998: 72, 84).

process (Staeck 1996; Knodt 1998), the Spanish government completely monopolized access to European funds (Morata and Muñoz 1997). This has changed only in recent years, when the central state and *Comunidades Autónomas* started to cooperate in the formulation and implementation of Community programs (Conejos 1993), a development which can also be observed in fisheries policy (Jones 2000).

While (re)distributive policies can have regulatory effects which affect regional autonomy, regulatory policies often entail distributive elements. European environmental policy is a case in point. As we saw in the policy study, Cohesion Fund money sometimes covers between 50–80% of the costs that the *Comunidades Autónomas* face in implementing expensive European environmental policies, such as the Urban Waste Water Treatment Directive. The distinction between regulatory and (re)distributive policies often becomes blurred.

I have not systematically compared the Europeanization of different policy areas. I can, therefore, ultimately not prove my claim that the uneven distribution of "say and pay" as well as the adaptational strategy by which the regions respond to it apply to the territorial institutions of a member state irrespective of policy area. Yet, the broad participation of the *Länder* and the *Comunidades Autónomas* in European policy-making, which comprises about 20 different policy areas, demonstrates the general effect of Europeanization on the interests and strategies of the regions in both countries. Moreover, the literature on the Europeanization of other policy areas in Germany and Spain lends credibility to the assumption that the differences between the domestic institutions of the two member states are more relevant in mediating the domestic impact of Europe than differences between policy areas within one member state (Cowles *et al.* 2001; Héritier *et al.* 2001).

Institutional dependency and beyond: Some suggestions for future research

The major categories of institution dependency are broad enough to allow for its application to other dimensions of domestic institutions, such as state–society relations or judicial structures. Maria Green Cowles and Vivien Schmidt, for instance, find that the pluralist structure of the European system of interest intermediation fits the pluralist UK system but challenges both statist business–government relations in France and corporatist patterns of interest intermediation in Germany. At the same time, German and French business have adopted different strategies in responding to new opportunities and constraints of Europeanization, giving rise to different forms of institutional adaptation (Schmidt 1999; Cowles

2001; cf. Lehmkuhl 1999). Anne-Marie Burley and Walter Mattli argued that the European system of judicial review (Art. 177 ECT) empowers lower domestic courts to circumvent their superior courts by directly addressing the European Court of Justice for a ruling on the compatibility of European and national law (Burley and Mattli 1993; cf. Stone Sweet and Brunell 1998). It may also empower citizens who can litigate against their states if domestic law violates rights conferred on them by European legislation. Such judicial review of legal acts is alien to both the UK State – where Parliament enjoys full sovereignty and, hence, its decisions are not subject to scrutiny by domestic courts – and the French State – where only the *Conseil Constitutionnel* can review laws between their passage in parliament and their promulgation by the president. The European system of judicial review, by contrast, is similar to the German judicial structures, where any citizen has the right to have a law judicially reviewed if he/she can claim that it violates his/her constitutional rights. Moreover, Lisa Conant's work shows that the response of both domestic courts and citizens to these new opportunities varies considerably across member states, depending on their capacity for acting on such claims and on the judicial culture of the country, respectively (Conant 2001).

Although my model is generalizable enough to be applied to different forms and dimensions of domestic institutions, it does not constitute a theory of either Europeanization or institutional change. The Institution Dependency Model identifies just one causal mechanism by which Europeanization may lead to domestic institutional change. And it specifies the conditions under which such changes are likely to occur and what degree of change we might expect. But institutional mismatch coupled with strategy changes through a gradual process of experiential learning triggered by rising costs of adaptation are only one route by which Europeanization can cause domestic institutional change. European policies can also play an important role in bringing about domestic institutional change. They do not always pose specific requirements for institutional adaptation at the domestic level. But as European norms, rules, and procedures can challenge those at the domestic level, European policies can also contradict domestic regulations, resulting in significant pressure for adaptation to which different domestic actors may respond in a wide variety of ways (Börzel 1998a; Héritier 2001; Héritier *et al.* 2001; Knill and Lenschow 2001).

Europeanization not only affects resources and strategies of domestic actors, but it can also challenge and change their preferences and identities. The socialization of domestic actors into new European norms and practices constitutes a major source of domestic institutional change (Olsen 1996, 1997). Socialization is compatible with the Institution

Dependency Model. I argue that instrumentally motivated changes of actors' strategies, which lead to formal institutional change, are likely to affect shared meanings of appropriateness in the long run. The newly established formal rules and procedures of intergovernmental cooperation do not correspond to the institutional culture of Spanish regionalism. As the *Comunidades Autónomas* increasingly interact within these new institutions, the experience of positive feedback may give rise to a new understanding of appropriate behavior.

Instrumental and cognitive adaptation or learning are not mutually exclusive.[129] Future research should therefore explore the relationship between institutional changes that follow an instrumental logic of cost–benefit calculations and those that are guided by a logic of appropriateness. My study presents one possible link between the logic of consequentiality and the logic of appropriateness.[130] The logic of appropriateness rather than the logic of consequentiality guides actors' initial response to environmental changes, such as Europeanization. While they face different strategy options, depending on their resources (action capacity), actors tend to follow certain standard operating procedures and rules of appropriateness, which evolve from experiences with similar situations in the past. The initial strategy choice is unlikely to be the result of a conscious calculation of the costs and benefits of alternative strategies at hand. Actors start to consider alternative strategies only if their initial strategy proves to be ineffective in pursuing their interests. Such instrumentally motivated strategy changes are likely to feed back to the logic of appropriateness.

External pressure for adaptation and actors' (changing) response to it are only one causal mechanism of institutional change. (Domestic) institutions may change as a result of internal dynamics, such as institutional aging, internal conflict, intentional reform, reinterpretation of rules and meaning, or institutional contradiction (cf. March and Olsen

---

[129] See for instance Knodt 1998; Kohler-Koch 1998; Checkel 2001; Knill and Lenschow 2001; Risse 2001.

[130] March and Olsen distinguish four possible relationships between the two logics. First, a clear logic dominates an unclear logic, i.e. when preferences and consequences are clear and identities or their rules are ambiguous, the logic of consequentiality prevails, or vice versa. Second, one logic establishes the fundamental constraints within which the other is used in order to make "refinements", that is rules and identities are seen as the preconditions of calculation, or vice versa. Third, the relationship between the two logics is sequential, i.e. actors may enter a relationship for instrumental reasons and then develop identities and rules as a result of their new experience. Finally, either logic is a special case of the other. Rules and identities are instruments of prior calculation, or interest calculation is one particular rule that is associated with specific identities and situations (cf. March and Olsen 1998). The theoretical model developed in this book is related to the last two interpretations.

1989, 1996; Friedland and Alford 1991; Powell 1991). Yet, in analyzing and explaining the domestic impact of Europe, it seems plausible to conceive of Europeanization as a (potential) external source of domestic institutional change.

Pressure for adaptation also provides another angle on the question of whether Europeanization leads to institutional convergence (Kastendiek 1990; Burnham and Maor 1995; Page and Wouters 1995; Rometsch and Wessels 1996; Weale *et al.* 1996; Aguilar Fernández 1997; Héritier *et al.* 2001). Institutional convergence, or institutional isomorphism, occurs among institutions which are exposed to the same environment (DiMaggio and Powell 1991). As argued earlier, similar pressure for adaptation gives rise to similar outcomes of institutional adaptation. Regions which have comparable resources suffer similar losses and are likely to opt for similar institutional solutions in order to redress the balance of power. This is not to say that there is only one optimal institutional outcome. Rather, actors appear to learn from each other as the Austrian and the Spanish regions did by imitating the German model of intrastate participation in 1993 and 1994, respectively. By now, the resourceful regions of Europe mobilize "through rather than beyond the established structures of the member states" (Jeffery 2000: 2). As pressure for adaptation varies according to the "goodness of fit", we are likely to see convergence within certain clusters of member states whose domestic institutions (policies, identities) face comparable pressure for adaptation. In order to explore the proposition of "clustered convergence", one would have to compare systematically groups of member states that vary in the degree of pressure for adaptation that their domestic institutions face.

Europe of the regions: Europe of the citizens?

If the proposition of clustered convergence holds, the findings of my study on the effect of Europeanization on the territorial institutions of the member states not only suggest a shift toward cooperative regionalism in the five highly decentralized member states. It also casts serious doubts on the "Europe of the Regions" as an institutional solution to the democratic deficit of the European Union.

First, the prevailing, or maybe even increasing, relevance of intrastate participation of the regions in European policy-making is undercutting the prospects of the regions for developing into a "third level" of government, alongside the member states and the European institutions. There appears to be a certain "disenchantment" with the idea of the "Europe of the Regions" among the institutionally well-entrenched regions. The Spanish *Comunidades Autónomas* and the German *Länder* are increasingly skeptical about the effectiveness of the collective representation of regional interests at the European level. The regions, which have the necessary resources to act as independent political actors in the European policy arena, tend to rely on their cooperation with the central state and on their offices in Brussels in order to channel their interests into the European policy process. The Committee of the Regions is only one of many strings that the resourceful regions can pull in European policy-making. The support of the strong regions, however, is crucial for promoting the institutionalization of the "third level" (e.g. by strengthening the rights of the Committee of the Regions) because they have the domestic resources (e.g. veto power) to push the issue onto the European agenda.

Second, intrastate participation of the regions promotes executive dominance in the European Union and thus exacerbates the existing problems of lacking accountability and transparency in European policy-making. Regional co-decision rights in formulating and representing the national bargaining position provide effective compensation for regional loss of competencies caused by Europeanization. But these compensatory co-decision powers are exercised by the regional governments, which, at best, inform and consult their parliaments on important European issues. Unlike in domestic policy-making, the regional parliaments do not have any formal powers in the formulation and decision-making of European policies. The disempowerment of regional parliaments reinforces the general trend of deparliamentarization at the domestic level as a consequence of Europeanization (cf. Rometsch and Wessels 1996).

The problems of decreasing political accountability and transparency are sharpened by the increasing sectorization of European policy-making, which result in the proliferation of interadministrative networks spanning all levels of government. While such networks can facilitate intergovernmental coordination and may promote the emergence of collectively shared understanding and practices among administrative elites (Lewis 1995; Joerges and Neyer 1997; Olsen 1997; Kohler-Koch *et al.* 1998), they have their own institutional dynamics and are difficult to govern (Benz 1995; Rhodes 1997). Most importantly, policy networks can serve as mechanisms of exclusion and "organized irresponsibility"; membership of networks is highly selective and the activities of networks are often not transparent and not subject to public scrutiny.

Intrastate participation may effectively redress the territorial balance of power between the central state and the regions. The cooperation of the central state and regional governments should also improve effective implementation of European policies. However, by providing an institutional solution to one challenge of Europeanization (centralization and effective implementation), intrastate participation appears to reinforce another: the lack of transparency and accountability of European policy-making. Intrastate participation not only undermines the prospects of the "Europe of the Regions", which has been celebrated as a potential remedy for the democratic deficit of the European Union (Bullmann 1994; Hierl 1995; Tomuschat 1995; Meehan 1997),[131] but it also contributes to problems of lacking accountability and transparency by promoting regional deparliamentarization, sectorization, and interlocking politics (*Politikverflechtung*) in the European system of multilevel governance.

The integration of the regional level into the European system of governance is no longer a problem. The major challenge for the European Union is the weak role of legislature at all levels of government. Highly decentralized states face problems of executive dominance. Yet, their institutions usually provide for a counterbalance through the effective representation of functional interests (cf. Börzel and Hosli 2000). In Germany, for instance, the vertical system of party integration ensures ample representation of citizens' interests in the policy process. While Europeanization promotes deparliamentarization, the European Union largely lacks effective mechanisms of political representation. The participation of the regions in European policy-making exacerbates rather than solves the problem. The regions have their place in Europe, but a "Europe of the Regions" is not necessarily a "Europe of the citizens". The European Union will have to find new ways of increasing its responsiveness to and representation of societal interests.

---

[131] See also the "Resolution on Transparency and Democracy in the Community" of the European Council in Birmingham on 18 October 1992 (Conclusion of the Presidency, Appendix 1: Point 4), the speech of the Federal Chancellor before the *Bundestag* given on 13 December 1991 (Europa-Archiv 47, 1: D 110–117 (114)), and the Eurobarometer of October/November 1991; 21 August 1992 edited by the Commission of the European Communities, Directorate General XVI: Info-Background, "No Europe Without Regions", Brussels 1992.

Appendix: The major EU environmental policies of the policy study

The directive on the quality of water on human consumption (drinking water directive) (80/778/EEC)

The Directive on the Quality of Water on Human Consumption (Drinking Water Directive),[131] adopted by the Council on 15 July 1980, is one out of three Directives that regulate water for human consumption.[132] The Drinking Water Directive applies to all water that is required for direct human consumption (drinking water) and for food production. It imposes legally binding, substantive standards to reach a certain level of drinking water quality. The member states must fix values for each of the parameters indicated in the Directive, within the scope set by the guiding and mandatory values.[133] The Directive also prescribes how often and by what means authorities have to monitor the water quality and it specifies a method of analysis for each parameter.

The directive on the combating of air pollution from industrial plant (84/360/EEC) and the directive on the limitation of emissions of certain pollutants into the air from large combustion plants (88/609/EEC)

There are two Directives which are of particular importance for the EU policy on the combating of air pollution: the Directive on the Limitation of Emissions of Certain Pollutants into the Air from Large Combustion Plants and its "mother directive", the Directive on the Combating of Air Pollution from Industrial Plants.

---

[131] OJ L 129, 30/8/80.

[132] The other two Directives are the Directive on the Quality of Surface Water 75/440 (OJ L 194, 15/7/75) and the Directive on Medicinal Waters and Mineral Waters 80/777 (OJ L 299/1, 30/8/80).

[133] The water intended for direct human consumption is subject to all mandatory values of maximum admissible concentration in the Directive. For the water used in food production, only the toxic and microbiological parameters are mandatory. The member states are free to set their own values for the organoleptic and physiochemical parameters as well as for undesirable substances.

The Industrial Plant Directive, which the Council adopted on 28 June 1984,[134] provides framework legislation for preventing and reducing air pollution caused by industrial plants. The Directive does not set any substantive emission standards but establishes an administrative framework that contains procedural requirements for the authorization of the operation of any new industrial plant and the substantial modification of existing plants. From July 1, 1987, the authorization of a new plant, or of the substantial modification of an already existing plant, must only be granted if:

1. all appropriate preventive measures against air pollution were taken, including the application of the best available technology not entailing excessive costs;
2. the emission of the plant will not cause any significant air pollution, especially with regard to those polluting substances listed in Annex II of the Directive; and
3. none of the emission or air quality limit values applicable will be exceeded.

The member states are to ensure that applications for authorization and the respective decision of the competent authority are made available to the public concerned. The member states must implement measures in order to have existing plants gradually adapt to the best available technology. This adaptation of existing plants is to be carried out by taking into account the technical characteristics of the plant and the nature and volume of its polluting emissions. Adaptation, however, must not impose excessive costs on the plant concerned. The Directive finally stipulates the possibility for the Council to fix "emission limit values", based on the best available technology not entailing excessive costs (BATNEEC), but only if it appears to be strictly necessary and if it is approved by the unanimous vote of the member states.

The first time the Council set emission limit values was four years later when it adopted the Directive on Large Combustion Plants.[135] Combustion plants with an output of more than 50 MW have to apply the best available technology not entailing excessive costs (BATNEEC) to reduce their emissions. Measuring methods for monitoring compliance also have to meet BATNEEC requirements. For large combustion plants with a thermal output greater than 50 MW, which enter operation after July 1, 1987, the Directive defines binding emission values for three pollutants: sulphur dioxide (SO_2), dust, and nitrogen oxides (NO_x). New

[134] OJ L 188, 16/7/84.
[135] OJ L 336, 7/12/88.

plants have to comply not only with these emission limit values but they must also use BATNEEC to reduce air pollution. Old plants are not subject to emission standards as such, but the member states have to reduce their total annual emissions progressively. For this purpose, they are expected to develop national programs setting out the timetable and the implementing procedures for the emission reduction. By applying the best available technology, the member states should ensure the reduction of their total emission for SO_2 and NO_x by an increasing percentage over 1980 levels in three phases: 1993, 1998, and 2003. The emission ceilings to be achieved (national bubbles) vary, however, among the member states according to their economic, energy, and environmental situation.

The directive on environmental impact assessment (85/337/EEC)

The 5th Environmental Action Programme indicated a change in European environmental policy-making (1992–97). The principle of shared responsibility between state authorities, industry, consumers, and the general public is to complement the traditional command and control approach. The Directive on Environmental Impact Assessment[136] is one of the first policies to implement this new approach. It constitutes an instrument of procedural regulation, which assesses in a systematic and cross-sectoral way the potential impact of certain public and private projects on the environment. Any project that is likely to have significant effects on the environment is subject to an environmental impact assessment prior to authorization by the competent authority. The developer of a project has to provide the authorities with information on the characteristics of the project, the measures envisaged in order to avoid, reduce and remedy adverse effects, and the data required to identify and assess the main potential effects of the project. The member states can establish a procedure, in which the competent authority and the developer informally agree upon the precise scope of the required information (scoping procedure). All information shall be forwarded to public authorities that are likely to be concerned by the project. It must also be made available to the public. The public concerned has the right to make allegations. Finally, the competent authorities have to consider the information, together with the public allegations made, and to decide on the positive or negative environmental impact of a solicited project. Authorities have to inform the public about their final decision as well as the reasons and considerations on which they based their decision.

[136] OJ L 175, 5/7/85.

The directive on freedom of access to information on the environment (90/313/EEC)

The difficulties of monitoring and enforcing the growing number of European environmental policies motivated the Commission to take measures that render information on the environment more easily available to the citizen. The most important directive in this area is the Directive on Freedom of Access to Information on the Environment (AI Directive).[137] The Directive is based on the idea that broader access to environmental information increases transparency and openness, thereby encouraging citizens to participate more actively in the protection of the environment. Any ordinary or legal person – irrespective of nationality or concern – has the right to request information that environmental authorities, or bodies with public responsibility for the environment, hold on the environment. The Directive only allows for refusal if the request concerns information that affects public security, the confidentiality of the proceedings of public authorities, international relations, national defence, matters that are under legal inquiry, commercial and industrial confidentiality, the confidentiality of personal data, material voluntarily supplied by third parties, unfinished documents and internal communications of the administration, and where disclosure of the information may damage the environment. Authorities can also deny a request when the request is manifestly unreasonable or formulated in too general a manner. The public must have the possibility to seek judicial and administrative review against the refusal of, or failure to provide, requested information. Apart from the obligation to make environmental information available upon request, member states are called upon actively to provide general information to the public.

The directive concerning urban waste water treatment (91/271/EEC)

The Urban Waste Water Treatment Directive[138] sets up a comprehensive system for controlling the quality of urban waste water treatment and discharges from most areas that are populated. It regulates waste water discharges from 11 types of industry to waste water collection systems and treatment plants. From January 1, 1994 onward, such discharges require a permit issued by the member-state authorities, which must comply with the requirements stipulated in Annex I of the Directive. Moreover, the Directive sets requirements for urban waste water treatment plants

---

[137] OJ L 158, 23/6/90.
[138] OJ L 135, 30/5/91.

and collection systems. Urban areas of different sizes are given a series of deadlines, spanning the dates December 1, 1995 and December 31, 2005, in order to establish or up-grade their collection systems and treatment plants so as to meet the requirements of the Directive. As a minimum, municipalities have to provide collection systems and a secondary, biological treatment for urban waste water. Finally, the member states had to identify sensitive areas (by December 31, 1993), to which specific discharge standards apply.

The eco-audit management and audit system regulation (1836/93/EC)

The Community Eco-Management and Audit Scheme (EMAS), established by a Regulation in 1993,[139] is a voluntary instrument that should provide incentives for enterprises to introduce an environmental management system for assessing and improving industrial activities and providing the public with adequate information. The Regulation requires the member states to establish a voluntary scheme that would identify industrial sites where firms had set up – within the framework of a company's policy – environmental management systems, including regular audits and public reports on environmental performance. The public, suppliers, and consumers are provided with information about the commitment of the company to improving its environmental performance and to reducing impact on the environment that results from operations at the site. The registration with Eco-Audit would bring public recognition that encourages industry to develop more environmentally friendly production procedures. Having direct effect, the EMAS Regulation does not require transposition into national law. However, member states are supposed to establish a system of registration for sites implementing EMAS, as well as accreditation of independent environmental inspectors and the supervision of their activities.

The directive concerning integrated pollution prevention and control (96/61/EC)

The 5th Environmental Action Programme lists the integrated pollution prevention and control (IPPC) as a priority area of action. It accounts for the integrated character of the environment where no one part is separate from another. The IPPC Directive[140] does not set any substantive policy

---

[139] OJ L 168, 10/7/1993.
[140] OJ L 257, 10/10/1996.

standards. Rather, it provides procedural regulations for the integrated authorization of new and the modification of existing industrial installations with respect to their compliance with air, water, and soil emissions. The IPPC Directive builds on the Industrial Plant Directive of 1984 and is more specific and demanding. All industrial installations listed in Annex I require a permit. The permit must set emission limit values based on what is achievable through the use of best available technology. The permit also contains suitable monitoring requirements that specify the measurement methodology, frequency, and evaluation procedure and an obligation to supply the competent authority with the data it needs to check compliance with the permit. Emission limit values must be set with the aim of ensuring that environmental quality standards are not infringed. While new installations have to comply with the IPPC regulations immediately, the modification of existing plants is subject to IPPC only from 2003. Finally, in 2007 permits for existing installations have to be re-evaluated in light of the BATNEEC requirement.

References

Abromeit, Heidrun. 1992. *Der verkappte Einheitsstaat.* Opladen: Leske + Budrich.

Agranoff, Robert. 1993. Intergovernmental Politics and Policy: Building Federal Arrangements in Spain. *Regional Politics and Policy* 3 (2): 1–28.

Agranoff, Robert, and Juan Antonio Ramos Gallarín. 1997. Toward Federal Democracy in Spain: An Examination of Intergovernmental Relations. *Publius* 27 (4): 1–38.

Aguilar Fernández, Susana. 1993. Corporatist and Statist Design in Environmental Policy: The Contrasting Roles of Germany and Spain in the European Community Scenario. *Environmental Politics* 2 (2): 223–247.

Aguilar Fernández, Susana. 1994a. Convergence in Environmental Policy? The Resilience of National Institutional Designs in Spain and Germany. *Journal of Public Policy* 14 (1): 39–56.

Aguilar Fernández, Susana. 1994b. Spanish Pollution Control Policy and the Challenge of the European Union. *Regional Politics and Policy* 4 (1): 102–117.

Aguilar Fernández, Susana. 1997. *El reto del medio ambiente. Conflictos e intereses en la política medioambiental europea.* Madrid: Alianza Universidad.

Aguilar Fernández, Susana, and Manuel Jiménez Sánchez. 1998. Spanish Coordination in the European Union: The Case of Exhaust Emission Directives. Manuscript, Madrid: Instituto Juan March.

Albertí Rovira, Enoch. 1986. *Federalismo y cooperación en la República Federal Alemania.* Madrid: Centro de Estudios Constitucionales.

Albertí Rovira, Enoch. 1990. La colaboración entre el Estado y la Generalidad de Cataluña. *Autonomies* 12: 51–63.

Albertí Rovira, Enoch 1991. La colaboración entre el Estado y las Comunidades Autónomas. In *El futuro de las Autonomías territoriales. Comunidades Autónomas: Balance y Perspectivas*, edited by Luis Martín Rebolle. Santander: Universidad de Cantabria IV, 201–217.

Albertí Rovira, Enoch. 1993. Los convenios entre Comunidades Autónomas. In *Las relaciones interadministrativas de cooperación y colaboración*, edited by Institut d'Estudies Autonòmics. Barcelona: Generalitat de Catalunya, Institut d'Estudies Autonòmics, 63–85.

Albertí Rovira, Enoch. 1998. Relaciones de colaboración con las Comunidades Autónomas. In *Informe Comunidades Autónomas 1997*, edited by Instituto de Derecho Público. Barcelona: Instituto de Derecho Público, 65–78.

Albertí Rovira, Enoch, E. Roig Moles, and J. Sort Jané. 1995. *La reforma constitucional del Senado*. Barcelona: Institut d'Estudis Autonòmics.

Andersen, Svein S., and Tom Burns. 1996. The European Union and the Erosion of Parliamentary Democracy: A Study of Post-Parliamentary Governance. In *The European Union: How Democratic Is It?*, edited by S. S. Andersen and K. A. Eliassen. London: Sage, 227–251.

Andersen, Svein S., and Kjell A. Eliassen, eds. 1993. *Making Policy in Europe: The Europeification of National Policy-making*. London, Thousand Oaks, New Delhi: Sage.

Anderson, Jeffrey. 1990. Sceptical Reflections on a Europe of the Regions: Britain, Germany, and the ERDF. *Journal of Public Policy* 10 (4): 417–447.

Bache, Ian. 1998. *The Politics of EU Regional Policy: Multilevel Governance or Flexible Gatekeeping?* Sheffield: Sheffield Academic Press.

Bache, Ian, Stephen George, and R. A. W. Rhodes. 1996. The European Union, Cohesion Policy and Sub-national Actors in the United Kingdom. In *Cohesion and European Integration: Building Multi-level Governance*, edited by L. Hooghe. Oxford: Oxford University Press, 294–319.

Balme, Richard. 1995. French Regionalization and European Integration: Territorial Adaptation and Change in a Unitary State. In *The European Union and the Regions*, edited by B. Jones and M. Keating. Oxford: Clarendon Press, 167–190.

Barcelo i Serramalera, Merce. 1993. *Die Europäische Gemeinschaft und Autonome Gemeinschaften*. Saarbrücken: Europa-Institut der Universität des Saarlandes.

Barschel, Uwe. 1982. *Die Staatsqualität der Länder. Ein Beitrag zur Theorie und Praxis des Föderalismus in der Bundesrepublik Deutschland*. Heidelberg, Hamburg: R. v. Decker's Verlag, G. Schenk.

Bell, Daniel. 1988. The World in 2013. *Dialogue* 3 (88): 2–9.

Bengoetxea, Joxerramon. 1994. La participación de las Autonomías en las instituciones comunitarias. *Revista Vasca de Administración Pública* 3 (40): 123–147.

Benz, Arthur. 1985. *Föderalismus als dynamisches System, Zentralisierung und Dezentralisierung im föderativen Staat*. Opladen: Westdeutscher Verlag.

Benz, Arthur. 1991a. Chancen und Grenzen einer Länderneugliederung in Deutschland. In *Die Zukunft des kooperativen Föderalismus in Deutschland*, edited by G. Hirscher. München: Hans-Seidel-Stiftung, 143–166.

Benz, Arthur. 1991b. Perspektiven des Föderalismus in Deutschland. *Die Öffentliche Verwaltung* 44 (14): 586–598.

Benz, Arthur. 1993a. Regionen als Machtfaktor in Europa. *Verwaltungsarchiv* 84 (3): 328–348.

Benz, Arthur. 1993b. Reformbedarf und Reformchancen des kooperativen Föderalismus nach der Vereinigung Deutschlands. In *Verwaltungsreform und Verwaltungspolitik im Prozeß der deutschen Einigung*, edited by W. Seibel, Arthur Benz, and Heinrich Mäding. Baden-Baden: Nomos, 454–473.

Benz, Arthur. 1995. Politiknetzwerke in der Horizontalen Politikverflechtung. In *Netzwerke und Politikproduktion. Konzepte, Methoden, Perspektiven*, edited by D. Jansen and K. Schubert. Marburg: Schüren, 185–204.

Benz, Arthur. 1998. Politikverflechtung ohne Politikverflechtungsfalle. Koordination und Strukturdynamik im europäischen Mehrebenensystem. *Politische Vierteljahresschrift* 39 (3): 558–589.

Benz, Arthur. 1999. Der deutsche Föderalismus. In *50 Jahre Bundesrepublik Deutschland. Rahmenbedingungen, Entwicklungen, Perspektiven,* edited by T. Ellwein and E. Holtmann. Opladen: Westdeutscher Verlag, 135–153.

Berger, Peter L., and Thomas Luckmann. 1966. *The Social Construction of Reality: A Treatise in the Sociology of Knowledge.* New York: Doubleday.

Bethge, Herbert. 1989. Die Rolle der Länder im deutschen Bundesstaat und ihre rechtlichen Einflußmöglichkeiten auf die nationale Gemeinschaftspolitik. In *Die Bundesrepublik Deutschland und das Königreich Spanien 1992. Die Rolle der Länder und der Comunidades Autonomas im europäischen Integrationsprozeß,* edited by H. A. Kremer. München: Bayerischer Landtag, 22–50.

Beyerlin, Ulrich. 1987. Umsetzung von EG-Richtlinien durch Verwaltungsvorschriften? *Europarecht* 2: 361–364.

Birke, Hans Eberhard. 1973. *Die deutschen Bundesländer in den Europäischen Gemeinschaften.* Berlin: Duncker & Humblot.

Blair, Philip. 1991. Federalism, Legalism and Political Reality: The Record of the Federal Constitutional Court. In *German Federalism Today,* edited by C. Jeffery and P. Savigear. Leicester and London: Leicester University Press, 63–83.

Blanke, Hermann-Josef. 1991. *Föderalismus und Integrationsgewalt. Die Bundesrepublik Deutschland, Spanien, Italien und Belgien als dezentralisierte Staaten in der EG.* Berlin: Duncker & Humblot.

Blume, Gerd, and Alexander Graf von Rex. 1998. Weiterentwicklung der inhaltlichen und personellen Mitwirkung der Länder in Angelegenheiten der EU nach Maastricht. Die Regierungskonferenz als Bewährungsprobe für die Ländermitwirkungsrechte. In *Europapolitik der deutschen Länder. Bilanz und Perspektiven nach dem Gipfel von Amsterdam,* edited by F. H. U. Borkenhagen. Opladen: Leske + Budrich, 29–49.

Böckenförde, Ernst-Wolfgang. 1980. Sozialer Bundesstaat und parlamentarische Demokratie. In *Politik als globale Verfassung. Aktuelle Probleme des nationalen Verfassungsstaates. Festschrift für Friedrich Schäfer,* edited by J. Jekewitz, Michael Melzer, and Wolfgang Zeh. Opladen: Westdeutscher Verlag, 182–199.

Borchmann, Michael. 1990. Konferenzen "Europa der Regionen" in München und Brüssel. *Die Öffentliche Verwaltung* 43 (20): 879–882.

Borchmann, Michael, and Wilhelm Kaiser. 1992. Die Mitwirkung der Länder im EG-Ministerrat. In *Die deutschen Länder in Europa. Politische Union, Wirtschafts- und Währungsunion,* edited by F. H. U. Borkenhagen, C. Bruns-Klöss, G. Memminger, and O. Stein. Baden-Baden: Nomos, 36–46.

Borkenhagen, Franz H. U., Christian Bruns-Klöss, Gerd Memminger, and Otti Stein, eds. 1992. *Die deutschen Länder in Europa. Politische Union, Wirtschafts- und Währungsunion.* Baden-Baden: Nomos.

Borras, Alegria. 1990. Die Mitgliedschaft Spaniens in der EG und ihre Auswirkungen auf die Autonomen Gemeinschaften. In *Föderalismus und Europäische Gemeinschaften unter besonderer Berücksichtigung von Umwelt und*

Gesundheit, Kultur und Bildung, edited by D. Merten. Berlin: Duncker & Humblot, 47–62.

Börzel, Tanja A. 1997. Does European Integration Really Strengthen the State? The Case of the Federal Republic of Germany. *Regional and Federal Studies* 7 (3): 87–113.

Börzel, Tanja A. 1998a. The Greening of a Polity? The Europeanisation of Environmental Policy-Making in Spain. *Southern European Society and Politics* 2 (1): 65–92.

Börzel, Tanja A. 1998b. Shifting or Sharing the Burden: The Europeanisation of Environmental Policy in Spain and Germany. *European Planning Studies* 6 (5): 537–553.

Börzel, Tanja A. 1999. The Domestic Impact of Europe: Institutional Adaptation in Germany and Spain. Department of Social and Political Science, European University Institute, Florence.

Börzel, Tanja A. 2000a. Why There is no Southern Problem: On Environmental Leader and Laggards in the EU. *Journal of European Public Policy* 7 (1): 141–162.

Börzel, Tanja A. 2000b. Improving Compliance Through Domestic Mobilisation? New Instruments and the Effectiveness of Implementation in Spain. In *Implementing EU Environmental Policy: New Approaches to an Old Problem*, edited by C. Knill and A. Lenschow. Manchester: Manchester University Press, 221–250.

Börzel, Tanja A. forthcoming. *On European Leaders and Laggards in Europe: Why There is (not) a Southern Problem*. London: Ashgate.

Börzel, Tanja A. and Thomas Risse. 2000. Who is Afraid of a European Federation. How to Constitutionalize a Multi-Level Governance System. In *What Kind of Constitution for What Kind of Polity? Responses to Joschka Fischer*, edited by C. Joerges, Y. Mény and J. H. H. Weiler. Florence: European University Institute, 45–59.

Brenner, Michael. 1992. Der unitarische Bundesstaat in der Europäischen Union. Zum Ausgleich unitarischer und föderativer Strukturen in der Bundesrepublik Deutschland vor dem Hintergrund eines vereinten Europas. *Die Öffentliche Verwaltung* 45 (21): 903–911.

Bullmann, Udo, ed. 1994. *Die Politik der dritten Ebene*. Baden-Baden: Nomos.

Bulmer, Simon. 1986. *The Domestic Structure of European Community Policy-Making in West Germany*. New York and London: Garland Publishing.

Bulmer, Simon, and William Paterson. 1987. *The Federal Republic of Germany and the European Community*. London: Allen & Unwin.

Burley, Anne-Marie, and Walter Mattli. 1993. Europe Before the Court: A Political Theory of Legal Integration. *International Organization* 47 (1): 41–77.

Burnham, Jane, and Mosche Maor. 1995. Converging Administrative Systems: Recruitment and Training in the EU Member States. *Journal of European Public Policy* 2 (2): 185–204.

Bustos Gisbert, Rafael. 1995. Un paso mas hacia la participación autonómica en asuntos europeos. El acuerdo de 30 de noviembre de 1994. *Revista Española de Derecho Constitucional* 15 (45): 153–172.

Cafruny, Alan, and Glenda Rosenthal, eds. 1993. *The State of the European Community II: The Maastricht Debate and Beyond.* Boulder, CO: Lynne Rienner.

Cameron, David R. 1992. The 1992 Initiative: Causes and Consequences. In *Europolitics: Institutions and Policy-making in the New European Community,* edited by A. Sbragia. Washington, DC: Brookings Institution, 23–74.

Cameron, David R. 1995. Transnational Relations and the Development of European Economic and Monetary Union. In *Bringing Transnational Relations Back In – Non-State Actors, Domestic Structures and International Institutions,* edited by T. Risse-Kappen. Cambridge: Cambridge University Press, 37–78.

Caporaso, James A., and Joseph Jupille. 2001. The Europeanization of Gender Equality Policy and Domestic Structural Change. In *Transforming Europe: Europeanization and Domestic Change,* edited by M. G. Cowles, J. A. Caporaso, and T. Risse, 21–43.

Casals, Juan Luis Diego. 1994. La participación de las Comunidades Autónomas en el proceso de la aplicación de decisiones de la Unión Europea. Un balance y una propuesta. *Revista Vasca de Administraciones Públicas* 3 (40): 149–167.

Casanovas y la Rosa, Oriol. 1989. Las competencias de las Comunidades Autónomas en la aplicación del derecho comunitario europeo. *Revista de Instituciones Europeas* 3 (16): 767–787.

Checkel, Jeffrey T. 2001. The Europeanization of Citizenship? In *Transforming Europe: Europeanization and Domestic Change,* edited by M. G. Cowles, J. A. Caporaso and T. Risse, 180–197.

Christiansen, Thomas. 1994. *European Integration Between Political Science and International Relations Theory: The End of Sovereignty.* Working Paper, Robert Schuman Centre for Advanced Studies 94/4. Florence: European University Institute.

Christiansen, Thomas. 1997. Reconstructing European Space: From Territorial Politics to Multi-level Governance. In *Reflective Approaches to European Governance,* edited by K. E. Jørgensen. London: Macmillan, 51–68.

Cienfuegos Mateo, Manuel. 1997. La intervención de las Comunidades Autónomas en cuestiones relativas a las Comunidades Europeas a través de la Comisión General de las Comunidades Autónomas y la Conferencia para asuntos relacionados con las Comunidades Europeas. *Autonomies* 22: 155–204.

Classen, Claus Dieter. 1993. Maastricht und Verfassung: kritische Bemerkungen Zum neuen "Europa-Artikel" 23 GG. *Zeitschrift für Rechtspolitik* 26 (3): 57–61.

Clement, Wolfgang. 1991. Auf dem Weg zum Europa der Regionen. In *Föderalstaatliche Entwicklungen in Europa,* edited by J. J. Hesse and W. Renzsch. Baden-Baden: Nomos, 15–26.

Clement, Wolfgang. 1995. Der Ausschuß der Regionen. Kritik und Ausblick: eine politische Bewertung. In *Mitsprache der dritten Ebene in der europäischen Integration. Der Ausschuß der Regionen,* edited by C. Tomuschat. Bonn: Europa Union, 94–115.

Clostermeyer, Claus-Peter. 1992. Die Mitwirkung der Länder in EG-Angelegenheiten. In *Die deutschen Länder in Europa. Politische Union,*

Wirtschafts- und Währungsunion, edited by F. H. U. Borkenhagen, C. BrunsKlöss, G. Memminger, and O. Stein. Baden-Baden: Nomos, 171–182.

Coleman, James S. 1986. Social Action Systems. In *Selected Essays,* edited by J. S. Coleman. Cambridge: Cambridge University Press, 85–136.

Collier, Ruth B., and David Collier. 1991. *Shaping the Political Arena: Critical Junctures, the Labor Movement, and Regime Dynamics in Latin America.* Princeton, NJ: Princeton University Press.

Commission of the European Communities. 1990. *Seventh Annual Report to the European Parliament on Commission Monitoring of the Application of Community Law, COM (90) 288 (final).* Brussels: Commission of the European Communities.

Commission of the European Communities. 1991. *Eighth Annual Report on Monitoring of the Application of Community Law (1990).* COM (91) 231 final. Brussels: Commission of the European Communities.

Commission of the European Communities. 1993a. *Report from the Commission of the Implementation of Directive 85/337/EEC on the Assessment of the Effects of Certain Public and Private Projects on the Environment.* Brussels: Commission of the European Communities.

Commission of the European Communities. 1993b. *Tenth Annual Report on Monitoring of the Application of Community Law (1992).* COM (93) 320 final. Brussels: Commission of the European Communities.

Commission of the European Communities. 1996. *Thirteenth Annual Report on Monitoring the Application of Community Law (1995).* COM (96) 600 final. Brussels: Commission of the European Communities.

Commission of the European Communities. 1998. *Fifteenth Annual Report on Monitoring the Application of Community Law (1997),* Vol. COM (98) 317 final. Brussel: Commission of the European Communities.

Commission of the European Communities. 1999. *Sixteenth Annual Report on Monitoring the Application of Community Law (1998).* COM (99) 301 final. Brussels: Commission of the European Communities.

Commission of the European Communities. 2000. *Seventeenth Annual Report on Monitoring the Application of Community Law (1999).* COM (2000) 92 final. Brussels: Commission of the European Communities.

Conant, Lisa Joy. 2001. Europeanization and the Courts: Variable Patterns of Adaptation among National Judiciaries. In *Transforming Europe: Europeanization and Domestic Change,* edited by M. G. Cowles, J. A. Caporaso, and T. Risse, 97–115.

Conejos, Jordi. 1993. Los Fondos Estructurales de las Comunidades Europeas. Aplicación en España y participación regional. In *Informe Comunidades Autónomas 1992,* edited by Instituto de Derecho Público. Barcelona: Instituto de Derecho Público, 327–342.

Cowles, Maria Green. 1995. Setting the Agenda for a New Europe: The ERT and EC 1992. *Journal of Common Market Studies* 33 (4): 611–28.

Cowles, Maria Green. 2001. The TABD and Domestic Business-Government Relations. In *Transforming Europe: Europeanization and Domestic Change,* edited by M. G. Cowles, J. A. Caporaso, and T. Risse, 159–179.

Cowles, Maria Green, James A. Caporaso, and Thomas Risse, eds. 2001. *Transforming Europe: Europeanization and Domestic Change*. Ithaca, NY: Cornell University Press.

Cuerdo Pardo, José Luis. 1995. *La Acción Exterior de las Comunidades Autónomas. Teoría y Práctica*. Madrid: Escuela Diplomática.

Dalmau i Oriol, Casimir de. 1997. Propuestas y aspiraciones de las Comunidades Autónomas sobre la articulación de mecanismos para garantizar la participación autonómica en la toma de decisiones en el seño de la Unión Europea. *Autonomies* 22: 87–99.

Dastis Quecedo, A. 1995. La administración española ante la Unión Europea. *Revista de Estudios Políticos* 90: 323–349.

Degen, Manfred. 1998. Der Ausschuß der Regionen. Bilanz und Perspektiven. In *Europapolitik der deutschen Länder. Bilanz und Perspektiven nach dem Gipfel von Amsterdam*, edited by F. H. U. Borkenhagen. Opladen: Leske + Budrich, 103–125.

Delors, Jacques. 1988. Arbeitsdokumente des Präsidenten der Kommission, Jacques Delors, für das Treffen mit den Ministerpräsidenten der deutschen Länder am 19.5.1988. *Europa-Archiv* 47 (3): D 341–343.

Desideri, Carlo. 1995. Italian Regions in the European Community. In *The European Union and the Regions*, edited by B. Jones and M. Keating. Oxford: Clarendon Press, 65–87.

Desideri, Carlo, and Vincenzo Santantonio. 1997. Building a Third Level in Europe: Prospects and Difficulties in Italy. In *The Regional Dimension of the European Union: Towards a Third Level in Europe?*, edited by C. Jeffery. London: Frank Cass, 96–116.

Dewitz, Lars von. 1998. Der Bundesrat. Bilanz der Arbeit im EU-Ausschuß seit 1992. In *Europapolitik der deutschen Länder. Bilanz und Perspektiven nach dem Gipfel von Amsterdam*, edited by F. H. U. Borkenhagen. Opladen: Leske + Budrich, 69–83.

Diaz-López, César Enrique. 1985. Centre-Periphery Structures in Spain: From Historical Conflict to Territorial Consociational Accommodation. In *Centre-Periphery Relations in Western Europe*, edited by V. Wright and Y. Mény. London: Allen and Unwin, 236–272.

DiMaggio, Paul J., and Walter W. Powell. 1991. The Iron Cage Revisited: Institutional Isomorphism and Collective Rationality in Organizational Fields. In *The New Institutionalism in Organizational Analysis*, edited by W. W. Powell and P. J. DiMaggio. Chicago and London: University of Chicago Press, 63–82.

Dyson, Kenneth. 1980. *The State Tradition in Western Europe: A Study of an Idea and Institution*. Oxford: Martin Robertson.

Dyson, Kenneth, ed. forthcoming. *European States and the Euro: Playing the Semi-Sovereignty Game*. Oxford: Oxford University Press.

Dyson, Kenneth, and Kevin Featherstone. 1996. EMU and Economic Governance in Germany. *German Politics* 5 (3): 325–355.

Dyson, Kenneth, and Kevin Featherstone. 1999. *The Road to Maastricht*. Oxford: Oxford University Press.

Eicher, Hermann. 1988. *Die Machtverluste der Landesparlamente. Historischer Rückblick, Bestandaufnahme, Reformansätze*. Berlin: Duncker & Humblot.

Einert, Günther. 1986. EG-Entwicklung unter Ländervorbehalt? In *Die deutschen Länder und die Europäischen Gemeinschaften*, edited by R. Hrbek and U. Taysen. Baden-Baden: Nomos, 41–59.

Ellwein, Thomas, and Jens Joachim Hesse. 1987. *Das Regierungssystem der Bundesrepublik Deutschland*. 6th ed. Opladen: Westdeutscher Verlag.

Engel, Christian. 1998. Das "Europa der Regionen" seit Maastricht. In *Europapoliti der deutschen Länder. Bilanz und Perspektiven nach dem Gipfel von Amsterdam*, edited by F. H. U. Borkenhagen. Opladen: Leske + Budrich, 153–178.

Engel, Christian, and Christine Borrmann. 1991. *Vom Konsens zu Mehrheitsentscheidungen. EG-Entscheidungsverfahren und nationale Interessenpolitik nach der Einheitlichen Europäischen Akte*. Bonn: Europa Union.

Engholm, Björn. 1989. Europa und die deutschen Bundesländer. *Europa-Archiv* 44 (12): 383–392.

Erbguth, Wilfried. 1991. Das UVP-Gesetz des Bundes. Regelungsgehalt und Rechtsfragen. *Die Verwaltung* 3: 283–323.

Escher, Hendrik. 1998. Ländermitwirkung und der Ausschuß der Ständigen Vertreter (AStV). In *Europapolitik der deutschen Länder. Bilanz und Perspektiven nach dem Gipfel von Amsterdam*, edited by F. H. U. Borkenhagen. Opladen: Leske + Budrich, 51–68.

Escobar Gómez, Gabriel. 1994. Evaluación de Impacto Ambiental en España: resultados prácticos. *Ciudad y Territorio* 2 (102): 585–595.

European Parliament. 1995. *European Affairs Committees of the Parliaments of the Member States*. Brussels: European Parliament.

Everling, Ulrich. 1993. Überlegungen zur Struktur der Europäischen Union und zum neuen Europa-Artikel des Grundgesetzes. *Deutsche Verwaltungsblätter* 108 (17): 936–947.

Falkner, Gerda. 2000. Effects of EU Membership on a New Member State. *Journal of Common Market Studies* 38 (2): 223–250.

Fastenrath, Ulrich. 1990. Die Länderbüros in Brüssel. *Die öffentliche Verwaltung* 45 (4): 125–136.

Featherstone, Kevin. 1988. *Socialist Parties and European Integration*. Manchester: Manchester University Press.

Fernández Farreres, Germán. 1993. Las conferencias sectoriales y los consorcios en las relaciones de colaboración entre el Estado y las Comunidades Autónomas. In *Las relaciones interadministrativas de cooperación y colaboración*, edited by Institut d'Estudies Autonómics. Barcelona: Generalitat de Catalunya, Institut d'Estudies Autonómics, 43–58.

Font, Nuria. 1996. La Europeización de la política ambiental en España. Un estudio de implementación de la directiva de evaluación de impacto ambiental. Ph.D. thesis, Departamento de Ciencia Política y Derecho Público, Universitat Autónoma de Barcelona, Barcelona.

Font, Nuria, and Francesc Morata. 1998. Spain: Environmental Policy and Public Administration: A Marriage of Convenience Officiated by the EU? In *Governance and Environment in Western Europe: Politics, Policy and Administration*, edited by K. Hanf and A.-I. Jansen. Harlow: Addison Wesley Longman, 208–229.

Friebe, Ingeborg, ed. 1992. *Die Landtage im europäischen Integrationsprozeß nach Maastricht. Vorschläge für eine Stärkung der europapolitischen Rolle. Gutachten für den Landtag von Nordrhein-Westfalen vom Institut für Europäische Politik.* Düsseldorf: Landtag von Nordrhein-Westfalen.

Friedland, Roger, and Robert R. Alford. 1991. Bringing Society Back In: Symbols, Practices, and Institutional Contradictions. In *The New Institutionalism in Organizational Analysis*, edited by W. W. Powell and P. J. DiMaggio. Chicago and London: Chicago University Press, 232–263.

Gamero Casado, Eduardo. 1993. Comunicación a la Ponencia Española. La estructura orgánica de las Comunidades Autónomas en relación con la ejecución del derecho comunitario europeo. In *La Comunidad Europea, la instancia regional, y organización administrativa de los Estados Miembros*, edited by Javier Barnes Vazquez. Madrid: Civitas, 195–215.

García de Enterría, Eduardo. 1991. La participación de las Comunidades Autónomas en la formación de las decisiones comunitarias. In *Comunidades Autónomas y Comunidad Europea. Relaciones jurídico-institucionales*, edited by Cortes de Castilla y León. Valladolid: Cortes de Castilla y León, 93–118.

García Morales, M. Jesús. 1993. Los convenios entre Cataluña y otras Comunidades Autónomas: Régimen jurídico y realidad en las relaciones de colaboración de la Generalidad con otras Comunidades. *Autonomies* 17: 99–119.

Garrett, Geoffrey, and Barry R. Weingast. 1993. Ideas, Interests, and Institutions: Constructing the European Community's Internal Market. In *Ideas and Foreign Policy*, edited by J. Goldstein and R. O. Keohane. Ithaca, NY: Cornell University Press, 173–206.

Gebers, Betty. 1993. Activities Concerning Access to Information. *Newsletter of the Environmental Law Network International (ELNI)* (1/1993): 3.

Gebers, Betty. 1996. Germany. In *Access to Environmental Information in Europe: The Implementation and Implications of Directive 90/313/EEC*, edited by R. Hallo. London, The Hague, Boston: Kluwer Law, 95–110.

George, Alexander L. 1979. Case Studies and Theory Development: The Method of Structured, Focused Comparison. In *Diplomacy: New Approaches in History, Theory and Policy*, edited by P. G. Lauren. London: Macmillan, 43–68.

George, Stephen. 1993. Intergovernmentalism and Supranationalism in the Development of the European Community. In *International Relations and Pan-Europe: Theoretical Approaches and Empirical Findings*, edited by F. Pfetsch. Münster and Hamburg: LIT, 159–171.

Gerster, Florian. 1993. Die Europaministerkonferenz der Länder. Aufgaben, Themen und Selbstverständnis. *Integration* 16 (2): 61–67.

Goetz, Klaus H. 1995. National Governance and European Integration: Intergovernmental Relations in Germany. *Journal of Common Market Studies* 33 (1): 91–116.

González Ayala, Maria Dolores. 1991. La jurisprudencia del Tribunal Constitucional en al aplicación del derecho comunitario por las Comunidades Autónomas. In *Comunidades Autónomas y Comunidad Europea. Relaciones jurídico-institucionales*, edited by Cortes de Castilla y León. Valladolid: Cortes de Castilla y León, 251–264.

González Encinar, José Juan. 1992. Ein asymmetrischer Bundesstaat. In *Der Staat der Autonomen Gemeinschaften in Spanien*, edited by D. Nohlen and J. J. González Encinar. Opladen: Leske + Budrich, 217–230.

Gourevitch, Peter. 1978. The Second Image Reversed: The International Sources of Domestic Politics. *International Organization* 32 (4): 881–912.

Grabitz, Eberhard. 1986. Die Rechtsbefugnis von Bund und Ländern bei der Durchführung von Gemeinschaftsrecht. *Allgemeines Öffentliches Recht* 111: 1–33.

Grande, Edgar. 1996. The State and Interest Groups in a Framework of Multi-level Decision-making: The Case of the European Union. *Journal of European Public Policy* 3 (3): 318–338.

Grau i Creus, Mireia. 2000. The Effects of Institutions and Political Parties Upon Federalism. The Channelling and Integration of the Comunidades Autonomas within the Central-Level Policy Processes in Spain (1983–1996). Ph.D. thesis, Department of Social and Political Sciences, European University Institute, Florence.

Greven, Michael. 1992. Political Parties between National Identity and Eurofication. In *The Idea of Europe*, edited by B. Nelson, D. Roberts, and W. Veit. Oxford: Berg, 75–95.

Haas, Evelyn. 1988. Die Mitwirkung der Länder bei EG-Vorhaben. Neuere Entwicklungen im Gefolge der Luxemburger Akte. *Die Öffentliche Verwaltung* 41 (15): 613–623.

Hailbronner, Kay. 1990. Die deutschen Bundesländer in der EG. *Juristenzeitung* 45 (2): 149–158.

Hall, Peter A. 1986. *Governing the Economy: The Politics of State Intervention in Britain and France*. Cambridge: Polity Press.

Hall, Peter A. 1993. Policy Paradigms, Social Learning, and the State. *Comparative Politics* 25: 275–96.

Hall, Peter A., and Rosemary C. R. Taylor. 1996. Political Science and the Three New Institutionalisms. *Political Studies* 44 (5): 936–957.

Hannaleck, Ilva, and Wolfgang Schumann. 1983. Die Beteiligung der Länder an der EG-Politik des Bundes. Probleme und Alternativen. *Zeitschrift für Parlamentsfragen* 14 (3): 362–371.

Hattam, Victoria C. 1993. *Labor Visions and State Power: the Origin of Business Unionism in the United States*. Princeton, NJ: Princeton University Press.

Held, Gerd. 1993. Föderalismus am Mittelmeer? Neue Problemlagen regionaler Modernisierung am Beispiel Kataloniens. *Aus Politik und Zeitgeschichte* B 20–21: 23–29.

Hellwig, Renate. 1987. Die Rolle der Bundesländer in der Europa-Politik. *Europa-Archiv* 42 (10): 297–302.

Herdegen, Matthias. 1992. Die Belastbarkeit des Verfassungsgefüges auf dem Weg zur Europäischen Union. *Europäische Grundrechtezeitschrift* 19 (24): 589–594.

Héritier, Adrienne. 1999. *Policy-Making and Diversity in Europe: Escape from Deadlock*. Cambridge: Cambridge University Press.

Héritier, Adrienne. 2001. Differential Europe: National Administrative Responses to Community Policy. In *Transforming Europe: Europeanization and*

Domestic Change, edited by M. Green Cowles, J. A. Caporaso and T. Risse, 44–59.

Héritier, Adrienne, Dieter Kerwer, Christoph Knill, Dirk Lehmkuhl, and Michael Teutsch. 2001. *Differential Europe: New Opportunities and Restrictions for Policy Making in Member States*: Lanham, MD: Rowman & Littlefield.

Héritier, Adrienne, Christoph Knill, and Susanne Mingers. 1996. *Ringing the Changes in Europe. Regulatory Competition and the Redefinition of the State: Britain, France, Germany*. Berlin, New York: De Gruyter.

Hesse, Jens Joachim. 1986. *Erneuerung der Politik "von unten"?* Opladen: Westdeutscher Verlag.

Hesse, Jens Joachim, and Wolfgang Renzsch. 1991. Zehn Thesen zur Entwicklung und Lage des deutschen Föderalismus. In *Föderalstaatliche Entwicklungen in Europa*, edited by J. J. Hesse and W. Renzsch. Baden-Baden: Nomos, 29–47.

Hesse, Konrad. 1962. *Der unitarische Bundesstaat*. Karlsruhe: Müller.

Hierl, Hubert, ed. 1995. *Europa der Regionen. Entstehung, Aufgaben, Perspektiven des Ausschusses der Regionen*. Bonn: Economica.

Hildebrand, Andreas. 1992. Die Finanzierung der Autonomen Gemeinschaften. In *Der Staat der Autonomen Gemeinschaften in Spanien*, edited by D. Nohlen and J. J. Gonzáles Encinar. Opladen: Leske + Budrich, 125–176.

Hoffmann, Stanley. 1966. Obstinate or Obsolete? The Fate of the Nation-State and the Case of Western Europe. *Daedalus* 85 (3): 865–921.

Hoffmann, Stanley. 1982. Reflections on the Nation-State in Western Europe Today. *Journal of Common Market Studies* 20 (1–2): 29–37.

Hoffmann, Stanley. 1989. The European Community and 1992. *Foreign Affairs* 68 (4): 27–47.

Hooghe, Liesbet, ed. 1996. *Cohesion Policy and European Integration: Building Multi-Level Governance*. Oxford: Oxford University Press.

Hooghe, Liesbet. 1995. Belgian Federalism and the European Community. In *The European Union and the Regions*, edited by B. Jones and M. Keating. Oxford: Clarendon Press, 135–166.

Hrbek, Rudolf. 1986. Doppelte Politikverflechtung: Deutscher Föderalismus und Europäische Integration. Die deutschen Länder im EG-Entscheidungsprozeß. In *Die deutschen Länder und die Europäischen Gemeinschaften*, edited by R. Hrbek and U. Thaysen. Baden-Baden: Nomos, 17–36.

Hrbek, Rudolf. 1987. Die deutschen Länder in der EG-Politik. *Außenpolitik* 38 (2): 120–132.

Hrbek, Rudolf and Sabine Weyand. 1994. *Betrifft: Das Europa der Regionen. Fakten, Probleme, Perspektiven*. München: Beck.

Instituto para la Política Ambiental Europea, Madrid. 1997. *Manual de Política Ambiental Europea: la UE y España*. Madrid: Fundación MAPFRE.

Ipsen, Hans Peter. 1972. *Europäisches Gemeinschaftsrecht*. Tübingen: Mohr.

Jachtenfuchs, Markus, and Beate Kohler-Koch. 1995. *The Transformation of Governance in the European Union*. Working Paper, AB III, Nr. 11. Mannheim: Mannheimer Zentrum für europäische Sozialforschung.

Jachtenfuchs, Markus, and Beate Kohler-Koch, eds. 1996. *Europäische Integration*. Opladen: Leske + Budrich.

Jänicke, Martin, and Helmut Weidner. 1997. Germany. In *National Environmental Policies. A Comparative Study of Capacity-Building*, edited by M. Jänicke and H. Weidner. Berlin *et al.*: Springer, 133–155.

Jaspert, Gunter. 1988. Die Beteiligung des Bundesrates an der europäischen Integration. In *Bundesländer und Europäische Gemeinschaft*, edited by S. Magiera and D. Merten. Berlin: Duncker & Humblot, 87–100.

Jeffery, Charlie. 1994. The Länder Strike Back: Structure and Procedures of European Integration Policy-making in the German Federal System. Discussion Papers in Federal Studies, FS 94/4. Leicester: University of Leicester.

Jeffery, Charlie. 1997a. Farewell to the Third Level? The German Länder and the European Policy Process. In *The Regional Dimension of the European Union. Towards a Third Level in Europe?*, edited by C. Jeffery. London: Frank Cass, 56–75.

Jeffery, Charlie. 1997b. Sub-National Authorities and European Integration. Moving Beyond the Nation-State? Paper presented at European Community Studies Association Conference, May 1997, Seattle, 29 May – 1 June 1997.

Jeffery, Charlie, ed. 1997c. *The Regional Dimension of the European Union: Towards a Third Level in Europe?* London: Frank Cass.

Jeffery, Charlie. 2000. Sub-National Mobilization and European Integration. *Journal of Common Market Studies* 38 (1): 1–23.

Jeffery, Charlie, and John Yates. 1993. Unification and Maastricht: The Response of the Länder Governments. In *Federalism, Unification and European Integration*, edited by C. Jeffery and R. Sturm. London: Frank Cass, 58–81.

Joerges, Christian, and Jürgen Neyer. 1997. From Intergovernmental Bargaining to Deliberative Political Processes: The Constitutionalisation of Comitology. *European Law Journal* 3 (3): 273–299.

John, Peter. 1997. Europeanization in a Centralizing State: Multi-Level Governance in the UK. In *The Regional Dimension of the European Union: Towards a Third Level in Europe?*, edited by C. Jeffery. London: Frank Cass, 131–144.

Johnson, Stanley P., and Guy Corcelle. 1995. *The Environmental Policy of the European Communities*. Second ed. London, The Hague, Boston: Kluwer Law International.

Jones, Barry, and Michael Keating, eds. 1995. *The European Union and the Regions*. Oxford: Clarendon Press.

Jones, Rachel. 2000. *Beyond the Spanish State: Central Government, Domestic Actors, and the EU.* Houndmills: Palgrave.

Kalbfleisch-Kottsieper, Ulla. 1993. Fortentwicklungen des Föderalismus in Europa: vom Provinzialismus zur stabilen politischen Perspektive? Ein Beitrag zur Rolle der Länder, Regionen und Autonomen Gemeinschaften bei den EG-Regierungskonferenzen und der Ratifizierung des Maastrichter Vertrags. *Die Öffentliche Verwaltung* 46 (13): 541–551.

Käppler, Birgit. 1996. Die deutschen Bundesländer im Europäischen Mehrebenensystem. Eine Fallstudie der Einflußnahme Bayerns auf die Europäische Wasserpolitik. Diplomarbeit, Fakultät für Politik- und Verwaltungswissenschaften, Universität Konstanz, Konstanz.

Kastendiek, Hans. 1990. Convergence or a Persistent Diversity of National Policies? In *The Politics of 1992: Beyond the Single European Market*, edited by C. Crouch and D. Marquand. Oxford: Basil Blackwell, 68–84.

Katzenstein, Peter J. 1984. *Corporatism and Change: Austria, Switzerland, and the Politics of Industry*. Ithaca and London: Cornell University Press.

Katzenstein, Peter J. 1985. *Small States in World Markets: Industrial Policy in Europe*. Ithaca and London: Cornell University Press.

Keating, Michael. 1996. *Nations against the State: The New Politics of Nationalism in Quebec, Catalonia and Scotland*. London: Macmillan.

Keating, Michael, and Howard Elcock. 1998. Devolution and the UK State. *Regional and Federal Studies*, Special Issue on the "Remaking of the Union: Devolution and British Politics in the 1990s" 8 (1): 1–9.

Keohane, Robert O. 1984. *After Hegemony: Cooperation and Discord in the World Political Economy*. Princeton, NJ: Princeton University Press.

Keohane, Robert O., and Helen Milner, eds. 1996. *Internationalization and Domestic Politics*. Cambridge: Cambridge University Press.

Kerremans, Bart, and Jan Beyers. 1997. The Belgian Sub-National Entities in the European Union: Second or Third Level Players? In *The Regional Dimension of the European Union: Towards a Third Level in Europe?*, edited by C. Jeffery. London: Frank Cass, 41–55.

Kewenig, Wilhelm A. 1990. Die Europäische Gemeinschaft und die bundesstaatliche Ordnung der Bundesrepublik Deutschland. *Juristenzeitung* 45 (10): 458–466.

Kitschelt, Herbert P. 1986. Political Opportunity Structures and Political Protest: Anti-Nuclear Movements in Four Democracies. *British Journal of Political Science* 16: 57–85.

Klatt, Hartmut. 1989. Forty Years of German Federalism: Past Trends and New Developments. *Publius* 19 (4): 185–202.

Klatt, Hartmut. 1991. Das föderale System der Bundesrepublik Deutschland als Rahmen für das Verhältnis von Zentralstaat und Ländern. In *Die Zukunft des kooperativen Föderalismus in Deutschland*, edited by G. Hirscher. München: Hans-Seidel-Stiftung, 41–82.

Kloepfer, Michael. 1984. Gesetzeslähmung durch fehlende exekutive Vorschriften im Abwasserabgabengesetz? *Natur und Recht* 7: 258–263.

Knill, Christoph. forthcoming. *The Transformation of National Administrations in Europe: Patterns of Change and Persistence*. Cambridge: Cambridge University Press.

Knill, Christoph, and Andrea Lenschow, eds. 2000. *Implementing EU Environmental Policy: New Approaches to an Old Problem*. Manchester: Manchester University Press.

Knill, Christoph, and Andrea Lenschow. 2001. Adjusting to EU Environmental Policy: Change and Persistence of Domestic Administrations. In *Transforming Europe: Europeanization and Domestic Change*, edited by M. G. Cowles, J. A. Caporaso, and T. Risse, 116–136.

Knodt, Michelle. 1998. *Tiefenwirkung europäischer Politik. Eigensinn oder Anpassung regionalen Regierens?* Baden-Baden: Nomos.

Kohler-Koch, Beate. 1996. The Strength of Weakness: The Transformation of Governance in the EU. In *The Future of the Nation State: Essays on Cultural Pluralism and Political Integration*, edited by S. Gustavsson and L. Lewin. Stockholm: Nerenius & Santerus, 169–210.

Kohler-Koch, Beate. 1998. Europäisierung der Regionen. Institutioneller Wandel als sozialer Prozeß. In *Interaktive Politik in Europa. Regionen im Netzwerk der Integration*, edited by B. Kohler-Koch *et al.* Opladen: Leske + Budrich, 13–31.

Kohler-Koch, Beate *et al.* 1998. *Interaktive Politik in Europa. Regionen im Netzwerk der Integration*. Opladen: Leske + Budrich.

Kooiman, Jan, ed. 1993. *Modern Governance: New Government-Society Interactions*. London: Sage.

Kössinger, Wilfried. 1989. *Die Durchführung des Europäischen Gemeinschaftsrechts im Bundesstaat, Bund-Länder Verhältnis und dem Europäischen Gemeinschaftsrecht*. Berlin: Duncker & Humblot.

Krasner, Stephen D. 1984. Approaches to the State: Alternative Conceptions and Historical Dynamics. *Comparative Politics* 16 (2): 223–46.

Krasner, Stephen D. 1988. Sovereignty: An Institutional Perspective. *Comparative Political Studies* 21: 66–94.

Kriesi, Hanspeter, Ruud Koopmans, Jan Willem Duyvendak, and Marco G. Giugni. 1992. New Social Movements and Political Opportunities in Western Europe. *European Journal of Political Research* 22: 219–244.

Ladrech, Robert. 1994. Europeanization of Domestic Politics and Institutions: The Case of France. *Journal of Common Market Studies* 32 (1): 69–88.

Le Galès, Patrick. 1994. Regional Economic Policies: An Alternative to French Economic Dirigisme? *Regional Politics and Policy* 4 (3): 72–91.

Lehmbruch, Gerhard. 1976. *Parteienwettbewerb im Bundesstaat*. Stuttgart: Kohlhammer.

Lehmbruch, Gerhard. 2000. Bundesstaatsreform als Sozialtechnologie? Pfadabhängigkeit und Veränderungsspielräume im deutschen Föderalismus. In *Jahrbuch des Föderalismus 2000*, edited by Europäisches Zentrum für Föderalismus-Forschung Tübingen. Baden-Baden: Nomos, 71–93.

Lehmkuhl, Dirk. 1999. *The Importance of Small Differences: The Impact of European Integration on the Associations in the German and Dutch Road Haulage Industries*. Amsterdam: Thela Thesis.

Lenschow, Andrea. 1997. The Implementation of EU Environmental Policy in Germany. In *The Impact of National Administrative Traditions on the Implementation of EU Environmental Policy. Preliminary Research Report for the Commission of the European Union, DG XI, April 1997*, edited by C. Knill. Florence: European University Institute, 46–107.

Lenz, Helmut. 1977. Die Landtage als staatsnotarielle Ratifikationsämter. *Die Öffentliche Verwaltung* 30 (5): 157–164.

Leonardy, Uwe. 1991. The Working Relationships between Bund and Länder in the Federal Republic of Germany. In *German Federalism Today*, edited by C. Jeffery and P. Savigear. Leicester and London: Leicester University Press, 40–62.

Lewis, Jeffrey. 1995. The European Union as a "Multiperspectivial Polity". Paper presented at the Forth Biannual International Conference of the European Community Studies Association, May 11–14, at Charleston, SC.

Lijphart, Arend. 1984. *Democracies: Patterns of Majoritarian and Consensus Government in Twenty-One Countries*. New Haven, CT: Yale University Press.

Linz, Juan J. 1973. Early State-Building and Late Peripheral Nationalism against the State: The Case of Spain. In *Building States and Nations*, edited by S. Eisenstadt and S. Rokkan. Beverly Hills, CA: Sage, 32–116.

López Guerra, Luis. 1993. La segunda fase de construcción del Estado de las Autonomías (1983–1993). *Revista Vasca de Administración Pública* 3 (36): 69–79.

Lowi, Theodore. 1972. Four Systems of Policy, Politics, and Choice. *Public Administration* 32 (4): 298–310.

Lübbe-Wolff, Gertrude. 1991. Die Bedeutung des EG-Rechts für den Grundwasserschutz. In *Umweltschutz in der Europäischen Gemeinschaft*, edited by P. Behrens and H.-J. Koch. Baden-Baden: Nomos, 127–156.

Magiera, Siegfried. 1988. Als Bundesstaat in der Europäischen Gemeinschaft. In *Bundesländer und Europäische Gemeinschaft*, edited by S. Magiera and D. Merten. Berlin: Duncker und Humblot, 11–19.

Majone, Giandomenico. 1993. The European Community between Social Policy and Social Regulation. *Journal of Common Market Studies* 11 (1): 79–106.

Majone, Giandomenico, ed. 1996. *Regulating Europe*. London and New York: Routledge.

Majone, Giandomenico. 1997. From the Positive to the Regulatory State: Causes and Consequences of Changes in the Model of Governance. *Journal of Public Policy* 17 (2): 139–167.

March, James G., and Johan P. Olsen. 1984. The New Institutionalism: Organizational Factors in Political Life. *American Political Science Review* 78: 734–749.

March, James G., and Johan P. Olsen. 1989. *Rediscovering Institutions*. New York: The Free Press.

March, James G., and Johan P. Olsen. 1995. *Democratic Governance*. New York: The Free Press.

March, James G., and Johan P. Olsen. 1996. Institutional Perspectives on Political Institutions. *Governance* 9 (3): 247–264.

March, James G., and Johan P. Olsen. 1998. The Institutional Dynamics of International Political Orders. *International Organization* 52 (4): 943–969.

Marin, Bernd. 1991. *Generalized Political Exchange: Antagonistic Cooperation and Integrated Policy Circuits*. Frankfurt am Main: Westview and Campus.

Marks, Gary. 1992. Structural Policy in the European Community. In *Europolitics: Institutions and Policymaking in the New European Community*, edited by A. Sbragia. Washington, DC: Brookings Institution, 191–224.

Marks, Gary. 1993. Structural Policy and Multilevel Governance in the European Community. In *The State of the European Community II: Maastricht Debates and Beyond*, edited by A. Cafruny and G. Rosenthal. Boulder, Co: Lynne Rienner, 391–410.

Marks, Gary. 1997. An Actor-centred Approach to Multi-level Governance. In *The Regional Dimension of the European Union: Towards a Third Level in Europe?*, edited by C. Jeffery. London: Frank Cass, 20–40.

Marks, Gary, Liesbet Hooghe, and Kermit Blank. 1996. European Integration from the 1980s: State-centric v. Multi-level Governance. *Journal of Common Market Studies* 34 (3): 341–78.

Marks, Gary, and Doug McAdam. 1996. Social Movements and the Changing Structure of Political Opportunity in the European Union. In *Governance in the European Union*, edited by G. Marks, F. W. Scharpf, P. C. Schmitter, and W. Streeck. London, Thousand Oaks, New Delhi: Sage, 95–120.

Marks, Gary, Francois Nielsen, Leonard Ray, and Jane Salk. 1996a. Competencies, Cracks and Conflicts: Regional Mobilization in the European Union. In *Governance in the European Union*, edited by G. Marks, F. W. Scharpf, P. C. Schmitter, and W. Streeck. London, Thousand Oaks, New Delhi: Sage, 40–63.

Marks, Gary, Fritz W. Scharpf, Philippe C. Schmitter, and Wolfgang Streeck, eds. 1996b. *Governance in the European Union*. London, Thousand Oaks, New Delhi: Sage.

Martín, Gerard. 1997. *El Tribunal Constitucional i el Medi Ambient*. Barcelona: Generalitat de Catalunya, Departament de Medi Ambient.

Martin, Steve, and Graham Pearce. 1999. Differential Multi-level Governance? The Response of British Sub-national Governments to European Integration. *Regional and Federal Studies* 9 (2): 32–52.

Mayntz, Renate, and Fritz W. Scharpf. 1995. Der Ansatz des akteurszentrierten Institutionalismus. In *Gesellschaftliche Selbstregulierung und politische Steuerung*, edited by R. Mayntz and F. W. Scharpf. Frankfurt am Main: Campus, 39–72.

Mazey, Sonia, and Jeremy Richardson, eds. 1993. *Lobbying in the European Community*. Oxford and New York: Oxford University Press.

Meehan, Elizabeth. 1997. The Citizen and the Region. *Regional and Federal Studies* 7 (1): 70–76.

Meier, Gert. 1987. Die Beteiligung der Länder an der Gesetzgebung der Europäischen Gemeinschaften: Ein Ende der Diskussion? *Zeitschrift für Rechtspolitik* 20 (7): 228–230.

Memminger, Gerd. 1992. Die Forderungen der Länder im Gefüge des Grundgesetzes. In *Die deutschen Länder in Europa, Politische Union, Wirtschafts- und Währungsunion*, edited by F. H. U. Borkenhagen, C. Bruns-Klöss, G. Memminger, and O. Stein. Baden-Baden: Nomos, 139–160.

Mény, Yves. 1987. France. In *Central and Local Government Relations. A Comparative Analysis of West European Unitary States*, edited by E. C. Page and M. J. Goldsmith. London: Sage, 88–106.

Mény, Yves. 1989. Formation et transformation des politiques communautaires: l'example français. In *Idéologie: partis politiques & groupes sociaux*, edited by Y. Mény. Paris: Presse de FNSP, 353–371.

Mény, Yves, Pierre Muller, and Jean-Louis Quermonne, eds. 1996. *Adjusting to Europe: The Impact of the European Union on National Institutions and Policies*. London: Routledge.

Merten, Detlef, ed. 1990. *Föderalismus und Europäische Gemeinschaften unter besonderer Berücksichtigung von Umwelt und Gesundheit, Kultur und Bildung.* Berlin: Duncker & Humblot.

Meyer, John W., and Brian Rowan. 1991. Institutional Organizations: Formal Structure as Myth and Ceremony. In *The New Institutionalism in Organizational Analysis,* edited by W. W. Powell and P. J. DiMaggio. Chicago and London: University of Chicago Press, 41–62.

Milward, Alan S. 1992. *The European Rescue of the Nation-State.* Berkeley, CA: University of California Press.

Ministerio para las Administraciones Públicas. 1993. *Régimen de distribución de competencias entre el Estado y las Comunidades Autónomas.* Madrid: Ministerio para las Administraciones Públicas.

Ministerio para las Administraciones Públicas. 1995. *La participación de las Comunidades Autónomas en los asuntos comunitarios europeos.* Madrid: Ministerio para las Administraciones Públicas.

Ministerio para las Administraciones Públicas. 1996. *Puesta en práctica de los Acuerdos Autonómicos de 1992 y sus efectos sobre el Estado Autonómico.* Madrid: Ministerio para las Administraciones Públicas.

Mitjans Perelló, Esther. 1993. Hacia una equiparación entre todas las Comunidades Autónomas: La amplificación de competencias de la Ley Orgánica 9/1992, de 23 de diciembre. *Autonomies* 17: 83–98.

Montoro Chiner, Maria Jesús. 1988. Die Beteiligung der Autonomen Gemeinschaften Spaniens an den Entscheidungen der Europäischen Gemeinschaft. In *Bundesländer und Europäische Gemeinschaft,* edited by S. Magiera and D. Merten. Berlin: Duncker & Humblot, 165–178.

Montoro Chiner, Maria Jesús. 1989. Rechtliche Konsequenzen aus dem Beitritt Spaniens zu den Europäischen Gemeinschaften. In *Aspekte der öffentlichen Verwaltung und Verwaltungswissenschaften in Spanien,* edited by C. Böhret. Speyer: Hochschule für Verwaltungswissenschaften Speyer, 49–61.

Montoro Chiner, Maria Jesús. 1990. Spanische Kompetenzverteilung im Bereich von Kultur, Bildung und Medien im Hinblick auf die EG-Rechtssetzung. In *Föderalismus und Europäische Gemeinschaften unter besonderer Berücksichtigung von Umwelt und Gesundheit, Kultur und Bildung,* edited by D. Merten. Berlin: Duncker & Humblot, 183–212.

Morass, Michael. 1994. *Regionale Interessen auf dem Weg in die Europäische Union.* Wien: Braumüller.

Morass, Michael. 1997. Austria: The Case of a Federal Newcomer in European Union Politics. In *The Regional Dimension of the European Union. Towards a Third Level?,* edited by C. Jeffery. London: Frank Cass, 76–95.

Morata, Francesc. 1987. *Autonomia Regional i Integració Europea.* Barcelona: Generalitat de Catalunya.

Morata, Francesc. 1995. Spanish Regions in the European Community. In *The European Union and the Regions,* edited by B. Jones and M. Keating. Oxford: Clarendon Press, 115–134.

Morata, Francesc. 1996. Barcelone et la Catalogne dans l'arène européenne. In *Les politiques du néo-régionalisme. Action collective régionale et globalisation,* edited by R. Balmes. Paris: Economica, 107–132.

Morata, Francesc, and Xavier Muñoz. 1997. Vying for European Funds: Territorial Restructuring in Spain. In *Cohesion Policy and European Integration: Building Multi-Level Governance*, edited by L. Hooghe. Oxford: Oxford University Press, 195–218.

Moravcsik, Andrew. 1991. Negotiating the Single European Act: National Interests and Conventional Statecraft in the European Community. *International Organization* 45 (1): 19–56.

Moravcsik, Andrew. 1993. Preferences and Power in the European Community: A Liberal Intergovernmentalist Approach. *Journal of Common Market Studies* 31 (4): 473–524.

Moravcsik, Andrew. 1994. *Why the European Community Strengthens the State: Domestic Politics and International Cooperation*. Working Paper, 52. Cambridge, MA: Harvard University.

Moravcsik, Andrew. 1997. Warum die Europäische Union die Exekutive stärkt. Innenpolitik und internationale Kooperation. In *Projekt Europa im Übergang? Staat und Demokratie in der Europäischen Union*, edited by K. D. Wolf. Baden-Baden: Nomos, 211–269.

Moravcsik, Andrew. 1998a. *The Choice for Europe: Social Purpose and State Power From Rome to Maastricht*. Ithaca, NY: Cornell University Press.

Moravcsik, Andrew. 1998b. Does International Cooperation Strengthen National Executives? The Case of Monetary Policy in the European Union. Paper presented at the conference "Europeanization and Domestic Political Change," Florence, 19 and 20 June.

Morawitz, Rudolf. 1981. *Die Zusammenarbeit von Bund und Ländern bei Vorhaben der Europäischen Gemeinschaft*. Bonn: Europa Union.

Morawitz, Rudolf. 1988. Die Zusammenarbeit von Bund und Ländern bei der Wahrnehmung von EG-Aufgaben. Erfahrungen und Reformbestrebungen. In *Bundesländer und Europäische Gemeinschaft*, edited by S. Magiera and D. Merten. Berlin: Duncker & Humblot, 45–60.

Morawitz, Rudolf, and Wilhelm Kaiser. 1994. *Die Zusammenarbeit von Bund und Ländern bei Vorhaben der Europäischen Union*. Bonn: Europa Union.

Moreno, Luis. 1994. Ethnoterritorial Concurrence and Imperfect Federalism in Spain. In *Evaluating Federal Systems*, edited by B. de Villiers. Cape Town: Juta, 162–193.

Moreno, Luis. 1997. Federalization and Ethnoterritorial Concurrence in Spain. *Publius* 27 (4): 65–84.

Müller, Edda. 1986. *Die Innenwelt der Umweltpolitik. Sozial-liberale Umweltpolitik – (Ohn)macht durch Organisation?* Opladen: Westdeutscher Verlag.

Müller-Brandeck-Bocquet, Gisela. 1996. *Die institutionelle Dimension der Umweltpolitik. Eine vergleichende Untersuchung zu Frankreich, Deutschland und der Europäischen Union*. Baden-Baden: Nomos.

Muñoz Machado, Santiago. 1985. La ordenación de las relaciones del Estado y las Comunidades Autónomas con la Comunidad Europea. *Revista Española de Derecho Constitucional* 5 (14): 9–76.

Muñoz Machado, Santiago. 1986. *El Estado, el Derecho interno y la Comunidad Europea*. Madrid: Civitas.

Nass, Klaus Otto. 1986. Nebenaußenpolitik der Bundesländer. *Europa-Archiv* 41 (21): 619–629.

Newton, Michael T. 1997. *Institutions of Modern Spain: A Political and Economic Guide.* Cambridge: Cambridge University Press.

North, Douglass C. 1990. *Institutions, Institutional Change, and Economic Performance.* Cambridge: Cambridge University Press.

Norton, Phillip, ed. 1996. *National Parliaments and the European Union.* London: Frank Cass.

OECD. 1997. *Environmental Performance Reviews: Spain.* Paris: OECD.

Olsen, Johan P. 1992. Analyzing Institutional Dynamics. *Staatswissenschaften und Staatspraxis* 3 (2): 247–271.

Olsen, Johan P. 1996. Europeanization and Nation-State Dynamics. In *The Future of the Nation State,* edited by S. Gustavsson and L. Lewin. London: Routledge, 245–285.

Olsen, Johan P. 1997. European Challenges to the Nation State. In *Political Institutions and Public Policy,* edited by B. Steunenberg and F. van Vught. The Hague: Kluwer Academic Publishers, 157–188.

Olsen, Johan P. and Guy Peters, eds. 1998. *Lessons from Experience: Experiential Learning in Administrative Reforms in Eight Democracies*: Oslo: Scandinavian University Press.

Oschatz, Georg-Berndt, and Horst Risse. 1988. Europäische Integration und deutscher Föderalismus. *Europa-Archiv* 43 (1): 9–16.

Oschatz, Georg-Berndt, and Horst Risse. 1989. Bundesrat und Europäische Gemeinschaften. Neue Verfahren der Bundesrats-Geschäftsordnung für EG-Vorlagen. *Die Öffentliche Verwaltung* 42 (12): 509–518.

Ossenbühl, Fritz. 1990. Landesbericht Bundesrepublik Deutschland. In *Föderalismus und Regionalismus in Europa,* edited by F. Ossenbühl. Baden-Baden: Nomos, 131–165.

Ostrom, Eleonor. 1990. *Governing the Commons.* Cambridge: Cambridge University Press.

Page, Edward C., and Linda Wouters. 1995. The Europeanization of National Bureaucracies? In *Bureaucracy in the Modern State: An Introduction to Comparative Public Administration,* edited by J. Pierre. Aldershot: Edward Elgar, 185–204.

Parejo Alfonso, Luciano. 1993. Las relaciones entre las administraciones públicas en el título I de la ley 30/1992, de 26 de noviembre, de régimen jurídico de las administraciones públicas y del procedimiento administrativo común. In *Las relaciones interadministrativas de cooperación y colaboración,* edited by Institut d'Estudis Autonòmics. Barcelona: Generalitat de Catalunya, Institut d'Estudis Autonòmics, 17–39.

Parri, Leonardo. 1989. Territorial Political Exchanges in Federal and Unitary Countries. *West European Politics* 12 (3): 197–219.

Patronat Català Pro Europa. 1988. *Catalunya a la Comunitat Europea: effects de l'adhesió i perspectives per al 1992.* Barcelona: Generalitat de Catalunya.

Patzig, Werner. 1981. *Die Gemeinschaftsfinanzierung von Bund und Ländern.* Bonn: Institut für Finanzen und Steuern.

Pérez González, Manuel. 1989. Die Rolle der Comunidades Autonomas im spanischen Staat und ihre rechtlichen Einflußmöglichkeiten auf die nationale Gemeinschaftspolitik. In *Die Bundesrepublik Deutschland und das Königreich Spanien 1992. Die Rolle der Länder und der Comunidades Autonomas im europäischen Integrationsprozeß*, edited by H. A. Kremer. Munich: Bayerischer Landtag, 51–71.

Pérez Sola, Nicolás. 1996. Problemas de delimitación competencial entre el Estado y las *CCAA* sobre medio ambiente y espacios protegidos. El caso andaluz. Paper presented at the I. Congreso Nacional de Derecho Ambiental. Comunicaciones, Seville, April.

Pietzcker, Jost. 1988. Zusammenarbeit der Gliedstaaten im Bundesstaat. Landesbericht Bundesrepublik Deutschland. In *Zusammenarbeit der Gliedstaaten im Bundesstaat*, edited by C. Starck. Baden-Baden: Nomos, 17–76.

Pizzorno, Alessandro. 1978. Political Exchange and Collective Identity in Industrial Conflict. In *The Resurgence of Class Conflict in Western Europe since 1968*, edited by C. Crouch and A. Pizzorno. London: Macmillan, 277–298.

Platzer, Hans-Wolfgang, and Walter Ruhland. 1994. *Welches Deutschland in welchem Europa? Demoskopische Analysen, politische Perspektiven, gesellschaftliche Kontroversen*. Bonn: Dietz Nachfolger.

Powell, Walter W. 1991. Expanding the Scope of Institutional Analysis. In *The New Institutionalism in Organizational Analysis*, edited by W. W. Powell and P. J. DiMaggio. Chicago and London: Chicago University Press, 183–204.

Powell, Walter W., and Paul J. DiMaggio, eds. 1991. *The New Institutionalism in Organizational Analysis*. Chicago and London: University of Chicago Press.

Przeworski, Adam, and Henry Teune. 1970. *The Logic of Comparative Social Inquiry*. New York: Wiley-Interscience.

Pueyo Losa, Jorge. 1989. Sobre el principio y los mecanismos de colaboración entre el gobierno central y las Comunidades Autónomas en asuntos relacionados con las Comunidades Europeas. *Revista de Instituciones Europeas* 16 (1): 29–74.

Pujol, Jordi. 1987. *L'Estatut d'Autònomia, pacte d'Estal. Discurs del President de la Generalitat al Parlament de Catalunya en el debat general sobre l'Estatut.* Barcelona: Les Corts de Catalunya.

Pujol, Jordi. 1995. In Richtung eines Europas der Regionen? In *Europa der Regionen. Eine Idee setzt sich durch: Ausschuß der Regionen*, edited by H. Hierl. Bonn: Economica Verlag, 48–59.

Putnam, Robert. 1988. Diplomacy and Domestic Politics: The Logic of Two-Level Games. *International Organization* 42 (2): 427–460.

Rau, Johannes. 1990. Geleitwort. In *Die Kräfte der Regionen. Nordrhein-Westfalen in Europa*, edited by U. v. Alemann, R. G. Henze, and B. Hombach. Baden-Baden: Nomos, 11–14.

Reinhardt, Michael. 1992. Abschied von der Verwaltungsvorschrift im Wasserrecht? Zu den Auswirkungen der neuen Rechtsprechung des EuGH auf den wasserrechtlichen Vollzug in der Bundesrepublik Deutschland. *Die Öffentliche Verwaltung* 3: 102–110.

Renzsch, Wolfgang. 1994. Föderative Problembewältigung. Zur Einbeziehung der neuen Länder in einen gesamtdeutschen Finanzausgleich ab 1995. *Zeitschrift für Parlamentsfragen* 25 (1): 116–138.

Renzsch, Wolfgang. 1995. Konfliktlösung im parlamentarischen Bundesstaat. Zur Regelung finanzpolitischer Bund-Länder-Konflikte im Spannungsfeld von Administration und Politik. Vorläufige Überlegungen. In *Der kooperative Staat. Krisenbewältigung durch Verhandlung?*, edited by R. Voigt. Baden-Baden: Nomos, 167–189.

Ress, Georg. 1986. Die Europäische Gemeinschaft und der deutsche Föderalismus. *Europäische Grundrechtezeitschrift* 13 (33): 549–558.

Rhodes, R. A. W. 1981. *Control and Power in Central-Local Government Relationships*. Farnborough: Gower.

Rhodes, R. A. W. 1986. *European Policy-Making, Implementation and Sub-central Governments*. Maastricht: European Institute of Public Administration.

Rhodes, R. A. W. 1997. *Understanding Governance: Policy Networks, Governance, Reflexivity and Accountability*. Buckingham and Philadelphia: Open University Press.

Risse, Thomas. 2001. A European Identity? Europeanization and the Evolution of Nation-State Identities. In *Transforming Europe: Europeanization and Domestic Change*, edited by M. G. Cowles, J. A. Caporaso, and T. Risse, 198–216.

Risse, Thomas, Maria Green Cowles, and James A. Caporaso. 2001. Europeanization and Domestic Change: Introduction. In *Transforming Europe: Europeanization and Domestic Change*, edited by M. G. Cowles, J. A. Caporaso, and T. Risse, 1–20.

Risse-Kappen, Thomas. 1996. Exploring the Nature of the Beast: International Relations Theory and Comparative Policy Analysis Meet the European Union. *Journal of Common Market Studies* 34 (1): 53–80.

Ritter, Ernst-Hasso. 1999. Zur Entwicklung der Landespolitik. In *50 Jahre Bundesrepublik Deutschland. Rahmenbedingungen, Entwicklungen, Perspektiven*, edited by T. Ellwein and E. Holtmann. Opladen: Westdeutscher Verlag, 343–362.

Rogers, Mary F. 1974. Instrumental and Infra Resources: The Basis of Power. *American Journal of Sociology* 79 (6): 1418–1433.

Rometsch, Dietrich, and Wolfgang Wessels, eds. 1996. *The European Union and the Member States: Towards Institutional Fusion?* Manchester and New York: Manchester University Press.

Rubio Llorente, Francisco. 1995. Les Comunitats Autònomes i la Comunitat Europea. *Autonomies* 20: 89–100.

Sandholtz, Wayne. 1993. Choosing Union: Monetary Politics and Maastricht. *International Organization* 47 (1): 1–39.

Sandholtz, Wayne. 1996. Membership Matters: Limits of the Functional Approach to European Institutions. *Journal of Common Market Studies* 34 (3): 403–429.

Sandholtz, Wayne, and John Zysman. 1989. 1992: Recasting the European Bargain. *World Politics* 42 (1): 95–128.

Sbragia, Alberta, ed. 1992. *Europolitics: Institutions and Policymaking in the New European Community*. Washington, DC: Brookings Institution.

Sbragia, Alberta. 2001. Italy Pays for Europe: Political Leadership, Political Choice, and Institutional Adaptation. In *Transforming Europe: Europeanization and Domestic Change*, edited by M. Green Cowles, J. A. Caporaso, and T. Risse, 79–98.

Scharpf, Fritz W. 1988. The Joint-Decision Trap: Lessons from German Federalism and European Integration. *Public Administration* 66: 239–278.

Scharpf, Fritz W. 1989. Der Bundesrat und die Kooperation auf der dritten Ebene. In *Vierzig Jahre Bundesrat. Tagungsband zum wissenschaftlichen Symposium in der Evangelischen Akademie Tübingen, 11.–13. April 1989*, edited by Bundesrat. Baden-Baden: Nomos, 121–166.

Scharpf, Fritz W. 1991. Entwicklungslinien des bundesdeutschen Föderalismus. *Leviathan* Sonderheft 12: 146–159.

Scharpf, Fritz W. 1992. Europäisches Demokratiedefizit und deutscher Föderalismus. *Staatswissenschaften und Staatspraxis* 3 (3): 293–306.

Scharpf, Fritz W. 1993. *Autonomieschonend und gemeinschaftsverträglich. Zur Logik der europäischen Mehrebenenpolitik.* Discussion Paper, 93/9. Köln: Max-Planck Institut für Gesellschaftsforschung.

Scharpf, Fritz W. 1997. *Games Real Actors Play.* Boulder, CO: Westview.

Scharpf, Fritz W. and Arthur Benz. 1991. *Kooperation als Alternative zur Neugliederung?* Baden-Baden: Nomos.

Scharpf, Fritz W., Bernd Reissert, and Fritz Schnabel. 1976. *Politikverflechtung, Theorie und Empirie des kooperativen Föderalismus in der Bundesrepublik Deutschland.* Kronberg/Ts.: Scriptor.

Schmidt, Vivien A. 1996. *From State to Market? The Transformation of French Business and Government.* Cambridge: Cambridge University Press.

Schmidt, Vivien A. 1999. National Patterns of Governance under Siege: The Impact of European Integration. In *The Transformation of Governance in the European Union*, edited by B. Kohler-Koch and R. Eising. London: Routledge, 155–172.

Schmitter, Philippe C. *1991. The European Community as an Emergent and Novel Form of Political Domination.* Working Paper No 26. Juan March Institute, Madrid.

Schmitter, Philippe C. 1992. Representation and the Future Euro-Polity. *Staatswissenschaften und Staatspraxis* 3 (3): 379–405.

Schneider, Erich. 1986. Europäische Einigung. Erwartungen der Landesparlamente, Beitrag der Länder. In *Die deutschen Länder und die Europäischen Gemeinschaften*, edited by R. Hrbek and U. Thaysen. Baden-Baden: Nomos, 57–68.

Schneider, Volker. 2001. Institutional Reform in Telecommunications: The European Union in Transnational Policy Diffusion. In *Transforming Europe: Europeanization and Domestic Change*, edited by M. G. Cowles, J. A. Caporaso, and T. Risse, 60–78.

Schönberg, Christoph. 1998. Europabeauftragte in den deutschen Bundesländern. *Die Öffentliche Verwaltung* (16): 665–672.

Schröder, Meinhard. 1986. Bundesstaatliche Erosionen im Prozeß der europäischen Integration. *Jahrbuch des öffentlichen Rechts, n.F.* 35: 83–102.

Schultze, Rainer-Olaf. 1993. Statt Subsidiarität und Entscheidungsautonomie Politikverflechtung und kein Ende. Der deutsche Föderalismus nach der Vereinigung. *Staatswissenschaften und Staatspraxis* 4 (2): 225–255.

Schwanenflügel, Matthias. 1993. Die Richtlinie über den freien Zugang zu Umweltinformationen als Chance für den Umweltschutz. *Die Öffentliche Verwaltung* (3): 95–102.

Scott, W. Richard. 1991. Unpacking Institutional Arguments. In *The New Institutionalism in Organizational Analysis*, edited by W. W. Powell and P. J. DiMaggio. Chicago and London: Chicago University Press, 164–182.

Scott, W. R., and J. W. Meyer. 1994. *Institutional Environments and Organizations.* Thousand Oaks, CA: Sage.

Simeon, Richard, ed. 1979. *Confrontation and Collaboration: Intergovernmental Relations in Canada Today.* Toronto: The Institute of Public Administration of Canada.

Smyrl, Marc. E. 1997. Does EC Regional Policy Empower the Regions? *Governance* 10 (3): 287–309.

Sontheimer, Kurt. 1990. *Deutschlands politische Kultur.* München and Zürich: Piper.

Späth, Lother. 1989. *Der Traum von Europa.* Stuttgart: Deutsche Verlags-Anstalt.

Staeck, Nicola. 1996. *Politikprozesse im Mehrebenensystem der Europäischen Union. Eine Policy-Netzwerkanalyse der europäischen Strukturfondspolitik dargestellt am Bundesland Niedersachsen.* Baden-Baden: Nomos.

Stein, Arthur A. 1983. Coordination and Collaboration: Regimes in an Anarchic World. In *International Regimes*, edited by S. D. Krasner. Ithaca, NY: Cornell University Press, 115–140.

Steinmo, Sven, Kathleen Thelen, and Frank Longstreth, eds. 1992. *Structuring Politics. Historical Institutionalism in Comparative Analysis.* Cambridge: Cambridge University Press.

Stöger, Fritz. 1988. Aufgaben und Tätigkeit des Beobachters der Länder bei den Europäischen Gemeinschaften. In *Bundesländer und Europäische Gemeinschaft*, edited by S. Magiera and D. Merten. Berlin: Duncker & Humblot, 101–120.

Stoiber, Edmund. 1987. Auswirkungen der Entwicklung Europas zur Rechtsgemeinschaft auf die Länder der Bundesrepublik Deutschland. *Europa Archiv* 42 (19): 543–552.

Stone Sweet, Alec, and Thomas Brunell. 1998. The European Court and the National Courts: A Statistical Analysis of Preliminary References, 1961–95. *Journal of European Public Policy* 5 (1): 66–97.

Stone Sweet, Alec, and Wayne Sandholtz, eds. 1998. *Supranational Governance: The Institutionalization of the European Union.* Oxford: Oxford University Press.

Streinz, Rudolf, and Matthias Pechstein. 1995. The Case of Germany. In *National Administrative Procedures for the Preparation and Implementation of Community Decisions*, edited by S. A. Pappas. Maastricht: European Institute of Public Administration, 133–160.

Strohmeier, Rudolf. 1988. Möglichkeiten der Einflußnahme auf den Entscheidungsprozeß der Europäischen Gemeinschaften durch die deutschen

Bundesländer nach Einrichtung von Länderbüros in Brüssel. *Die Öffentliche Verwaltung* 41 (15): 633–637.

Sturm, Roland, and Charlie Jeffery. 1993. German Unity, European Integration and the Future of the Federal System: Revival or Permanent Loss of Substance? In *Federalism, Unification and European Integration*, edited by C. Jeffery and R. Sturm. London: Frank Cass, 164–176.

Tarrow, Sidney. 1995. Mass Mobilisation and Elite Exchange: Democratization Episodes in Italy and Spain. *Democratization* 2 (3): 221–245.

Taylor, Paul. 1991. The European Community and the State: Assumptions, Theories and Propositions. *Review of International Studies* 17 (1): 109–125.

Teufel, Erwin. 1992. Föderalismus in der Bewährung. In *Föderalismus in der Bewährung. die deutschen Länder vor der Herausforderung fortschreitender EG-Integration*, edited by B. Vogel and G. Oettinger. Köln: Deutscher Gemeindeverlag und Kohlhammer, 3–8.

Thaysen, Uwe. 1985. Sicherung der Länder-Eigenstaatlichkeit und Stärkung der Landesparlamente, Vorschläge einer von den Fraktionsvorsitzendenkonferenzen von CDU/CSU, SPD und FDP berufenen interfraktionellen Arbeitsgruppe. *Zeitschrift für Parlamentsfrage* 16 (2): 179–182.

Thelen, Kathleen, and Sven Steinmo. 1992. Historical Institutionalism in Comparative Politics. In *Structuring Politics: Historical Institutionalism in Comparative Analysis*, edited by S. Steinmo, K. Thelen and F. Longstreth. Cambridge: Cambridge University Press, 1–32.

Tofarides, Maria. 1997. Cities and the European Union: An Unforseen Alliance? European Policy Process Occasional Papers, 30. Colchester: University of Essex.

Tomuschat, Christian. 1988. Bundesstaats- und Integrationsprinzip in der Verfassungsordnung des Grundgesetzes. In *Bundesländer und Europäische Gemeinschaft*, edited by S. Magiera and D. Merten. Berlin: Duncker und Humblot, 21–43.

Tomuschat, Christian. 1995. *Mitsprache der dritten Ebene in der europäischen Integration: Der Ausschuß der Regionen*. Bonn: Europa Union.

Tornos i Más, Joaquín. 1991. Algunos problemas competenciales en la ejecución interna de directivas comunitarias. *Autonomies* 13: 31–43.

Tsebelis, George. 1990. *Nested Games: Rational Choice in Comparative Politics*. Berkeley, CA: University of California Press.

Van der Eijk, C., M. Franklin, et. al. 1996. *Choosing Europe? The European Electorate and National Politics in the Face of Union*. Ann Arbor, MI: Michigan University Press.

Vitzthum, Wolfgang Graf. 1990. Der Föderalismus in der europäischen und internationalen Einbindung der Staaten. *Allgemeines Öffentliches Recht* 115 (2): 281–307.

Viver i Pi-Sunyer, Carles. 1990. Conflictos de competencias entre el Estado y la Generalidad de Cataluña. *Autonomies* 12: 43–49.

Voß, Dirk Hermann. 1989. *Regionen und Regionalismus im Recht der Mitgliedstaaten der Europäischen Gemeinschaft. Strukturelemente einer Europäischen Verfassungsordnung*. Frankfurt am Main: Peter Lang.

Wallace, Helen, and William Wallace, eds. 1996. *Policy-Making in the European Union*. Oxford: Oxford University Press.

Waskow, Siegfried. 1997. *Betriebliches Umweltmanagement. Anforderungen nach der Audit Verordnung der EG und dem Umweltauditgesetz*. Second ed. Heidelberg: C. F. Müller.

Weale, Albert, Geoffrey Pridham, Andrea Williams, and Martin Porter. 1996. Environmental Administration in Six European States: Secular Convergence or National Distinctiveness? *Public Administration* 74: 255–274.

Wiedmann, Thomas. 1992. Föderalismus als europäische Utopie. Die Rolle der Regionen aus rechtsvergleichender Sicht. Das Beispiel Deutschlands und Frankreichs. *Zeitschrift für Allgemeines Öffentliches Recht* 117 (1): 46–70.

Wincott, Daniel. 1995. Institutional Interaction and European Integration: Towards an Everyday Critique of Liberal Intergovernmentalism. *Journal of Common Market Studies* 33 (4): 597–609.

Windhoff-Héritier, Adrienne. 1991. Institutions, Interests and Political Choice. In *Political Choice. Institutions, Rules and the Limits of Rationality*, edited by R. Czada and A. Windhoff-Héritier. Frankfurt am Main, and Boulder, CO: Campus and Westview, 27–52.

Wolf, Joachim. 1992. Die Kompetenz der Verwaltung zur "Normsetzung" durch Verwaltungsvorschriften. *Die Öffentliche Verwaltung* (20): 849–860.

Wright, Vincent. 1994. Reshaping the State: The Implications for Public Administration. In *The State in Western Europe: Retreat or Redefinition*, edited by W. C. Müller and V. Wright. London: Frank Cass, 102–137.

Wuermling, Joachim. 1993. Das Ende der "Länderblindheit". Der Ausschuß der Regionen nach dem neuen EG-Vertrag. *Europäisches Recht* 28 (2): 196–207.

Ziller, Gebhard. 1986. Die EG-politische Mitwirkung des Bundesrates. In *Die deutschen Länder und die Europäischen Gemeinschaften*, edited by R. Hrbek and U. Thaysen. Baden-Baden: Nomos, 89–103.

Zürn, Michael. 1996. Über den Staat und die Demokratie im europäischen Mehrebenensystem. *Politische Vierteljahresschrift* 37 (1): 27–55.

Index